D1244659

Printed
Poison

◆ ◆ ◆

Printed Poison

◆　◆　◆

*Pamphlet Propaganda, Faction Politics,
and the Public Sphere in Early
Seventeenth-Century France*

Jeffrey K. Sawyer

UNIVERSITY OF CALIFORNIA PRESS
Berkeley　Los Angeles　Oxford

University of California Press
Berkeley and Los Angeles, California

University of California Press, Ltd.
Oxford, England

© 1990 by
The Regents of the University of California

Library of Congress Cataloging-in-Publication Data

Sawyer, Jeffrey K.
    Printed poison : pamphlet propaganda, faction politics, and the
public sphere in early seventeenth-century France / Jeffrey K.
Sawyer.
        p.   cm.
    Includes bibliographical references.
    ISBN 0-520-06883-1 (alk. paper)
    1. France—History—Louis XIII, 1610–1643—Pamphlets. 2. Public
opinion—France—History—17th century. 3. Despotism—France—
History—17th century. 4. Pamphleteers—France—Political
activity—History—17th century. I. Title.
DC123.3.S39 1990
944'.032—dc20   89-49051
                                                                              CIP

Printed in the United States of America

9   8   7   6   5   4   3   2   1

The paper used in this publication meets the minimum requirements of
American National Standard for Information Sciences—Permanence of Paper
for Printed Library Material, ANSI Z39.48-1984. ⊗

CONTENTS

ACKNOWLEDGMENTS

Many friends and colleagues helped make this book possible. Above all I want to thank Lynn Hunt for her understanding, encouragement, and criticisms from beginning to end.

My research in France was greatly facilitated by several colleagues. Bernard Barbiche was enormously helpful; special thanks also are in order to Alfred Soman and François Fossier. Keith Luria, James Farr, and Harriet Lightman provided valuable tips. I had the privilege of brief but useful interviews early in my research with Denis Richet, Roger Chartier, Louis Marin, Roland Mousnier, and Henri-Jean Martin, and somewhat later with Yves-Marie Bercé and Hubert Carrier. Hélène Duccini, whose *thèse de troisième cycle* anticipated parts of this book, generously shared with me her unpublished work and her thoughts about what remained to be done. I have recently had the pleasure of getting to know Christian Jouhaud and of learning much from his encounters with the pamphlet literature of the Fronde.

My work at the Newberry Library was made a great deal more fruitful through conversations with George Huppert, John Tedeschi, Harvey Graff, and Donald Bailey. Since moving east I have depended a great deal on the Baltimore-Washington historians of the Old Regime, an ideal community of scholars and friends. I especially want to thank Joseph Klaits, Timothy Tackett, Sharon Kettering, Orest Ranum, Jack Censer, Robert Kreiser, and James Collins for their support. Thanks to Nancy Roelker and J. M. Hayden for their suggestions and encouragement along the way.

Lloyd Moote, Sarah Hanley, Niel Larkin, Julie Hayes, and Raymond Hilliard provided incisive and learned comments on an early draft of the manuscript, for which I am very grateful.

Much-needed financial assistance was provided by the Newberry Library, the Mabel McLeod Lewis Memorial Fund, the University of California, the University of Richmond, and the Yale Gordon Endowment at the University of Baltimore. Both Richmond and Baltimore have been good places to work, thanks in large measure to the following colleagues, librarians, and administrators: Sheldon Wettack, John Rilling, Ernest Bolt, Jr., Martin Ryle, John Gordon, Emory Bogle, Hugh West, John Treadway, Denis Robison, Littleton Maxwell, Sue Ratchford, Mebane Turner, Catherine Gira, Richard Swaim, Thomas Jacklin, John Mayfield, Alfred Guy, Donald Mulcahey, Larry Thomas, Joy Chapper, Donald Haynes, Garrett Van Meter, Wayne Markert, and Carol Vaeth.

I can only begin to acknowledge the many intangible debts that I accumulated in the course of writing this book. I owe much to all of my teachers at Berkeley, especially Thomas Barnes, Arthur Quinn, Martin Jay, Gene Brucker, William Bouwsma, and Thomas Conley. The support of my family—Webster, Margery, Carl, Alan, and Anne Sawyer—was beyond the call of love or duty. To Piet van der Wallen Mijnlief, Fred Foley, Patricia Crouse, John and Gwynne Tysell, Scott Bergren, William Smith, Kathy Yusavage, Dallas Clouatre, William Crisman, Mark McFadden, Thomas Sloane, Marie-Annick Cabrillac and family, Demetrios and Connie Mavroudis, David Evans and family, William and Althea Wagman, George Rawson, and Wendy Smith, thank you.

Finally, it has been a pleasure to work with the University of California Press. I am grateful to two anonymous readers for recognizing the unusual nature of my arguments (as well as my sentences) and especially to Sheila Levine, Betsey Scheiner, Mark Jacobs, and Kristen C. Stoever.

ABBREVIATIONS

A.N.   Archives Nationales
Annales: E.S.C. *Annales: Economies, Sociétés, Civilisations*
B.N.   Bibliothèque Nationale

f. (ff.)   folio page(s)

EDITORIAL NOTE

Seventeenth-century documents were the primary sources for this study. Effective editing and translating of these texts are difficult owing to the irregularities of seventeenth-century French. Whenever an original text has been cited, I have generally sought to provide an English translation as close as possible to the original in meaning, tone, and level of diction. In problematic cases, philological precision was sacrificed to readability. The major exception to the translation rule is pamphlet titles, which have generally been left untranslated. In cases where the original text has been reproduced untranslated, I generally retained the original orthography, capitalization, punctuation, and diacritical marks except where this would cause confusion. Where appropriate, I have substituted 'v' for 'u' (e.g., 'souverain' for 'souuerain'), 'j' for 'i' (e.g., 'jamais' for 'iamais'), 'et' for '&' and so forth. Such changes have been kept to a minimum; for example, I saw no need to change 'Roy' to 'Roi,' 'mesme' to 'même' or 'estat' to 'état'.

CHRONOLOGY

Notable developments in publishing and censorship ($^{++}$)

Pamphlet Campaigns (**)

1583–1594   Worst years of the Holy League

** Bitter pamphlet polemics take place between Protestants and Catholics. Printers in Paris and Lyon publish hundreds of pamphlets in favor of the League

1594   Coronation of Henry IV

1598   Edicts of pacification protecting civil rights of Protestants are signed at Nantes

1600   Marriage of Henry IV to Marie de Médicis

$^{++}$ Twenty-four official members of the booksellers guild are under the jurisdiction of the University of Paris. About sixty others are doing business in the capital more or less without regulation

1601   Birth of Louis XIII

1602   Henry IV has maréchal Biron executed for treason

1603   Henry IV allows the return of Jesuit colleges to Paris, but maintains a foreign policy of alignment with the Protestant powers—England, the United Provinces, and the Swiss Cantons

** Important pamphlet exchanges concerning Henry IV's political and religious policies

1610   Assassination of Henry IV by Ravaillac

Louis XIII is coronated, but his authority is exercised by Marie de Médicis, the queen mother and sole regent

    ** Outburst of pamphlets lamenting the loss of Henry IV; accusations of a conspiracy behind the assassination

    ++ The Châtelet (basic royal court for the Paris region) enacts a *règlement* designed to regulate the book trades (November); "prohibited books" and "seditious pamphlets" cited as a major reason for the law, but the matter is removed to the higher sovereign court of the Parlement of Paris

1610–1614   ++ Parlement of Paris condemns and reconfirms the suppression of many Jesuit publications allegedly condoning "tyrannicide." Huguenot tracts are also condemned and suppressed. The archbishop of Sens's court condemns as heretical a Gallican tract, which judgment the Parlement of Paris refuses to quash

1611   Restructuring of the king's councils; Sully (Protestant minister of finance) resigns; ultramontane faction gains influence

    ** *Mercure françois* appears—a year-by-year narrative summary of political news also containing many excerpts from pamphlet literature

1612   ++ *Mercure françois* temporarily suppressed by the Parlement of Paris (August)

1613   Concini (an Italian favorite of the queen regent) elevated to the position of maréchal of France and given other honors and offices; Guise family coalition at court outmaneuvering the Bourbon-Soissons coalition in the struggle for patronage

    ** *Mercure françois* receives a new royal privilege (1 May)

1614   Revolt of a coalition of the great nobility led by the third prince de Condé (Henri II de Bourbon) against Marie de Médicis

    ** Initial exchange of pamphlets between rebellious princes and the government of the queen regent; (February–May) Condé publishes a letter of protest against the queen regent's administration

Announcement of an Estates General (June)

    ** Exchange of pamphlets in preparation for the Estates General (June–October)

++ Arrest and trial of several Parisian booksellers dealing in pamphlets (July); several dealers suffer fines and banishment; sixteen pamphlets condemned by name

++ The Châtelet and the Parlement condemn the publishing of any book or pamphlet without royal permission

Louis XIII celebrates his majority and appoints Marie de Médicis "head of his councils" (20 October)

Opening of the Estates General (27 October)

** Several exchanges of pamphlets concerning the revolt of the princes and the Estates General

1615   Closing of the Estates General (24 March)

Parlement of Paris agitated about the *Paulette,* which Marie de Médicis quietly extends for four more years

** Exchange of pamphlets concerning the royal government's continuing failure to address the grievances drawn up at the Estates General

++ Marie de Médicis scolds a delegation from the Parlement for lack of initiative in stemming the tide of pamphlet literature

Second revolt of the great nobility led by Condé

** New barrage of pamphlets following Condé's publication of a manifesto and his initiation of military efforts to obstruct the marriage ceremony of Louis XIII (June–November)

++ Two letters sent over the signature of Louis XIII to Henri de Mesmes (*lieutenant civil* in the Châtelet) complaining of the unabated flow of pamphlets

++ Parlement of Paris condemns several pamphlets

Marriage of Louis XIII to Anne of Austria at Bordeaux

** Many pamphlets celebrate the marriage

1616   Struggle between the rebellious nobles and the government enters a phase of truce and negotiations

** Negotiations between the administration of Marie de Médicis and rebellious nobles discussed at length in the pamphlet literature (February–May)

Revolt of the great nobility and their Protestant supporters is brought to a close by the Peace of Loudun (3 May)

The prince de Condé is active in the king's councils (July–August)

** Pamphlet literature regularly attacks Concini

++ *Lieutenant civil* of Paris fines three colporteurs; orders book and pamphlet sellers to return to their places in the University quarter (especially those working the Pont-Neuf)

Condé arrested (1 September); Concini's house pillaged in Paris; the princes leave Paris again

** Third major exchange of pamphlets between rebellious nobles and the government begins in September and continues until April 1617

++ Parlement of Paris forbids publication of any "books, writings, pamphlets, letters or other publications of any kind" without permission (September)

Concini arranges the dismissal of Henry IV's old ministers (Villeroy, Jeannin, Brûlart de Sillery); new ministry formed from among Marie de Médicis's confidants (Mangot, Barbin, and Luçon—the future Cardinal Richelieu)

Revolt of the great nobility evolves into civil war in the provinces

1617   Concini is killed by Louis XIII's bodyguards while being taken prisoner at the king's direction

** Outburst of pamphlets celebrating the death of Concini and the heroism/liberation of Louis XIII

The queen mother's advisers are dismissed and she is exiled to Blois; Henry IV's ministers recalled; Charles Albert de Luynes, the king's favorite, struggles to manage the royal councils

An Assembly of Notables is convoked at Rouen in an effort to strengthen Luynes's government

1618–1619   Marie de Médicis encourages her partisans to defy the authority of Louis XIII in her effort to regain influence in the king's councils; military maneuvers follow

** Pamphlet wars between the supporters of Louis XIII and those of Marie de Médicis

++ Enactment of a great *règlement* governing the book trades by *lettres patentes* of the king (9 July 1618). Stringent prohibitions against printing or distributing "prohibited" books and "seditious" pamphlets; anything published in Paris must be affixed with a notice of royal permission obtained in advance of publication

++ Death sentences passed in a criminal procedure before the king's council against two pamphleteers (Sity and Durand) associated with Marie de Médicis (July)

1619 ++ Efforts to enforce the *Règlement* of 1618 lead to an attempt to arrest all unlicensed booksellers in Paris (January); Parisian officials publish their intention to initiate criminal proceedings against any printer or book dealer selling any material without royal permission (March)

++ The author Vanini burnt in Toulouse (April); opposition pamphleteers such as Mathieu de Morgues flee France

1620 Louis XIII's government forcibly reestablishes Catholic church in Navarre and Béarn, former strongholds of Protestantism

** Outburst of pamphlets on Protestant issue

** Pamphlet campaign against Luynes begins

++ An extensively annotated version of the *Règlement* of 1618 is published by the Parisian lawyer M. L. Bouchel

1621 War against the Protestants; Luynes dies during siege of Montauban

** Pamphlet campaign against the Protestants intensifies

++ Jean Fontanier, author of the "heretical" *Tresor inestimable,* is ordered burnt alive in Paris; persecution of Théophile de Viau begins

++ *Règlement* of 1618 is republished

1622–1625 Disorganizaton within king's councils; rural uprisings in the provinces; the queen mother returns to Paris and participates in government; Richelieu named cardinal and brought into king's councils

** Exchanges of pamphlets focus on France's religious, economic, and social problems; others that concentrate on political scandal help to disgrace successive ministries of Brûlart and La Veuville, assisting in Richelieu's rise to power

++ King's council appoints its own board of censors consisting of four doctors of theology (May 1623)

++ Richelieu recruits a band of writers to take over the direction of royal propaganda (1624)

** *Mercure françois*, now taken over by Père Joseph with Richelieu's support, begins to cover events of Thirty Years' War in great detail

** Pamphlet campaign regarding France's international politics intensifies

++ Royal *lettres patentes* demand enforcement of the *règlement* of 1618

1626   An Assembly of Notables convoked in Paris to strengthen the reorganized administration of Louis XIII and Marie de Médicis; Richelieu and Marillac are principal ministers.

1627–1628   Siege of La Rochelle; the Protestant stronghold surrenders in October 1628

** Pamphlet campaigns focus on war against the Protestants (which the Parlement of Paris tries to actively censor)

++ Richelieu begins enforcing provisions of 1618 *règlement* against pamphlets throughout France

++ The chancellor's office begins sponsoring the editing and publication (by T. Godefroy and others) of collections of royalist tracts

1629   The French army prepares to engage the Spanish in northern Italy; Richelieu is directing foreign policy

++ A comprehensive codification of royal law, the *Code Michau*, containing stringent censorship provisions is registered by the Parlement of Paris under protest

1630   "Journée des Dupes"; Marillac is disgraced; Richelieu now principal minister of state; Marie de Médicis exiled again; rural uprisings against poverty and taxes; *Code Michau* is dead letter

France committed to an anti-Hapsburg policy; toleration of the Protestants only within strict limitations

1631   Gaston d'Orléans (Louis XIII's younger brother) revolts against Richelieu's administration; more rural uprisings

++ *Règlement* of 1618 is republished again; *lettres patentes* again demand enforcement

** The long pamphlet campaign attacking Richelieu and his policies begins

$^{++}$ Sponsored by Richelieu, the *Gazette* is founded by Théophraste Renaudot in part to counteract the pamphlet campaigns against the government's policies

1632   The duc de Montmorency leads a revolt in Languedoc against Richelieu's administration and is executed; rural uprisings continue

$^{++}$ Cardin Le Bret publishes the absolutist treatise, *De la Souveraineté du Roy*

1632–1634   ** Height of the pamphlet campaign against Richelieu by partisans of Marie de Médicis such as Mathieu de Morgues

$^{++}$ Decision by the prévôt of Paris fixes the number of legal colporteurs in Paris at fifty (March)

1635 $^{++}$ Foundation of the *Academie française*

$^{++}$ Richelieu's propagandists are working on several projects, notably official histories of Louis XIII's reign and the cardinal's own memoirs

1635–1640 $^{++}$ Under Chancellor Seguier, censorship is more effective than ever

1636   Major uprising of peasants and small farmers (*croquants*) in western France

1636–1642   Several plots against Richelieu are exposed and suppressed

1637 $^{++}$ Descartes's *Discours de la méthode* is published

1642   Richelieu dies; Mazarin takes his place

1643   Louis XIII dies; Anne of Austria acts as regent for their son Louis XIV (until 1651); Cardinal Mazarin in charge of the king's councils; Parlement of Paris agitates against Mazarin

$^{++}$ Ordinance of the *prévôt* of Paris forbids printing presses in private homes

1648   Uprising of the Parlement of Paris against Mazarin and Anne of Austria; suppression (short-lived) of the intendants; Anne of Austria flees Paris with Louis XIV

Peace of Westphalia ends the Thirty Years' War

1649   Prince de Condé, called "the Great Condé" (Louis II, son of Henri II de Bourbon, third prince de Condé, mentioned above), distinguished general of the Thirty Years' War, leads a loyal army against the *frondeurs* of Paris

   ** Massive pamphlet campaign against Mazarin; pamphlets recount the events of the Fronde for four years

1650–1652   Military forces of the Fronde are defeated; Louis XIV returns to Paris

   ++ Parlement of Paris reissues *arrêts* against defamatory pamphlets

1654   Louis XIV crowned

1661   Mazarin dies; Fouquet is disgraced; Colbert enters king's councils; Louis XIV takes personal control of the councils

1685   Revocation of the Edict of Nantes

   ** Sporadic pamphlet campaigns in opposition to Louis XIV

   ** Recurrent pamphlet campaigns for and against Louis's foreign policy

1715   Death of Louis XIV

Introduction

❖   ❖   ❖

Political pamphlets were produced on a remarkable scale in seventeenth-century France. One inventory of the Bibliothèque Nationale in Paris lists 3,417 titles from the reign of Louis XIII (1610–1643) and 4,503 titles from the reign of Louis XIV (1643–1715).[1] These pamphlets constituted the political press of the age, and historians of the Old Regime have long recognized their importance.[2] Yet a convincing explanation of the concrete purposes and functions of these pamphlets has not emerged.

By later standards the production of pamphlets in the seventeenth century was slow and distribution poorly organized. Rates of functional literacy were low, especially outside large urban centers. There were few opportunities for the general population, or even the elite reading public, to respond directly to pamphlets by engaging in the national political process. And in the world of the Old Regime, there were many means of coercion and manipulation besides the printed word whereby powerful men and women could achieve their political goals.

What, then, did the authors and sponsors of these pamphlets hope to accomplish? How effective were their efforts? What audience, or public, did they reach? How do the pamphlets fit in the broader context of political discourse and culture? This book offers answers to these questions based on a close analysis of pamphlet production, pamphlet rheto-

1. *Catalogue de l'Histoire de France* (1968 ed.); see Duccini, "Regard sur la littérature pamphlétaire," 313–337.

2. Leber, *L'Etat réel de la presse*, 96–97; Martin, *Livres*, 1:197–274; and Chartier, "Pamphlets et gazettes," 1:407. The holdings of several major research libraries in the United States are catalogued in Lindsay and Neu, *French Political Pamphlets*, and published in the extensive microfilm collection, *French Political Pamphlets*.

ric, and political dynamics during the course of a particular national conflict—the struggle for domination of Louis XIII's government from 1614 to 1617.

Propaganda has a long history in early modern Europe.[3] In Old Regime France, government ministers routinely sponsored and disseminated printed material for political purposes, as the work of Joseph Klaits, Myriam Yardeni, and others has shown.[4] The mid-eighteenth century marked a new stage of development, especially when the views of the *philosophes* began to echo a Lockean preoccupation with the connections between public opinion and political consent.[5] Such enlightened thinking helped to precipitate the crisis of political authority that led to the Revolution of 1789 and the end of the Old Regime. Before the eighteenth century, however, a simpler and more traditional view prevailed. Propaganda aimed to help the government control the *impressions* (perceptions) of its subjects in order to secure better compliance with its policies.

The 1614–1617 conflict in France is a particularly revealing context for investigating the use of printed propaganda in early modern politics. In this introduction, I seek to explain why this is so. Preliminary remarks about method are also in order, as are comments about the relationship of this book to recent work on the history of printing, popular culture, and the world of books. I also indicate why this study has larger implications for our understanding of the politics of absolutism.

The 1614–1617 crisis, which brought down the government of Louis XIII's mother, Marie di Médicis, has a special significance in the history of French politics and pamphleteering. Not only was it one of the more important political upheavals of the century, but it also set a pattern of political disobedience for later rebellions. The presence of a minor king and a regency government was always destabilizing for the Old Regime because it exposed the conventions of monarchical government to public discussion and embarrassing legal scrutiny. The normal ties of personal allegiance to the king were attenuated, and the precise boundaries of sovereign royal authority became more difficult to enforce. Only during the Fronde (in Louis XIV's minority), and possibly during the brief religious wars of the 1620s, did such a flood of printed propaganda challenge the royal government as that of 1614–1617.

3. Roelker, "Impact of the Reformation Era," 2:41–84; Lewis, "War-propaganda and Historiography," 1–21; and Hale, "War and Public Opinion," 18–36.

4. Klaits, *Printed Propaganda under Louis XIV,* 3–34; Yardeni, *Conscience nationale en France;* and in addition to the sources cited below for the seventeenth century, Kaiser, "Abbé de Saint-Pierre," 618–643.

5. Much was borrowed from the views of John Locke. Baker, "Politics and Public Opinion under the Old Regime: Some Reflections," 204–246; and Ozouf, "L'Opinion publique," 419–434.

Some features of these pamphlet wars have already been studied. J. M. Hayden has analyzed the content and production patterns of the pamphlets surrounding the Estates General of 1614.[6] Denis Richet analyzed a sample of pamphlets published from 1612 through 1615 in an investigation of the presence of historical consciousness in the political argument of the times.[7] The most comprehensive study to date was undertaken by Hélène Duccini, who provided the first effective overview of pamphlet production in the seventeenth century and a more detailed view of the 1614–1617 campaigns.[8] The present investigation is based in part on this earlier work, but it also analyzes pamphlets from a new perspective, emphasizing the place of the printed word in the political process as a whole.

The early seventeenth century was a period of fundamental and complex transition in France. The steady growth of the state transformed the monarchy, but centralized royal power was frequently undermined by financial weakness, popular revolts, and self-interested obstructionism on the part of the king's own officials. Religious war no longer dominated political culture, but fearsome memories remained. The highly emotional factionalism of the later years of the Holy League (1585–1594) still played an important part in local and national politics. Secularization was strong in many quarters but was less influential on the whole than the efforts of the *dévôts* to revitalize Catholicism.[9] Intellectual life in general was also moving from the metaphorical world of the late Renaissance and baroque periods to the syllogistic world of seventeenth-century classicism; political discourse reflected this change.[10] Dense analogical reasoning *à la* Jean Bodin increasingly gave way to more straightforward legal argumentation in the style of Charles Loyseau and Cardin Le Bret.

Absolutism is a central theme for historians of this period; but as a term, it is the subject of some debate.[11] The term *absolutism* has come to mean so many things that one specialist has suggested it be abandoned altogether.[12] A solution less neat but perhaps more realistic is to accept it as common currency but to remain alert to its changing value in different contexts. In a widespread, generic sense, *absolutist* describes any highly centralized European state like the one over which Louis XIV

---

6. Hayden, "Uses of Political Pamphlets," 143–165; and Hayden, *France and the Estates General*, 90–92, 99, 107–113, 142–144, and 164–171.

7. Richet, "Autour des Etats-Généraux," 151–194.

8. Duccini, "La Littérature pamphlétaire."

9. Cf. Church, *Richelieu and Reason of State.*

10. Thuau, *Raison d'état et pensée politique.*

11. Bonney, "Absolutism," 93–117.

12. Hanley, *"Lit de Justice" of the Kings of France*, 226–227.

presided.[13] More specific meanings are used to designate particular developments in early modern Europe that contributed to making absolutist states possible.

Studies of French absolutism usually emphasize one of four areas—(1) political institutions, (2) ideological change, (3) social structures, or (4) cultural life. First, even within the extended apparatus of the royal government, military, administrative, and fiscal functions were increasingly centralized in the hands of the king or a few ministers and their agents.[14] Second, an expanding ideology of unchallengeable royal power was built out of a mixture of juridical ideas in opposition both to representative government and to moral restraints on political authority coming from the church.[15] Third, state centralization and its ideological justifications grew out of a social reality in which the greater share of economic resources was concentrated in the hands of royal officials or classes of merchants and financiers who were able to maintain effective relationships with those officials.[16] Fourth, the government succeeded in part because it presented itself as a necessary result of France's immutable legal, moral, and social order wherein all authority emanated from an eternal hierarchy originating in the will of God and extended downward through the monarchy.[17] An important expression of these developments was the staging of state ceremonials and public rituals affirming the monarchs' position within the state.[18]

All of these elements of absolutism were at work in early seventeenth-century France, but periodization is a problem.[19] If we take the political institutions of the later Middle Ages as our reference point, the government of France under Francis I (1515–1547) or Henry II (1547–1559) appears to be moving toward absolutism in many ways.[20] Yet perhaps an even clearer example is the remarkably centralized and effective government built up by Henry IV (1589–1610) after the breakdown of royal authority under Henry III (1574–1589).[21] However, if we take the probable epitome of absolutism as our starting point—the power of Louis

13. For example, Anderson, *Lineages of the Absolutist State,* 15–42; and Behrens, *Society, Government, and the Enlightenment,* 10–40.

14. Parker, *French Absolutism,* 46–117; Bonney, *Political Change in France;* and Major, *Representative Government in Early Modern France.*

15. See Bonney, "Absolutism," 95–99, for an overview; and Mousnier, "Exponents and Critics of Absolutism," 4:104–131.

16. Beik, *Absolutism and Society in Seventeenth-Century France,* 3–33; and Giesey, "State-Building in Early Modern France," 191–207.

17. Basdevant-Gaudemet, *Charles Loyseau, 1564–1627.*

18. Giesey, "Models of Rulership in French Ceremonial," 41–64.

19. This is Hanley's main objection to the term in *"Lit de Justice,"* 226–227. See also Rowen, "Louis XIV and Absolutism," 302–305.

20. Knecht, *Francis I and Absolute Monarchy,* 7–9, 27–29.

21. Salmon, *Society in Crisis,* 309–328.

XIV's government from about 1660 to approximately 1700—the governments of Henry IV and even Louis XIII (1610–1648) look relatively undeveloped.[22]

From the present perspective, it is less important to determine which king had more real power than to understand how the forces of centralization worked. Why was it increasingly difficult to oppose the government in the political sphere? To this end, our analyses of the various means of coercion, manipulation, and persuasion that supported royal power need to be integrated into a broader cultural framework of investigation.[23] The power of the monarchy did not rest, ultimately, on the ability of the king and his officials to impose their will on local subjects through violence (the repression of popular revolts notwithstanding).[24] In the process of centralization, the king's ministers were often forced to undermine opponents through short-term concessions, financial rewards, and other benefits.[25] The exact relationship between local and central authority remained ambiguous in many situations.

The trend toward absolutism also involved psychological factors, and the contribution of printing in this regard is of primary importance. The technology of movable type certainly meant that uniform messages could be sent to a large population that was geographically and socially diverse.[26] Did printing thus provide the basis for a more homogeneous national political culture? Could the government use printed communications more effectively to reinforce patterns of obedience? It now seems improbable to historians specializing in the field that printing alone caused the cataclysmic mental and cultural revolution envisioned by Marshall McLuhan.[27] But printing brought a new awareness of ideology to many social strata. In combination with other social and cultural developments, this new awareness gradually altered the meaning of political conflict and the scale of public participation in national politics.[28]

Governments sought to control the printing press from the beginning.[29] It is well known that this effort broke down in the sixteenth century, once pamphlets began to be used systematically as weapons in the arsenal of Protestant reformers. A. G. Dickens concludes that "between 1517 and 1520, Luther's thirty publications probably sold well over

---

22. But cf. Lossky, "Absolutism of Louis XIV," 1–15.

23. Baker, "Introduction," xi–xxiv. Cf. Tucker, "Culture," 173–190.

24. Cf. Tilly, "History of European State-Making," 24–37; Anderson, *Lineages*, 95–101; and Porchnev, *Soulèvements populaires en France*.

25. Beik, *Absolutism and Society*, 3–31; Richet, *France moderne*, 79–105; Hickey, *Coming of French Absolutism*, 3–13; and Collins, *Fiscal Limits of Absolutism*, 6, 65–107, 214–215.

26. Eisenstein, *Printing Press as an Agent of Change*.

27. McLuhan, *Gutenberg Galaxy*. Cf. Martin, "Culture écrite et culture orale," 225–282.

28. Kelley, *Beginning of Ideology*, 215–251.

29. Ibid.

300,000 copies."[30] From the point of view of established governments and the church, such publications were seditious and heretical—something to be suppressed.[31] But censorship was relatively ineffective, and the forces of law and order, most notably royal governments and the Catholic church, were compelled to compete with the opposition in the same public arena. The decrees of the Countil of Trent (fundamental to the Counter-Reformation) sanctioned popular religious polemic as well as the censorship of "heretical" publications.[32] Our modern term for propaganda probably stems from the Latin phrase *propaganda fide*, part of the name of a Catholic missionary congregation devoted to spreading the Catholic faith around the world.[33]

New research has helped to elucidate the social dimensions of this expansion of printing. In France the work of Henri-Jean Martin and others has demonstrated that the early decades of the seventeenth century were pivotal.[34] The production of preapproved editions by official and semiofficial publishers increased dramatically. New regulations brought the printer's guild under greater government control.[35] A more enforceable system of censorship on the one hand and official patronage on the other gave the government new economic controls over publishing. The system of policing and privileges so well exposed by Robert Darnton and so hated by the intellectuals of the eighteenth century was largely invented between 1618 and 1635.[36] The production of popular literature did not fall outside this regime. The inexpensive popular books known as the *bibliothèque bleue* began to reach a broad audience of rural as well as urban folk in the later decades of the seventeenth century.[37] But there is no evidence that this type of popular literature contained much overt political news or commentary.[38]

30. Eisenstein, *Printing Press*, 303, citing A. G. Dickens, *Reformation and Society in Sixteenth-Century Europe* (New York, 1968), 51.

31. The "Index" of prohibited books is discussed in Grendler, *Roman Inquisition and the Venetian Press, 1540–1605*, 63–181.

32. Pallier, "Impressions de la Contre-Réforme," 215–273.

33. *New Catholic Encyclopedia*, 11:839–840.

34. Martin, *Livres*, 1:197–274. Much of the best recent research is elegantly summarized in Martin and Chartier, eds., *Histoire de l'édition*, vols. 1 and 2.

35. Martin, *Livres*, 1:51–57, 460–466; and Barbiche, "Régime de l'édition," 1:367–377. On the attitudes of magistrates toward censorship and legal proceedings, see the excellent article by Soman, "Press, Pulpit, and Censorship," 439–463.

36. Ibid., and Darnton, *Great Cat Massacre*, 145–189.

37. Mandrou, *Culture populaire aux XVIIe et XVIIIe siècles*.

38. Ibid. Mandrou's original conclusions in this respect have been sustained. See Marais, "Littérature et culture populaires," 65–105; Martin, "Culture écrit et culture orale," 225–282; Davis, "Printing and the People," 189–226; and Chartier, "Stratégies éditoriales et lectures populaires" and "*Bibliothèque bleue* and Popular Reading," in Chartier, *Cultural Uses of Print*, 145–182 and 240–257.

For fresh political information and opinion, the seventeenth-century French reader had few publications from which to choose. The first periodical, the stilted, semiofficial *Gazette,* did not appear until the 1630s.[39] More serious histories and chronologies were available, such as the *Mercure françois,* but these rarely appeared sooner than a year or two after the events they covered.[40] In short, political pamphlets both official and clandestine were the only significant printed source of news and commentary.[41] A good print shop could turn out more than one thousand sixteen-page pamphlets in a day's work, and many printers turned out dozens of pamphlets during years of political crisis.

Pamphlets were not the only, best, or quickest source of news, nor did they make oral and handwritten forms of communication obsolete. Personally delivered letters and messages could be sent more quickly by royal post from centers of power such as Paris to other parts of the country. But a printed pamphlet could follow upon an important event in a matter of days to inform an extended public about political activity that they were unable to witness firsthand. More important, pamphlets described events in detail and gave stories a "spin" or "slant" (in today's media jargon) or the imprimatur of some government or church official. Such published information was especially significant in part because of France's size. People far removed geographically from actual events and centers of power used pamphlets to determine the local political meaning of distant occurrences. The most dramatic example of immediate pamphlet production as journalism occurred during the Fronde—a four-year (1648–1652) political struggle that produced more than five thousand different political pamphlets (*mazarinades*) that regularly recapitulated events in a journalistic fashion for regionally specific audiences.[42]

39. Chartier, "Pamphlets et gazettes," 413–419.

40. The *Mercure françois* was a chronological narrative of important political, religious, and international news edited by the Parisian publisher, Jean Richer, first appearing in 1611. It appeared almost annually well into the 1630s and often gave relatively full accounts of important political events and pamphlet campaigns, complete with excerpted passages from important pamphlets. Its publishing history is complex and, to my knowledge, has never been fully reconstructed. It appears from the front matter of later editions that the first four volumes were reprinted more than once between 1617 and 1627.

41. Bellanger et al., eds., *Histoire générale de la presse française,* 1:63–79. Censer and Popkin provide a very useful introduction to more recent research, "Historians and the Press," 1–74.

42. On the *mazarinades* as journalism, see Grand-Mesnil, *Mazarin, la Fronde et la presse.* According to Carrier, the world's libraries contain about five thousand pamphlets from the years of the Fronde—many more than are listed in the catalogue of the Bibliothèque Nationale; see his "Souvenirs de la Fronde en U.R.S.S.," 27–50. On the regional character of these pamphlets see Jouhaud's work, n. 46 below.

The first modern investigation of seventeenth-century pamphlets was conducted at the turn of the century by Gustave Fagniez. His work showed how Père Joseph and other influential clergymen (many eventually allied with Cardinal Richelieu) used pamphlets to help build public support for a strong (Catholic but independent) state aggressively involved in the Thirty Years' War.[43] The link between public opinion and state power appeared self-evident to Fagniez, as it has to many students of propaganda. "If there is one dogma of political science that can be accepted by everyone in this age," he observed in 1900, "it is that the only governments with a future are those that have the support of public opinion."[44] Fagniez's approach was sensible and ahead of its time. But it lent itself to an essentially one-way analysis of "producers" and "consumers" of propaganda, that is, of government agents manipulating an undifferentiated public. Students of the media have strongly challenged this approach to the political press because it leaves relatively unexplored the problematic connections among public discourse, political attitudes, and patterns of behavior.[45] These connections are no longer self-evident. How does public opinion function as a source of political stability or instability? What are the links between collective psychology and the social reality of power?

Christian Jouhaud's recent work on the *mazarinades* and other seventeenth-century pamphlets is a vital new contribution to this enterprise.[46] Focusing on the pamphlet campaigns of the Fronde, especially those dealing with developments in Bordeaux, Jouhaud makes new sense out of the strategies and tactics of pamphleteers. Whereas the older studies tend to view pamphlets as an "expression" of partisan points of view or a "reflection" of political mentality more generally, Jouhaud emphasizes that the production and dissemination of a pamphlet was first of all a type of political "action" that must be understood in the monthly and even weekly context of political events.[47]

The problem of persuasion and its purposes, however, cannot be put

43. Fagniez, *Le Père Joseph et Richelieu, 1577–1638;* "Le Père Joseph et Richelieu," 470–521; "L'Opinion publique et la polémique au temps de Richelieu," 442–484; "L'Opinion publique et la press politique," 352–401; and "Fancan et Richelieu," 107:59–78 and 108:75–87.

44. Fagniez, "L'Opinion publique et la press politique," 352.

45. Cf. McQuail, "Influence and Effects of Mass Media," 36–53; and L. John Martin, "Moving Target," 3:249–294.

46. Jouhaud, "Ecriture et action au XVIIe siècle," 42–64; and *Mazarinades: la Fronde des mots,* which takes up (in the context of the Fronde) some of the themes I address in this study, although not always from the same perspective. See also Jouhaud's "Imprimer l'événement. De La Rochelle à Paris," 381–438.

47. Emphasized by Jouhaud in "Ecriture et action," 43–53, and "Imprimer l'événement."

aside, nor can it be easily formulated. Where does persuasion stop and manipulation or coercion begin? We need to study very precisely the strategic purposes of pamphleteering as part of more general attempts to encourage or inhibit specific kinds of organized political action.[48] Pamphlets often targeted well-defined groups for political mobilization. They used specific rhetorical forms in an effort to motivate these groups into action or to placate them into passivity. A more comprehensive view of this partisan, tactical function of pamphlets can be formed by patiently exploring these processes.

The cultural and linguistic turns in the recent historiography of early modern Europe have helped us to view words and actions in the political sphere in more complex and more enlightened ways. A rich variety of methods now pervades the analyses of verbal expression and political behavior. The result does not appear to be a new paradigm that will dominate research, but rather a rich cross-fertilization of ethnographic, interpretive, and sociological techniques for investigating the uses of discourse in historical context. Taken as a whole, these divergent approaches to discourse have greatly broadened our understanding of the "vocabulary of power," for example.[49] Along these lines Natalie Zemon Davis, Emmanuel Le Roy Ladurie, Robert Darnton, and others steeped in the cultural approach to history have sensitized us to the layered complexity of political behavior in Old Regime France.[50] Politics was about government, but it was also about playing games, maintaining one's social status, and representing one's self-image to the world and to God. Sarah Hanley's work on the *lit de justice* royal ceremony exemplifies the value of the cultural approach to the study of long-term political and constitutional development in early modern France, as does Lynn Hunt's reinterpretation of the political culture of the French Revolution.[51]

Yet with respect to national political conflicts in the prerevolutionary period, the cultural approach has some significant limitations. To the extent that one envisions politics as ritual, one tends to depreciate the strategic importance of discourse. Verbal polemic in the Old Regime was more than a by-product of politics. A primary purpose of public discourse was to generate power by influencing organized violence. However shaped by deep cultural patterns, this was also an arena in which people consciously risked their lives and fortunes for very specific pur-

48. See my review of Jouhaud's *Mazarinades,* in *Journal of Modern History* 58, no. 4 (1986): 933–935.

49. Pocock, *Machiavellian Moment;* Foucault, *History of Sexuality,* 81–102, and *Power/ Knowledge,* 78–145; and Skinner, *Foundations of Modern Political Thought.*

50. Davis, *Fiction in the Archives;* Darnton, *Cat Massacre;* and Le Roy Ladurie, *Carnival in Romans.*

51. Hanley, *"Lit de Justice";* and Hunt, *Politics, Culture, and Class.*

poses. Persuading others to act in concert with these purposes was a concrete medium, not merely a dramatization, of this struggle.[52]

This study makes use of several techniques of historical investigation. Classical models of propaganda analysis were employed in the initial stages of research, but none of these provided a comprehensive framework for the project as a whole.[53] The emphasis on "communicative action" and the "public sphere" owes much to the work of the German philosopher Jürgen Habermas.[54] Both the formation and expression of public opinion require the presence of specific institutions that enable discourse. Habermas has emphasized that many of these institutions exist apart from the formal state apparatus and have a history of their own. Habermas's formulation of the problem has helped historians to relate the study of public opinion to changing social and cultural structures beyond the context of representative government. A fundamental thesis of this book is that during the 1614–1617 conflict, France possessed a broadly accessible sphere of public, politically oriented communications. We can clearly identify a public acting and reacting in this sphere to political news and public debate. This process in turn greatly influenced the possibilities for political action on the part of local officials and the royal government. In later periods, notably the 1630s, the public's access to political discourse and information was greatly restricted.

In addition to the pragmatics of power, there is also the important issue of legitimation. The use of pamphlets to help justify the consolidation of royal power over the longer term is explored in the final two chapters of this book. Historians should remain circumspect about public opinion in this context. We can do little to reconstruct empirically the aggregate of individual attitudes in seventeenth-century France, and

52. Habermas, "Arendt's Communicative Concept of Power," 3–24.

53. Macdougall, *Understanding Public Opinion*, describes a framework that has been widely used to generate and analyze political propaganda. Cf. Laswell, *Propaganda Techniques in World War I*. This basic method has been sharpened over the years in three important ways, (1) by more rigorous quantitative analysis, (2) by the addition of a more subtle psychology of motivation, and (3) by more attention to the social and cultural dimensions of "communications." The literature on the media and "verbal behavior" in politics is now vast. Among the studies I found most useful were George, *Propaganda Analysis;* Ellul, *Propaganda and the Formation of Men's Attitudes;* Meuller, *Politics of Communication;* and Pye, "Introduction," 3–23.

54. Baker has called Habermas's work "the indispensible analysis" on the subject of the public sphere in "Politics and Public Opinion." He has in mind especially Habermas's *Strukturwandel der Öffentlichkeit,* 42–69, 76–101, 112–127, 278–294. See also Hohendahl, "Jürgen Habermas: 'The Public Sphere' (1964)," 45–47 (followed by a translation of Habermas's own summary of his theory, pp. 49–55); and "Critical Theory, Public Sphere and Culture," 89–118. Habermas now considers *Strukturwandel der Öffentlichkeit* an early work differing markedly from his current philosophical concerns; see Habermas, *Autonomy and Solidarity,* 149–189.

even if we could, many problems would remain. How can the opinions of a public manipulated by those in power be counted as authentic? Can those who were excluded from political life have had "public opinions" in any significant sense? The concept of "the public sphere" holds an important advantage over that of public opinion because it addresses the more concrete framework of communication and patterns of discourse that guided and sanctioned political behavior.

Any investigation of the specific functions of printed propaganda presupposes a method of interpreting texts. My own approach is best characterized as rhetorical. The emphasis is not on style and figures of speech, but on the ways in which pamphlets were designed to influence the perceptions and manipulate the behavior of an audience.[55] My analysis of pamphlet discourse is intended more to reconstruct the communicative relationship between pamphleteers and their readers than to delineate the conceptual universe of popular political thought as a whole. What this means, exactly, will be better illustrated in the chapters that follow. There were in fact many genres of seventeenth-century pamphlets. Harangues, discourses, letters of advice, and other forms of polemic can be classified and analyzed as arguments in the formal sense. These texts can be profitably sifted through the grids of classical rhetorical theory and modern theories of argument.[56] Other pamphlets, often in verse or in a satirical vein, are better classified as literary productions, less calculated to persuade than to entertain. The use of rhetorical and poetic devices in the pamphlets is wide-ranging and skillful, and interpretation requires careful attention to authorial strategies and exact contexts. For help in sorting out such matters, I have often found helpful the work of Louis Marin, Stanley Fish, and other modern theorists.[57]

This book steers away from the analysis of political events as a sequence of development. My primary concern is not with political or ideological change over time, even though I believe pamphlets played an important role in the long-term political development of France. I emphasize the basic point that I believe is essential to further investigation—namely, that the production and dissemination of print were fun-

55. The following practical and theoretical works have been especially useful: Brandt, *Rhetoric of Argumentation;* Auerbach, *Mimesis;* Burke, *Counter-Statement* and *Rhetoric of Motives;* Duncan, *Language and Literature in Society;* Booth, *Rhetoric of Fiction;* and Hirsch, Jr., *Validity in Interpretation.*

56. Perelman, *Champ de l'argumentation,* and with Olbrechts-Tyteca, *New Rhetoric.* See also Toulmin, *Uses of Argument.* See Angenot, *Parole pamphlétaire,* 9–14, 28–45, 145ff., for a theoretical differentiation among three basic strategies of persuasion—polemic, invective, and satire. An adaptation of Angenot's categories to seventeenth-century French pamphlets by Walker, *Typologische und terminologische,* came to my attention too late for integration into this study.

57. Marin, *Récit est un piège,* and *Portrait du Roi;* Fish, *Self-Consuming Artifacts.*

damental to the political process in France long before the age of periodicals and newspapers. In a national political struggle to influence the personnel and policies of royal government, publishing strategies and tactics were essential.

In order to clarify how Frenchmen understood the public dimension of their political system, chapter 1 explores the conceptual framework and social context of pamphleteering in the early seventeenth century. Chapter 2 explains more specifically the political dynamics of the 1614–1617 conflict and the strategic role played by pamphlets in the struggle for power. Chapters 3 and 4 focus on production, distribution, and censorship in order to clarify to whom and to what extent pamphlets were accessible. In these two chapters I seek to integrate recent work on the history of the publishing business (distribution, the cost of pamphlets, and the social status of readers) with my own archival study of distribution networks, the mechanics of censorship, and local politics. Chapters 5 and 6 explore from two different perspectives the audience and its reaction to the pamphlet campaigns. Chapter 5 investigates the use of invective and satire for persuasive purposes. Chapter 6 unravels some of the formal arguments about the alleged absolute power of the king and explores how absolutist rhetoric dominated the political arguments in the 1614–1617 pamphlet wars.

The final chapter concludes with an analysis of the long-term significance of the processes at work in the 1614–1617 crisis, and the government's reactions. This part of the argument is obviously haunted by our recognition that something "went wrong" in the Old Regime. Already by the middle of the eighteenth century the *philosophes* were regularly and openly criticizing the closure of the French political system.[58] With eyes often on England, they were intrigued by a freer press and representative assemblies. The importance of public opinion was asserted with increasing intensity after 1770 and was ultimately translated into the radical demands in 1789 for full freedom of the press and a republican form of government.[59]

In his analysis of the *ancien régime* several decades after the Revolution of 1789, Alexis de Tocqueville had the insight to focus on some important details of public political participation and to ask why "despotic" centralized power and the elimination of a public political sphere went hand in hand. The answer, he concluded, was that people were so completely prohibited from taking part in politics and from political expres-

---

58. Ozouf, "L'Opinion publique," 424–426.
59. "Declaration of the Rights of Man and of the Citizen" (1789), article 11. See also the analysis in Baker, "Politics and Public Opinion."

sion that they hardly had any legitimate political opinions. "In no other country of Europe," wrote Tocqueville, "had all political thought been so thoroughly and for so long stifled as in France: in no other country had the private citizen become so completely out of touch with public affairs and so unused to studying the course of events."[60] Tocqueville felt that without a functioning political sphere in which to "practice" politics, even the elites of the Old Regime could not organize into effective political pressure groups or influence government policy through the mobilization of public opinion.[61] When the effort to restore a truly public political sphere was finally made during the Revolution, the result was so chaotic precisely because the new class of leaders lacked political experience.

This insight into the weaknesses of the public sphere is essential to understanding the Old Regime and must be read back into our interpretation of its political development. There was a public, and it had opinions. But what did it matter? The history of pamphleteering helps explain at least part of the story. For roughly three hundred years pamphlets were a principal vehicle for public political discourse in Old Regime France. Understanding how they functioned, on the one hand, as instruments of manipulation and oppression and, on the other, as a medium of authentic public debate that expanded and contracted under different circumstances should tell us a great deal about political power.

60. Tocqueville, *Old Regime and the French Revolution*, 205.
61. Ibid.

ONE

◆ ◆ ◆

The Public Sphere in
Early Seventeenth-Century France

The slander of those who are employed in the management of public affairs is a sweet and agreeable poison that slips easily into our minds. And, once they are so contaminated, it is very difficult for our minds to admit the truth.

Pierre Jeannin, one of Marie de Médicis's principal councillors, published the above remarks in a 1615 pamphlet. His reply was part of an exchange initiated by the duc de Bouillon, who had published a pamphlet impugning the trustworthiness and fiscal policies of the queen mother's government.[1] Jeannin's response, in essence, accused the duke of publishing propaganda to serve his own ends. The queen's councillor used a telling metaphor in his counterattack—slander is described as a "poison" capable of "contaminating" (or "infecting") the minds of the people.

Although seventeenth-century Frenchmen had no exact synonym for our modern term "propaganda," they were deeply aware of the manipulative power of words and information. The far-reaching effects of this genuine respect for and fear of political discourse, and the resulting impact on political behavior, have not been clearly understood. An awareness of the power of discourse profoundly affected the intense national conflict from 1614 to 1617. It is impossible to grasp the motives and intentions of the pamphlet authors and sponsors involved without a better appreciation of the conceptual world in which they worked.

It was common in the seventeenth century to view politics as a process whereby one gained or lost influence through managing the perceptions (*impressions*) of others. In their efforts to position themselves as highly as possible in the sociopolitical hierarchy, political elites were greatly preoccupied with public display—where they sat, stood, or walked in public ceremonies, what they wore, and the splendor of their public appear-

1. *Mercure françois* 4 (1617):90–110, summarizes the exchange of pamphlets in June 1615, and gives extensive quotations.

ances.[2] There is abundant testimony to the seventeenth-century belief that manipulating public perceptions through the printed word was especially effective, and therefore perilous. One author expressed the danger this way in 1615.

> There is nothing these disturbers of the public peace have not tried; no means have they failed to set in motion, nor tricks have they failed to employ in order to succeed in their pernicious designs. The easiest way to arrive at their ends, they imagined, was to denigrate the administration of [government] affairs through slanderous pamphlets [*libelles diffamatoires*], which contain as many capital crimes as words, and whose . . . authors merit nothing less than the flames.[3]

Reputations were ruined by scandal and disgrace, just as they were enhanced by the right kind of discourse. A good name protected one's power and influence. In a chapter of Cardinal Richelieu's *Testament politique* devoted to the analysis of power (*puissance*, not *pouvoir*, which is better translated as 'authority'), we read that "the Prince ought to be powerful through his reputation. . . . Reputation is so necessary to a prince that he of whom one has a good opinion does more with his name alone than those who are not well thought of [can do] with armies."[4] The measure of a prince's power was the extent of his glory (*gloire*).[5]

Obsessed with their public images, seventeenth-century Frenchmen developed elaborate tactics to create and reinforce their reputations.[6] They struggled to establish a good name (*nom*), and worked to suppress any rumors (*bruits*) or slanders (*médisances*) that might undermine their prestige. There were deep cultural and psychological links between this view of one's public image and the study of rhetoric. The fashionable predilection for rhetoric among educated men and women in the seventeenth century is well known, but the association of rhetoric with ceremonial orations and *belles lettres* has in some ways concealed the impact of this training on the politics of the age. A rhetorical conception of language carried with it important implications about communication. By definition, rhetoric was the strategic use of language for the purpose of achieving a desired impact on one's listeners or readers. Political discourse self-evidently fit into such a conception. Not so self-evident was

2. See Giesey, "Models of Rulership"; Hanley, *"Lit de Justice"*; Bryant, *King and the City*, 21–50, 99–124; and Jackson, *Vive le roi!*, 3–23, 115–173, 206–215.

3. *Avertissement à la France touchant les libelles* (1615), 5–6.

4. Richelieu, *Testament politique*, 373; "La réputation est d'autant plus nécessaire à un prince que celui duquel on a bonne opinion fait plus avec son seul nom que ceux qui ne sont pas estimés avec des armées."

5. Cf. Ranum, *Artisans of Glory*, 103–277; and Marin, *Portrait du Roi*, 49–115.

6. Jouhaud, "Duc et l'archevêque," 1017–1039.

the deeply rooted tendency to view the world of political action in rhetorical terms.[7] Politics, like rhetoric, had a necessarily public dimension, and was composed of strategies perpetrated upon audiences.

RHETORIC AS POLITICAL ACTION

Witnesses to the propaganda campaigns of the early seventeenth century were particularly disturbed by the quantity and viciousness of the pamphlets. Responding to pamphlets attacking some great noblemen in the period from 1614 to 1617, one author wrote, "one has never seen written such an hysterical attack on the honor of the Princes. A single day does not go by that does not bring forth some little book full of injuries and slander [*médisance*]."[8] The author continued, "What ink has not been used to stain and blacken their reputation?. . . What devices and fabrications have not been used to give a bad impression of their rights and praiseworthy intentions?"[9] Supporters of the other side had the same complaint, as illustrated by the passage from Jeannin's pamphlet quoted at the outset of this chapter.

The seventeenth-century vocabulary for describing these publishing practices reveals a complex interplay of rhetorical concepts on the one hand and legal notions akin to defamation and seditious libel on the other. Politicians and pamphlet authors commented frequently on the calculated dissemination of *bruits* and *libelles diffamatoires* and worried about the *mauvaises impressions* that these caused among the people. *Bruit* was a general term, frequently used to refer to political rumors or disturbances; it referred especially to public clamors or outcries, common tales, and the talk among the people.[10] The phrases *faire courir un bruit* and *semer un bruit* were commonly used to describe the acts of spreading political news or rumors with the potential to create a public disturbance, but did not necessarily refer to printed propaganda.[11] Another common

---

7. Brown, "Language as a Political Instrument."

8. *Discours sur les calomnies* (1614), 9.

9. Ibid., 5.

10. Cotgrave, *Dictionarie of the French and English Tongues*, s.v. *bruit*.

11. In a letter to Cardinal de Sourdis, 29 February 1614, Pontchartrain wrote, "Le vice-senechal est ung tres mauvais homme d'avoir faict courir les bruicts que vous mandez" (Pontchartrain's spelling), B.N. Ms. fr. 6379, f. 189. In a letter from the queen regent to many provincial governors and lieutenants sent 13 February 1614, Marie mentions that "les bruits qui s'espandent et augmentent a ceste occasion pouroient produire de mauvais effects dans les provinces au prejudice du repos public," in *Correspondance de la mairie de Dijon*, 3:128. I owe this reference to James Farr, who assisted me greatly with archival work in Dijon. An anonymous pamphlet from 1615 mentions "tous les faux bruits qu'on a semez contre . . . [le] gouvernement," *Discourse*, B.N. Lb36. 878.

phrase, *publier un libel,* also referred to spreading false information either orally or in printed form.

Pieces of printed propaganda—leaflets, posters, pamphlets, or small books—were occasionally designated by neutral terms such as *billets, affiches,* or *livrets.*[12] But pamphlets were generally referred to as *libels* or *libelles diffamatoires.* Seditious and defamatory pamphlets were potent weapons of disorder, and politicians were thus often eager to punish the authors and printers of such literature. A special provision against pamphleteering was included in one section of a wide-ranging "peace treaty" reached in 1616 between the leader of a faction of rebel nobles and the government of Marie de Médicis. The section mandated a penalty of death for the authors of any "memoires, libelles diffamatoires, lettres, escrits, et livrets injurieux et scandaleux" of a political nature.[13] The article also expressly forbade the printing or offering for sale of any such material.

Such severe measures were usually softened, however, by a convenient double standard that left room for patronage and protection. The same article that stipulated the death penalty for the authors of pamphlets bowed to this double standard by granting amnesty to anyone guilty of writing, printing, or selling propaganda during the previous two years. The loophole was obviously designed to protect loyal writers on both sides who had been active in the recent pamphlet campaigns, many of whom, after all, were high-ranking clergymen and important advisers.

Attitudes toward pamphleteering clearly reflected the general opinion about public discourse and its place in political life—views rooted in both political experience and academic training. Especially for the generation of Frenchmen who had survived the Holy League (1583–1594), political oration was a powerful, even deadly, weapon. Nicolas Pasquier, a respected intellectual and thoughtful student of *éloquence,* wrote the following bitter indictment shortly after the assassination of Henry IV in 1610.

> The ability of a preacher to speak well is an attractive and valuable gift of nature which, augmented and cultivated by extensive use and study, provides clarity and beauty to the fair conceptions of his mind. . . . But, if he decides to abuse the sweetness of his language, there is no more terrible plague on a Kingdom than this well-spoken preacher . . . his tongue becomes a weapon of violence on which depends the life or death of those for whom and against whom he uses it.[14]

12. Hubert Carrier suggested to me that a *billet* was probably a handbill or leaflet and that an *affiche* was most likely something posted.

13. Article 42, Edict of Loudun, Bouchitté, ed., *Négotiations,* 738–739.

14. Pasquier, *Remonstrances tres-humbles* (1610), 44–45.

This lament and warning suggests that respect for the power of the printed and spoken word stemmed mainly from personal experience. The writings of Guillaume Du Vair, another student of rhetoric who had survived the years of the League, confirm this view. Political oratory of the wrong sort could "strangely deform, and even ruin, the whole of civil society."[15] Eloquence was one thing; demagoguery was quite another.

At the same time, Pasquier, Du Vair, and other students of rhetoric believed order, truth, and civic virtue in the realm of discourse would help support a realm of politics embodying the same qualities. Belief in the good of public discourse was borrowed in part from the Stoic authors (especially Cicero), whose treatises on rhetoric were then circulating widely in France.

Every educated person of the early modern era was familiar with the fundamentals of rhetoric as a discipline taught in the schools. The Renaissance inspired a great resurgence of interest in classical rhetorical theory and its implications for *belles lettres,* philosophy, and history.[16] Rhetoric was an important part of the curriculum of higher education; a year of rhetoric was often the finishing touch on five or six years of secondary education.[17] It was a subject for more advanced contemplation as well. The notion of *éloquence* was fundamental to the work of l'Academie français from the beginning.[18] Marc Fumaroli's massive study of treatises on rhetoric demonstrates how extensively sixteenth- and seventeenth-century scholars investigated the process of persuasion and the characteristics of *éloquence.*[19] Students of the subject devoted much time to the classical treatises—Aristotle, Cicero, Quintilian, and their followers, especially St. Augustine.[20]

The interest in rhetoric went well beyond aesthetics. The value of persuasion was obvious to the leaders of the Catholic church, who hoped to reconvert Protestants. And from still another angle, the study of rhetoric was important for developing what we might today call "social skills." In early modern elite society, where witty conversation, elegant letter writing, and effective public speaking were expected, *l'art de bien dire*

15. Du Vair, *De l'éloquence françois,* 151. Cf. Ranum, *Paris in the Age of Absolutism,* 35–47.

16. Seigel, *Rhetoric and Philosophy in Renaissance Humanism,* and Struever, *Language of History.* For sixteenth-century France, see Kelley, *Foundations of Modern Historical Scholarship.* For the seventeenth century, see France, *Racine's Rhetoric,* and *Rhetoric and Truth in France.* For England, see Shapiro, *Probability and Certainty.*

17. France, *Rhetoric and Truth,* 4, and Huppert, *Public Schools in Renaissance France,* 51–54.

18. Davidson, *Audience, Words, and Art,* 3–4.

19. Fumaroli, *L'Age de l'éloquence.*

20. Professor Fumaroli traces these influences throughout his book and provides an extensive bibliography of classical treatises printed toward the end of the sixteenth century and the beginning of the seventeenth century.

and *l'art de persuader* were important skills for any ambitious person to cultivate.[21]

When circumstances required it, a good citizen had a duty to use his understanding of rhetoric to move his fellow citizens into the proper state of mind by speaking out or publishing for the public good. Du Vair boasted that during the last years of the Holy League, Henry IV had asked him to compose an anti-League pamphlet favorable to the king's cause, which he did "under the name of an inhabitant of Paris, and in language suitable to this condition."[22] It was not unusual for Du Vair to exploit the somewhat complex rhetorical strategy of fictionalized political voice. He used the persona of a Parisian bourgeois in part because the League had used the same strategy with evident success to mobilize the Parisians against Henry. Rhetorical calculations of this kind generated an entire repertoire of stylistic and argumentative devices that were a central part of pamphlet warfare in the seventeenth century.[23] Rhetorical posture was as important as ideological content in conveying political messages. Persuasion, in the usual sense of convincing an audience of the truth of a particular proposition, was often less important than moving an audience to identify with the general worldview of a pamphlet as conveyed through its literary qualities.

A man such as Du Vair perceived his own use of rhetoric (in pamphleteering or public oratory) in high-minded Stoic terms, just as he envisioned his involvement in politics as arising out of transcendental values—goodness, justice, honor, and duty. The Stoic tradition, however, rested on an idealistic conception of the power of the virtuous orator to influence the political nation. This was as evident to many of Du Vair's contemporaries as it is to us, and they made fun of him later in his career as a deluded idealist fond of making great speeches but naive and ineffective in the world of ministerial politics. Yet French political culture was not amenable to Machiavellian strategies either. The author of *The Prince* hailed the importance of reputation as a basis of power and observed that in many cases a false reputation could function almost as well as a true one.[24] This kind of cynicism was generally rejected, or at least suppressed, in France, but no one rejected the notion of the political efficacy of a prince's reputation.[25] On the contrary, the need for princes, noblemen, and ministers to cultivate the affections of the people was

21. France, *Racine's Rhetoric*, 12.

22. Du Vair, *Les Oeuvres* . . . , 400–401.

23. Discussed more fully in chapters 2, 5, and 6.

24. Machiavelli, *The Prince*, quoted in *Machiavelli: The Chief Works and Others*, 3 vols., trans. Allan Gilbert (Durham, N.C., 1965), 1:57–68 (chapters 15–19).

25. Kelley, "Murd'rous Machiavel in France," 545–559.

taken to be a virtually self-evident political reality. The following passage, taken from a pamphlet published in 1614, illustrates the point.

> For even though they [nobles in opposition to the government] are princes [of France's royal house], so are they in some fashion subject to the people, and their prestige [*nom*] depends upon the esteem in which they are held. . . . So that I hold it necessary for all our princes [including the king] to communicate in a familiar way [*communiquer familièrement*] with their peoples, and from time to time appear before them in public actions where their virtue and skill can be seen.[26]

This passage also makes clear that the power of political communication depends not only on its eloquence but also on its strategic appropriateness. The rhetorical tradition shaped political discourse, in this context, by providing a way of strategically analyzing communicative practices embedded in French culture and society.

POLITICAL DISCOURSE IN THE PUBLIC SPHERE

The idea of a public sphere of discourse was hardly alien to French political thought of the time. Even Jean Bodin, the strident apologist for a strong, unified monarchy, clearly believed any viable commonwealth would have to contain a public sphere that was separate from the immediate jurisdiction of the sovereign.[27] This sphere, which he linked with civic life, was made up of many elements. The seventeenth-century English translation of Bodin's treatise provides a fascinating enumeration of these public institutions.

> But beside that soveraigntie of government thus by us set downe, as the strong foundation of the whole Commonweale; many other things besides are of citisens to be had in common among themselves, as their markets, their churches, their walks, ways, lawes, decrees, judgements, voyces, customs, theaters, wal[l]s, publick buildings, common pastures, lands, and treasure; and in briefe, rewards, punishments, su[i]tes, and contracts: all which I say are common unto all the citisens together, or by use and profit; or publick for everyman to use, or both together.[28]

26. *Le Serviteur Fidelle* (1614), 13–14.
27. Bodin, *Six Bookes of a Commonweale*, 203–210.
28. Ibid., 11. The French edition of 1583 reads as follows:

Mais outre la souveraineté, il faut qu'il y ait [dans une Republique] quelque chose de commun, et de public: comme le dommaine public, le thresor public, le pourpris de la cité, les rues, les murailles, les places, les temples, les marchés, les usages, les loix, les coustumes, la justice, les loyers, les peines, et autres choses semblables, qui sont ou communes, ou publiques, ou l'un et l'autre ensemble. (Bodin, *Six Livres de la République*, 14.)

Many things besides the power of the sovereign defined a common-wealth, and a commonwealth in which such public institutions and public "voyces" did not exist could scarcely be imagined.

Excessive license of speech was perceived as dangerous and would be curtailed in a well-run commonwealth.[29] But few (if any) political thinkers writing before the 1630s could envision a French state in which the king and his council would have complete control over all public communication. Such a view was possible in the mid-seventeenth century but virtually unthinkable in the age of Bodin, or of Pasquier and Du Vair.[30] In spite of the tendency of political theorists to envision the structure of monarchical political authority as a smoothly functioning, hierarchical chain of command emanating downward from the will of the king, they emphasized that the primary purpose of monarchical institutions was the good of the people.[31] To maintain his authority, a monarch had to act in accordance with reason and Christian morality, and to respect the traditions of the kingdom and the needs of the people. An anonymous pamphleteer writing in 1615 put it this way: "Kings, Princes, and Sovereign Powers have no more certain foundation for the establishment of their power and the safety of their persons than the affection and good will of their subjects."[32]

This view was much more than a platitude. Effective government depended at least in part, and in very concrete ways, on the goodwill of the governed. History had demonstrated this, and nowhere more clearly than in France during the decades of the religious wars. One of the great lessons drawn from the demise of Henry III was that a prince could not afford to alienate the affection of his subjects. When this happened, when the king's "reputation" was destroyed, he lost his ability to govern.[33]

Regardless of the monarchy's theoretical underpinnings, consultation with some subjects was often necessary in order for the king and his council to govern effectively. The hierarchical chain of command had to be interrupted periodically so that superiors could obtain the advice and consent of their inferiors. The convocation of regional estates, national estates (Estates General), assemblies of notables, and special meetings of the sovereign courts was often interpreted in this way—as consultative

---

29. Bodin, *Six Bookes of a Commonweale*, 543–544, 638, 642–645.

30. See the concluding chapter of this book.

31. Parker, "Law, Society and the State," 253–285; Mousnier, "Participation des gouvernés," 231–262; Richet, *La France moderne*, 37–59; and Keohane, *Philosophy and the State in France*, 79–82.

32. *Le Censeur, discours d'estat* (1615), 3.

33. One Parisian, Pierre L'Estoile, collected more than three hundred pamphlets against Henry III. Bellanger et al., eds., *Histoire générale de la presse française*, 1:67.

political assemblies convoked by the Crown to deal with particular problems of taxation, religion, and local discipline.[34] Such assemblies, despite their ambiguous constitutional status, provided a political forum for those who were not part of the central royal government.

The opportunity of advising the king, however, was perceived rather more as a privilege sanctioned by customary law than as a political right. (Even the claims of the nobility to political power were seen to rest more on their public office as seigneurs and military officials than on their birthright.)[35] The privilege of consultation was enjoyed by certain men because of their membership in corporate bodies—regional government, a town council, a sovereign court, the church, and so on. However, most opportunities to participate in the making of public policy through consultation were understood to be ad hoc—special opportunities brought about by specific political crises. This was especially true of meetings of the great national assemblies—the Estates General and Assemblies of Notables—where participation was increasingly limited to a few notables and magistrates of one kind or another. This select group was always aware of its mission to serve the local community (however defined) but did not see itself as representing the will of the people in a democratic sense. Just like the monarch, elites looked out for their own interests as well as those of the "realm," and for the "common good" or "the public good," in a general sense.[36]

Such views did not amount to anything like a commitment to freedom of political expression in the later, eighteenth-century sense. In fact the trend was in the opposite direction—because control of political perceptions was essential to the stability of the state, government control of information was vital.[37] Truth and candor in political discourse nevertheless had a certain value, and censorship had its limits. Again, the views of Bodin help to illustrate the constellation of attitudes. Despite his commitment to a strong monarchy and even to the basic principles of royal censorship, Bodin drew back from advocating the creation of an office of censor backed by royal power and authority. He states explicitly that the power of such a censor could become an instrument of tyranny.[38]

No one writing about politics in the early seventeenth century was comfortable either with the idea that government agents should control all manner of public expression, or with the notion that public speech should be completely free. One pamphleteer expressed this ambiguity in 1617 in the following way: he did not wish to be seditious, he claimed, but

34. Major, *Representative Government in Early Modern France*, 160–200.
35. Basdevant-Gaudemet, *Charles Loyseau*, 162–204.
36. Mousnier, "Participation des gouvernés," 231–262.
37. Soman, "Press, Pulpit, and Censorship," 439–441.
38. *Six Bookes of a Commonweale*, 646.

felt "obliged" to publish his "discourse of complaints" because it might help to bring an end to the "public calamities," explaining: "everyone [has] an interest in contributing to the public cause."[39] The "public cause" was a common theme for authors of pamphlets. Many claimed it was their sense of duty (as opposed to their individual or partisan interests) that forced them to criticize those in power. Another pamphlet started out in this vein:

> I freely confess that it is not my usual profession to take my complaints before the deliberations of the powerful, nor to discuss their plans and resolutions; nor do I here plan to speak of these matters except according to the laws of honor and modesty. But I am a Frenchman, through and through a Frenchman, who loves his King and the Queen Mother, . . . and it is in consideration of this love that I believe I am free of blame and crime if I speak a bit freely. I cannot dissimulate in the least concerning what I think ought to be discussed among good and natural subjects of a State.[40]

Clearly disingenuous on one level, such preambles suggest on another the genuine uneasiness about the boundaries of legitimate discussion. To discuss political matters that concern everyone was one thing the same author suggested. To pretend to put oneself on an equal footing with those in power was presumptuous and in bad taste. To insult those in power was, at the very least, slanderous and, mostly likely, seditious. Yet, the same author observed, it was equally irresponsible to not warn others of real dangers to the state or to mislead the powerful with falsehoods or banalities.[41]

PAMPHLETS IN THE PUBLIC SPHERE

Since the reign of Francis I it had been more or less illegal to publish pamphlet-type literature in France whenever religion or politics was involved. As pamphlet propaganda intensified during the religious wars, efforts to control it escalated accordingly, and the laws became increasingly specific.[42] During the reign of Francis II, a royal edict declared that "all producers of placards, handbills, and pamphlets that could tend to move the people to sedition, [including] printers, disseminators, and sellers of the said placards" should be considered "enemies of the Crown and of the public tranquility, guilty of lese majesty."[43] In 1571 a fairly

---

39. *Remonstrances faictes à Messieurs les Princes* (1617), 2.
40. *Discours sur les conferences faites* (1615), 4.
41. Ibid., 4–5.
42. Kelley, *Beginning of Ideology*, 213–251.
43. Much of this history is available in B.N. Ms. fr. 22061; the Edict of 1560 is excerpted in items #17, #18.

comprehensive ordinance regulating the printing industry was enacted. Article 23 of the edict called for the election of two master printers and four of the twenty master booksellers officially recognized by the University of Paris to supervise the "community." One of their jobs was to ensure that heretical, inflammatory, and libelous material not be printed.[44]

By 1614, therefore, censorship legislation had been on the books for more than half a century, although the legislation had proved generally unenforceable. The leaders of the publishing community were neither willing nor able to police their colleagues effectively. Suppression of printed material generally had to be initiated by the Crown or the sovereign courts, and during the conditions of civil war, censorship was partisan and irregular. Effective control of the printing industry did not begin until the 1620s, when Richelieu was finally able to enforce the law.[45] The key piece of legislation, interestingly enough, was a general *règlement* sponsored by the Parlement of Paris, that became law in 1618. The passage of this *règlement* was in part a direct response to the flood of pamphlets following the assassination of Henry IV and to the pamphlet campaigns of 1614–1617.

The concern with pamphlets suffuses the wording of censorship legislation of the 1610–1618 period. The attempt in 1610 to introduce a new regime of censorship resulted from the theological and political pamphlet wars of Henry IV's reign.[46] The importance of the 1618 legislation was not the novelty of its provisions—most of which had been established in one form or another in earlier edicts—but that for the first time the Crown, the Parlement, the university, the Châtelet, and the leaders of the printing trades had cooperated in establishing mechanisms to regulate and police the industry. Later, Cardinal Richelieu was able to extend the provisions of the Parisian edict to cover all of France during the course of the 1620s and 1630s. The 1618 *règlement* thus became the central piece of censorship legislation for rest of the seventeenth century.[47]

Meanwhile, the manufacture and dissemination of royal propaganda in pamphlet form was becoming a routine government function. Pamphlet literature was, in many respects, another avenue for reasserting the political commonplaces of royal propaganda—the dignity of royal persons, the excellence of the French monarchy, and other themes of the ancient mythology of kingship.[48] The general effort to strengthen royal

44. A printed copy of the edict intended for circulation in Paris, B.N. Ms. fr. 22061, item #25.

45. Martin, *Livres*, 1:54–57, and Barbiche, "Régime de l'édition," 1:369–375.

46. B.N. Ms. fr. 22061, item #47.

47. Martin, *Livres*, 1:54–57, 271, 441.

48. Bloch, *Royal Touch*, 198.

governments and legitimate their policies generated all kinds of propaganda—printed words and images, elaborate public ceremonies, painted
and sculpted images, sermons, funeral orations, ballets, and so forth.[49]

But pamphlets also constituted a literature of direct political engagement and an important medium of resistance to royal power. The anonymity of print afforded some protection against reprisal, and authors
were usually able to conceal themselves when they wished to do so.
Pamphlets thus provided a significant opportunity for public political
expression of ideas that otherwise would have been censored. It is hardly
surprising, then, that pamphlets accompanied every major political and
religious upheaval in seventeenth-century France.

Pamphlet wars were intense in France for many of the same reasons as
elsewhere in Europe. France's political press was more like England's
than has often been assumed. Partisans of the Gallican and Anglican
churches alike used much the same kind of polemical literature in their
struggle against Rome.[50] Religious nationalism and absolutism were
closely linked in both countries. The participation of highly motivated
and well-educated clergymen contributed to the double-edged use of
political pamphlets as a means both to legitimate and to criticize the
policies of the monarchy.[51] Religion was not, however, the only theme of
discontent. Foreign policy, fiscal policy, and social problems were woven
into pamphlet discourse.

The campaigns of the Fronde, during which the country was frequently on the verge of a civil war, were the most spectacular of the Old
Regime pamphlet wars, but they were hardly unique. Similar ones had
occurred periodically since the sixteenth century. Vicious and volumi-
nous pamphlet wars took place during the years of the Holy League,
when militant Catholics could dictate terms to Parisian printers. During
the reign of Henry IV important campaigns were waged over religious
matters, foreign policy, and Henry's treatment of the great nobility. As
noted earlier, Henry's assassination provoked a flood of pamphlet literature about him, his reign, and the possibility of an assassination conspiracy. The 1614–1617 pamphlet wars were brought about, as we shall see,
largely by a political revolt of great nobles. Still more barrages broke out
in 1619 and throughout the 1620s and 1630s. None of these earlier

49. Bardon, *Portrait mythologique;* and Hanley, "*Lit de Justice.*"

50. Salmon, "Gallicanism and Anglicanism," 155–188.

51. An excellent example of this duality is provided by the later years of the religious
wars in France. Robert Harding explores the themes of criticism in "Revolution and Reform in the Holy League," 379–416, and Myriam Yardeni looks into the themes of legitimation in *Conscience nationale en France.* On the earlier use of pamphlets, see Bellanger et
al., eds., *Histoire générale de la presse française,* 1:29–76; Febvre and Martin, *L'Apparition du
livre,* 412–455; Kingdon, *Geneva and the Coming of the Wars of Religion in France;* and Seguin,
L'Information en France de Louis XII à Henri II.

PAMPHLET PRODUCTION
1611–1653

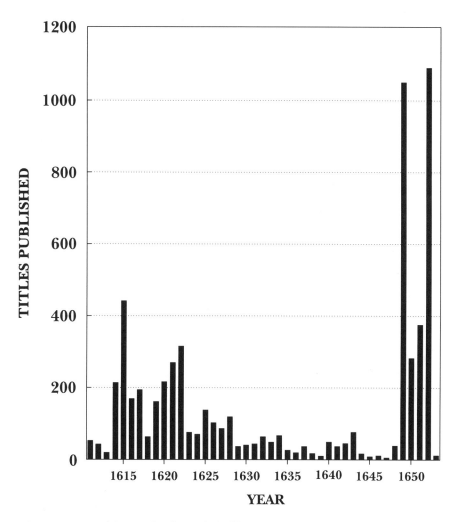

Figure 1. Pamphlet Production, 1611–53
This graph illustrates the relative intensity of pamphlet production by year. Each bar represents the largest number of pamphlets currently held in any single archival collection published in the year indicated, according to the following sources: Bibliothèque Nationale, *Catalogue de l'histoire de France;* Hélène Duccini, "Regard sur la littérature pamphlétaire en France au XVIIe siècle," *Revue historique* 260 (1978): 313–337; the microfilm collection *French Political Pamphlets* (Woodbridge, Conn.: Research Publications, Inc., 1979–1980); J. M. Hayden, "The Uses of Political Pamphlets: The Example of 1614–15 in France," *Canadian Journal of History* 21 (1986): 143–165.

pamphlet campaigns churned out as much paper and ink as did the Fronde, but many were as intense in other respects, including, for example, the severity of their attacks on government policy.

Some telling statistics about pamphlet production in the seventeenth century are illustrated in Figure 1. Pamphlet production corresponds very closely to the degree of political conflict at the national level. This relationship is also clear from the monthly and weekly fluctuations that Figure 1's annual tabulations do not show. Even within a particularly active year, production rose and fell in relation to major political occurrences.[52] These variations obviously reflected the efforts of pamphlet authors and their sponsors to achieve specific political goals. We begin, in the following chapter, to explore more carefully how in the specific context of 1614–1617 the production of pamphlets complemented and helped to form concrete, short-term strategies of political action.

52. Cf. Jouhaud, "Ecriture et action," 42–64.

TWO

◆ ◆ ◆

Political Tactics
and Rhetorical Strategies

So here [seditious pamphlets] is the wickedness they use to alter the desires of the people. They disparage the government of the State, and make the simple-minded believe that matters are in such a state of extremity—as if their writings were as true as they are calumnious!—that it would be legitimate for a subject to throw off the yoke of obedience that we owe our King. . . . This is the usual pretext of those who make trouble in the States.

—AVERTISSEMENT À LA FRANCE TOUCHANT LES LIBELLES (1615), 6

At the heart of the 1614–1617 political conflict was a contest for control of the king's councils, the central organs of royal power. The contestants were great nobles, powerful clergymen, and court favorites—Marie de Médicis and her supporters on one side, and the prince de Condé and his associates on the other.[1] Often, such struggles during the Old Regime were not national or even public political events, but personal contests for power among already formidable individuals.[2] The vast majority of Frenchmen did not ordinarily participate in such struggles, which would remain among the hundreds of court intrigues played out in the semi-private culture of the Louvre. The events of 1614–1617 were transformed into a national crisis by both sides, which sought to move the struggle beyond immediate, personal factions and to mobilize larger coalitions of political supporters. The opposition raised troops, took over provincial towns, and tried to generate support in the provinces. The ruling faction tried to prevent such developments by working hard to maintain the allegiance of key nobles, powerful royal officials, and the important provincial towns. Long-standing antagonisms between Protestants and Catholics complemented and intensified this process.

These political coalitions were formed for the explicit purpose of

1. The struggle up to the spring of 1615, with extensive discussion of economic and foreign policy, is analyzed by Hayden, *France and the Estates General*, 8–173. A detailed narrative account of politics at the French court during these years can be found in Zeller, *Minorité de Louis XIII*, and *Louis XIII*, both based heavily on diplomatic correspondence in Italian archives. On the dynamics of the king's council, see Mousnier, "Conseil du roi de la mort de Henri IV," 141–178; and Pagès, "Conseil du roi sous Louis XIII," 283–324. Among the primary sources listed in the bibliography, see especially Phelypeaux de Pontchartrain, *Mémoires concernant les affairs de France;* duc de Rohan, *Mémoires;* Bouchitté, ed., *Négotiations.* The *Mercure françois*, vols. 3 and 4, is indispensable.

2. Cf. Beik, *Absolutism and Society*, 59–116; Mettam, *Power and Faction*, 1–44.

dominating the state's political resources. It is true that great nobles and key officials stood at the head of extensive networks of private patronage and that these networks could be mobilized in a struggle for power.[3] However, the private political resources of even the most powerful nobles were meager compared with the vast resources of the state. Great personal power resulted from the ability of an individual and his network of clients and allies to dominate the machinery of government. Even the power of the Crown depended on such political networks. The king or the acting head of state could direct government only with the cooperation of great nobles, key ministers, provincial leaders, and royal officials. In effect, the monarchy governed through a ruling coalition whose members traded "service to the king" for the opportunity of monopolizing particular governmental operations. When this system broke down, monarchical government ceased to function.[4]

The strategy of the prince de Condé in 1614 and the other noble challengers was to precipitate a disintegration of Marie de Médicis's government by upsetting her ruling coalition. The minority of Louis XIII was an important backdrop to this challenge. A minor king and a regency government did not project the same kind of authority as an active, adult, unquestionably sovereign king. Condé had been trying to exploit this situation to his advantage. As "first prince of the blood," perhaps he even hoped to replace Marie de Médicis, queen mother and regent, as the king's principal adviser and acting head of state.

Condé had good reason to be resentful of royal power and eager to take part in political affairs. His father (Henry IV's cousin) and grandfather had been among the great Bourbon chiefs of the Huguenot party, whose victories on the battlefield had helped to make Henry a king. However, Condé was quite young when Henry abjured (1593) and became king of France at Chartres on 27 February 1594. While king, the older Henry IV never seems to have shown the young Condé much deference. In 1609 the prince felt obliged to flee to Spanish territory in Flanders to keep his young and attractive wife away from the attentions of Henry. Upon returning to Paris after Henry's assassination, he found himself more or less under the tutelage of his much older uncle, Charles de Bourbon, compte de Soissons. In turn, when Soissons died in 1612, Condé was somewhat isolated at Marie's court.

Eager to claim the political legacy of his family, Condé became increasingly impatient with court politics in 1613, when he perceived his

3. Kettering, *Patrons, Brokers, and Clients;* McKennan, "Gaston d'Orléans and the Grands."

4. Such dysfunction was, of course, a major cause of the prolonged civil wars following the death of Henry II, and the principal reason for the fate of Henry III; Ranum, *Paris in the Age of Absolutism,* 25–47.

Bourbon faction losing power. His views can be gathered from his notes for a speech that he hoped to deliver before Louis XIII at the assembled Estates General in 1614.

> [Upon my return to France following the assassination of Henry IV,] I found the Queen, your mother, in possession of the Regency, your person, and the Kingdom; I found the court divided into two factions and came to realize that the Queen, your mother, was from the beginning constrained for the health of your State to accord to the most powerful unjust benefits, contrary to your authority.[5]

He goes on to explain that he and the other members of the Bourbon family are members of the weaker faction and that the purpose of his actions is to restore a more appropriate balance to the councils.

More immediately, Condé and the challengers hoped to quickly mobilize enough public support to destroy the ruling coalition's sense of security, and hence its loyalty to the queen mother. Under these conditions key members might defect and the queen regent (and the faction at court that supported her) would yield to the challengers' demands, granting them more significant positions in the king's councils. Condé and his supporters believed such a turn of events would bring them greater personal political and financial opportunities, particularly enhancing their privileges and patronage powers as military governors of important provinces and towns.[6]

The defensive strategy of the ruling faction was somewhat different because its support network, in the form of the normal machinery of government, was already in place. The problem of the coalition in power was to maintain and reinforce its strength. There was no guarantee that the people "in the service of the king" would remain loyal if they began to view such loyalty as personally dangerous or as damaging to their political, social, and economic interests. The government therefore had to forward persuasive arguments and make political concessions. Equally important was the need to weaken the opposing coalition through intimidation, largess, and appeals to reason, religion, and principle.

5. "Harangue du Prince de Condé—1614," Musée de Condé, Chantilly, 1867/111.G.8 [Ms 910]. On the extensive power of Condé's rivals, the duc de Guise, his three brothers, and their allies, see Zeller, *Minorité de Louis XIII*, 88–118.

6. Condé and three of his five most important allies were governors of major provinces. Condé was governor of Guyenne; the duc de Nevers, of Champagne; the duc de Vendôme, of Brittany; and the duc de Longueville, of Picardie. Another sometime ally, the duc de Bouillon was a marshal of France, an even higher-ranking military office with functions much like those of a provincial governor. Harding's *Anatomy of a Power Elite* is essential for understanding the revolts of the great nobility in this period, giving more substance to the conventional view of the dissatisfaction among the great nobility following the death of Henry IV.

As part of this struggle to build and maintain coalitions, the production and dissemination of pamphlets functioned in several ways. One obvious way was as a channel of information. Both sides used pamphlets to inform potential supporters of essential political facts. In the initial stages of the conflict, key pamphlets put the public on notice that a struggle was indeed under way. Later, pamphlets conveyed information about the progress of the conflict—peace agreements, renewed fighting, the imprisonment of an important individual, the assassination of another. Just as important, pamphlets focused public attention on particular issues, actually defining or creating them in many instances.

Both major factions in the 1614–1617 conflict were competing for the loyalty or cooperation of large political interest groups, such as the Huguenots, the militant Catholics, the magistrates of the sovereign courts, the municipal elites of important towns, and the nobility. Both sides tried to represent themselves as having political intentions that would appeal to these specific groups by dramatizing issues, such as Louis XIII's marriage, in partisan ways. This was most obvious in Condé's recruitment of Protestants and in the efforts of the queen mother to mobilize strong Catholic support, but other interest groups were equally important. The most intense pamphleteering took place when both sides were preparing for the possibility of war. Pamphlets were used to help raise troops and the money necessary to field them and to gain the support of the provincial communities that would provide supplies.

Propaganda also affected the faction leaders. The existence of large numbers of widely circulated political pamphlets had an important impact on political calculations. The publication of Condé's manifestos of February 1614 and August 1615 had an enormous effect on the political elite. These publications, more than anything else, convinced those in control of the government of the seriousness of Condé's challenge. The style and content of Condé's propaganda also gave supporters of the queen mother, such as Villeroy, important clues as to the rebels' goals and how their challenge might be met. Pamphlet propaganda thus shaped and directed the struggle itself by influencing tactical planning.

Three features of the 1614–1617 campaigns illustrate the tactical uses of pamphlets especially well: (1) the relation of pamphlet production to key events, (2) the intensity of the rhetorical appeals used at key moments in the conflict, and (3) the tailoring of pamphlet rhetoric to appeal to various political interest groups. The political contest unfolded in a series of acts inseparable in meaning from the rhetorical contest in the pamphlet literature. Each important turn of events in the 1614–1617 struggle for power was rendered even more important by the significance invested in those events by pamphleteers.

GOING PUBLIC

In order to initiate their challenge, the princes, as they were called, left Paris in January and February 1614 to establish or renew political alliances in the provinces and to secure military control of some important towns and regions. Most of them headed for Champagne because the ducs de Nevers, Mayenne, and Bouillon had allies there. Their first act of organized violence was to force their way into the poorly garrisoned town of Mézières, a town within Nevers's military jurisdiction as governor of the province. Although technically a subordinate of Nevers, the captain of the garrison resisted the entry of the princes and their followers under direct orders from the local military governor of the town, an ally of the queen mother.

The prince's strategy at this point was to establish a base of military operations in the provinces that would pose a major political problem for Marie de Médicis. This threat would be used to force her to convoke an assembly of the Estates General and to grant other political concessions in exchange for a cessation of hostilities. Condé believed he and his allies would also be able to persuade the Estates General to endorse his usurpation of much of the queen mother's power. In particular, he hoped to convince the deputies at the Estates General to authorize a rearrangement of the composition of the king's councils, changes in foreign and domestic policies, and a postponement of the impending marriages of Louis XIII and his eldest sister, Elizabeth, respectively to Anne of Austria and Philip of Spain (Philip III's children).

With the deputies to the Estates General much in mind, Condé and his supporters publicized their revolt though a series of letters and pamphlets addressed to important people and centers of power. They attempted to favorably influence the public's perception of this protest by adopting the stance of political reformers concerned about the "good of the state" and "service to the king." *Double de la lettre escritte par monseigneur le prince de Condé, suivant le vray original. A la reyne regente, mere du roy, le 19. Fevrier mil six cens quatorze,* printed in Mézières, was the first pamphlet in this campaign.[7]

In sixteen pages Condé spelled out the reasons for his dissatisfaction with the political state of affairs in France, implying that the queen mother's indulgence (*bonté*) was the cause of many abuses. He said he was requesting a convocation of the Estates General because of these abuses. Condé called attention to his exalted nobility; he was in fact the highest-

---

7. There are several editions of *Double de la lettre* (1614). (Either the copy printed in Mézières or the original letter sent to Paris was quickly reproduced by several Parisian printers.)

ranking nobleman outside the immediate royal family. He suggested he was being excluded from his proper place in the government, which he characterized as being in the hands of a small faction that had usurped the king's authority with less of a claim to authority than he himself possessed. This faction, the prince asserted, had introduced dangerous innovations in foreign and domestic policy.

Condé's rhetoric was designed to appeal to a broad audience. He portrayed the queen mother's administration as scandalous, alleging that she and her advisers were in league with worthless financiers and judges: "men who enrich themselves without work on the blood of the people." Under their rule, "patronage, nepotism, and money" rather than merit "exercise all power." The queen mother's faction, the prince de Condé claimed, was overturning the wise and beneficial policies of Henry IV, a change in government policy that not only perverted the social order of the kingdom but also tarnished France's prestige among the other nations of Europe, a prestige that Henry had earned through his independent and tough-minded policies.

Condé's rhetoric anticipated the responses from the queen mother's pamphleteers. The pamphlet therefore warned that the government would portray the princes' actions as motivated by private interest. Condé anticipated that he would be called a rebel and thus underplayed the military dimension of his challenge to the government. He professed his loyalty and service to the king and the queen mother and sought to make a distinction between this personal loyalty and his legitimate grievances. The prince also tried to make a distinction between his duty to the king and the queen mother personally, and his challenge to those advisers, whom the pamphlet characterized as having usurped the king's authority and placed France in danger. The pamphlet also emphasized Condé's hoped for reform, not with arms in hand, but through the convocation of an Estates General. If the conflict escalated into a military confrontation, the pamphlet suggested, it would be the fault of the queen mother's pernicious advisers, not of Condé and his gentlemanly and princely associates.

Marie and her advisers moved quickly to fend off this challenge by keeping elements of their own coalition from joining the rebels.[8] In addition to concrete military measures, they responded in kind to Condé's pamphlet with a letter over the queen mother's signature, largely composed by Villeroy, the most experienced secretary of state and one of the

8. Hayden covers this thoroughly in *Estates General,* 54–73. The factionalism of the government's position is emphasized in a letter by Villeroy: "First of all take care that the Prince of Condé does not develop any authority in the council, nor any credit among the nobility," B.N. Ms. Colbert 17, f. 28 (see the following note).

most skillful diplomats of his age.[9] *Double de la responce de la royne regente, mere du roy, a la lettre escrite a sa majeste, par monseigneur le prince de Condé, le 19. Fevrier 1614* was first published as a pamphlet by two of the king's official printers and was afterwards reprinted a number of times by other printers.[10] A skillful piece of propaganda, it was designed at once to frighten people about Condé's challenge, defend the administration's policies, and undermine Condé's claim to be a champion of the public good.

Condé had claimed the royal government was in the hands of a self-serving faction; Villeroy asserted it was in the hands of people who right-fully represented the public interest and were working for the public good. Moreover, Villeroy suggested, the queen mother's principal advisers were the same men who had so skillfully aided Henry IV. He admitted there were many problems within the royal government and within France generally, but he questioned the rebels' commitment to reforms. If the regency had been such a disaster, why had Condé waited for four years to protest its policies? Moreover, could the prince be so naive as to believe that venality, for instance, had only just sprung up? If Condé and the other *grands* were interested in reforming the state, why were they out in the provinces causing more trouble? Why did they deprive the queen regent of their counsel, Villeroy asked, and force her into the humiliating position of having to bargain with or chastise her greatest subjects? As he argued along these lines, Villeroy tried to leave Condé with an honorable way to declare peace. He claimed the court recognized the good intentions of the princes and that the queen mother was eager to treat them in the manner fitting their rank.

Yet Villeroy also made it clear that Condé and his allies appeared to be engaged in nothing less than rebellion when they published letters criti-

---

9. For Villeroy's authorship of this pamphlet, see a second response proposed by Jean-nin, B.N. Ms. fr. 3712, ff. 73–80, which the copyist described as "a letter written in the name of the Queen Mother of the King, then Regent in France, by M. Jeannin to M. the Prince de Condé as a response to that which he wrote to Her Majesty in the month of February, 1614, on the subject of the disturbances then existing in France. This letter was not sent because M. Villeroy provided another which follows the present one." Villeroy also wrote two private letters of advice to the queen mother on how to handle the princes' challenge. Written very early in 1614, the first letter exists in three different copies—B.N. Ms. fr. 3712, ff. 1–12 verso; B.N. Ms. Colbert 17, ff. 28–31; and Bibliothèque Mazarine Ms. 2110, ff. 286–289 verso (none of the copies is in Villeroy's own hand). Mastellone has published the version at B.N. Ms. Colbert 17 in *Reggenza di Maria de Medici*, 229–234, reproducing the incorrect date "1611," which was erroneously written on the copy. Ville-roy's second letter of advice to the queen mother, dated 10 March 1614, exists in B.N. Ms. fr. n.a. 7260, ff. 123–129 verso, and has been published by J Nouaillac, "Avis de Villeroy," 79–89. On Villeroy's long, distinguished career, see Nouaillac, *Villeroy*.

10. Lindsay and Neu 3061. For nine other editions see 3062–3065, and 3072–3076.

cal of the government and tried to "give the subjects of the King a bad impression" of the regent's administration. Villeroy also exposed the duplicity of Condé's claim that he was angry with the advisers, not with the queen regent. Condé's attack on the loyal servants of the king, he implied, was an artifice employed to defame the regency and was thus an indirect attack on the very foundation of the government. Here Villeroy made clear that Condé really wanted much more than he claimed, and he was in fact trying to take control of the government by force.

Villeroy also tried to consolidate support for the queen mother's policies by rebutting Condé's attacks on her foreign and domestic policies. He defended the Spanish marriages as an alliance for peace, not a concession to Spanish power and Catholic militancy. He defended the regent's record of enforcing the edicts of pacification (which included the Edict of Nantes) protecting the Huguenots. The regent's primary political goal had been to keep France at peace and to maintain the king's state and his authority until he was old enough to govern himself. Any problems with the regency were unfortunate but necessary side-effects of this goal. Finally, Villeroy tried to ensure that Condé did not get credit for the convocation of the Estates General. He claimed the queen mother had intended to convoke the assembly in any case in conjunction with the king's coming of age later that year.

This initial exchange of pamphlets illustrates how much the assault on public opinion was an essential part of the political contest that dominated the next four years. We cannot follow, blow by blow, the ensuing charges and countercharges, but it will be useful to highlight some of the turning points in the campaigns. From beginning to end, both sides worked hard to project favorable impressions of the principal members of their factions, of their general policies, of their honesty, of their respect for the traditions of French political life, and so on. Both sides also shifted their strategies at key moments in an effort to maintain the upper hand in the battle for public opinion.

Initially, Condé hoped to capitalize on the ambiguity of his stance as a "loyal" challenger of the queen mother. By August 1615, however, after more than a year of trying to play by this set of rules, Condé hardened his position. In his campaign of 1615, Condé called attention much more directly to his effort to overthrow "this company of a few individuals who call themselves the King's council" and who had "usurped all the power in the Kingdom."[11] At this point he issued an open invitation to armed insurrection and stressed the need to oppose with force the completion

---

11. *Manifeste et justification* (1615), 18. *Declaration et justification* (1615), identical in content. The pamphlets are dated "à Coucy ce 19 jour d'Aout 1615." Jean Janon of Sedan was the original printer.

of Louis XIII's Spanish marriage.[12] He openly appealed to the Protestants and identified by name some of the individuals he wanted removed from the king's councils. The struggle had now escalated to a new level of violence in the sphere of public discourse; a concomitant escalation in the sphere of military activity would occur within several weeks.

Responding in kind, the queen mother's advisers published *Declaration du Roy contre le prince de Condé*, charging Condé and his associates with specific criminal and treasonous activities. Among the "treasonous" activities listed (in addition to forming a "faction" within the state, directing a "conspiracy" against the Crown, forming an army without the king's permission, and confiscating royal revenue) was the crime of having published "a scandalous manifesto tending to cause general sedition and revolt among our subjects."[13] At the same time, a large number of pamphlets celebrating the marriage was published in an effort to interest people in the new alliance between the two great Catholic monarchies and to fascinate the public with the pageantry of it all.[14] These promarriage broadsides were particularly well produced (high-quality printing on expensive paper) and must have done much to undermine Condé's attempt to block the marriage.

Having obtained one of her principal political goals, the queen mother became more flexible, and in early 1616 she allowed herself to be convinced by Villeroy that negotiations might be more to her advantage than continued civil war. A peace was declared, and pamphlets announcing the cessation of hostilities were published.[15] When the Treaty of Loudun (between the Crown and the rebels) was finally signed in 1616, pamphlets were also published that communicated much of the treaty's contents.[16] These pamphlets constituted a genuine campaign for peace and were designed more to demobilize the public—particularly the militant Catholics and Protestants, who were more interested in victory than in peace. For this reason, a series of pamphlets publicized the "confirma-

12. *Declaration de monseigneur, le prince* (1615), which came out several weeks later than the *Manifeste*, was a straightforward call to arms.

13. *Declaration du Roy*, 3 "Il publia un Manifeste scandaleaux et tendant à sedition et trouble general de nos subjects: et non content de ce, a faict et escrit en divers endroicts plusieurs lettres par laquelle il publie se vouloir armer pour s'opposer à nostredit voyage" (indicating the *Manifeste* of 1615 and the voyage to Bordeaux to accomplish the marriage).

14. The Bordelais printer Simon Millanges published more than a dozen such pamphlets; Desgraves, "Bulletins d'information," 31–33.

15. In January, *Ordonnance du roy* (1616). Then, from February through May a series of publications announced the prolongation of the "truce" and the continuing efforts to reach a lasting settlement at the conferences of Loudun; see Lindsay and Neu 3690, 3698, and 3703–3707.

16. In June, the settlement was announced in *Edict du Roy* (1616), followed by more pamphlets on the specific contents of the treaty.

tion" of the edicts of pacification that protected Protestants' civil rights and religious establishments.[17]

Each important turning point in the 1614–1617 political struggle was thus accompanied by a shift in pamphleteering strategy. The pamphlet campaigns were not a monolithic outpouring of traditional common-places, but purposefully designed verbal assaults intended to comple-ment overall political strategy. This careful maneuvering was especially evident as Condé tried first one approach and then another in his effort to gain credibility and support. The modulations in the government's propaganda were also important. These shifts in the tone, style, and content of pamphlets helped to structure the 1614–1617 conflict by de-fining and redefining the political issues in relationship to key interest groups.

AUDIENCE GROUPS AND RHETORICAL APPEALS

The pamphlet campaigns of 1614–1617 produced more than 1,200 ti-tles, some of which were printed in as many as eighteen editions.[18] Such a volume of words immediately raises the question of audience. Who read these pamphlets, and how were they read? These questions have to be approached from several directions. Obviously "technique"—the me-chanics of production, dissemination, and censorship—affected reader-ship in crucial ways. The technical aspects of the campaign, along with the problem of literacy, will be examined in chapters to follow. Much about the audience can also be learned from juxtaposing pamphlet rhet-oric with the strategic considerations discussed above. Pamphlets were *intended* to be read by certain audience groups.

In this section we shall focus on the intentions of pamphlet authors and their sponsors. This should help us to determine the politically signi-ficant target audiences. As has already been suggested, strategists tried both to politicize a broad, unspecified public and to mobilize (or placate) particular groups. What groups were envisioned as politically important during these struggles? What kinds of rhetoric were used to appeal to them? We can begin to form an idea from the letter of advice that Ville-roy wrote to Marie de Médicis on 10 March 1614. The aging secretary of state (a veteran of the civil wars of the sixteenth century) used a number of arguments to convince the queen mother that it would be wise to negotiate with Condé and the princes. Waging a war against them, he cautioned, might "put at great risk" the "authority and reputation" of the

---

17. *Declaration du roy sur les edicts de pacification* (1616).
18. Duccini, "Regard sur la littérature pamphlétaire."

king and her administration.[19] In the course of his letter, Villeroy enumerates the major interest groups that were still loyal to the queen mother's administration, and he advises the regent to be careful to keep them within her political coalition.

> [Your Majesty] . . . is faithfully assisted and served by a good number of great nobles, officers of the Crown, governors of provinces, gentlemen and lords of all conditions, as well as the Parlements, the other sovereign courts and royal officials, along with the magistrates and corporate organizations of the towns. [And] . . . you still have reason to hope that the Protestants as a body will not engage in these disturbances.[20]

These individuals and groups constituted Villeroy's political checklist of the most vital segments of the public, and he developed his political and propaganda strategies with them in mind. It was partly to maintain their allegiance in the face of Condé's challenge that Villeroy urged the queen mother to work for some genuine political reforms—cutting back on venal offices, suppressing the *droit annuel*, and restructuring the councils of the king.[21] In this way, Villeroy suggested, "you will give the public great satisfaction and reap the principal benefits" of public approval.[22]

The opposition faction of nobles had a similar conception of the politically important public. Among the closing lines of Condé's 1615 *Manifeste* was the following list of people and groups Condé hoped would join his efforts to "reform" the royal government and wrest control of the king's councils from the usurpers who ruled in the king's name.

> We pray and exhort all the princes, peers of France, officers of the Crown, seigneurs, *chevaliers*, governors, gentlemen, and others of whatever quality and condition they may be [as well as] all the Parlements, and all the orders and estates of this Kingdom, all the towns and communities, and generally all those who call themselves Frenchmen, and who are not yet joined with us, to come to our aid and assist us in a cause so just.[23]

Although Condé tried to catch everyone in this net and also devoted particular attention to groups within the nobility, the similarity between

19. Villeroy discusses at some length how the queen will best maintain her authority within the kingdom generally and especially over the subordinate institutions of the royal government; Ms. fr. n. a. 7260, ff. 125 and 127 verso (see n. 9 above).

20. Ibid., 123 verso.

21. Ibid., 129. Venality of office was widely detested, even within the judicial establishment which benefited from it; see Sawyer, "Judicial Corruption and Legal Reform," 95–117.

22. Ms. fr. n. a. 7260, 127; "[Il] servira grandement que Votre Majesté commence la premiere à mettre la main à ladicte reformation non en discourse et parolles seulement. . . . D'autaunt que vous contenterez grandement le public et recueillirez le principal fruict de ladicte reformation."

23. *Manifeste*, 37 (see n. 11 above).

the groups he identified specifically, and those mentioned by Villeroy, is striking. Those challenging the administration as well as the queen mother's advisers envisioned the politically important public as a composite of identifiable political interest groups whose support was necessary in order to gain or keep control the royal government and the state.

The pamphleteers working for both Condé and the queen mother therefore tailored their rhetoric to appeal to these designated interest groups.[24] The traditional nobility was an obvious target because of their importance to the military conflict and because of their chronic financial vulnerability.[25] An example of Condé's appeals to the nobility is evident in the following passage from his earliest pamphlet, the "letter" to the queen mother in February 1614.

> The nobility is impoverished by the *taille*, the salt tax, and extraordinary demands for money. All their revenues are burdened with tariffs. All their titles, even though lost and burned, are being investigated. The nobility, the foundation of France, . . . which once controlled the destiny of kings, is now taxed and banished from offices of justice and finance for lack of money. Their lives and their goods are under the control of others. They are deprived of the wages for the men of arms and the archers that they have traditionally maintained. And, they are now the slaves of their creditors.[26]

Such appeals to the nobility were countered by the queen mother's supporters in a number of ways. One was to remind the nobility how badly many of their families had fared during the civil wars of the sixteenth century. The author of *Le vieux Gaulois*, a proadministration response, had obviously read Condé's pamphlet and responded directly to his rhetoric.[27] "The nobility, which you exalt in order to win over through flattery" had no interest, the author asserted, in Condé's political program.[28] A true gentleman, the pamphlet claimed, didn't even pay the taxes mentioned in the prince's pamphlet.[29]

24. Despite Villeroy's urging that something be done about the venality of offices and the unanimous recommendation of all three orders at the Estates General that the *droit annuel* be suppressed, legislation renewing the *droit* was enacted in spring 1615, once the deputies had gone home. This was an obvious political concession to magistrates of the high sovereign courts, whose support the queen's administration badly needed.

25. The scramble for pensions and army commissions during these years was frantic. For example, a gentleman ally of Condé's (mentioned in chapter 4) was apparently willing to support the queen in May 1614 in exchange for a pension of two thousand écus and a commission in the royal army; B.N. Ms. Clair. 364, f. 131 (a letter from the bishop of Poitiers to Secretary of State Pontchartrain, 17 May).

26. *Double de la lettre* (1614), 8.

27. *Le vieux Gaulois* (1614).

28. Ibid., 9.

29. Ibid., 16; "Un seul vrayement Gentil-homme ne paye taille ny gabelle, si ce n'est qu'en acheptant le sel au prix que tout le monde l'achepte."

If it is true that debts have made the nobility slaves, it is also true that wars have been the cause of this. And if one considers their obligations and contracts, it might be found that the past League and rebellions against their rulers have been the cause [of their ruin], just as you [the princes] would like to happen again with your requests that they mortgage their lands for your defenses and their freedom for your [selfish] designs.[30]

Other pamphlets carried on in this same vein. In an appeal to any young nobles who might be attracted to the faction of the princes for the sake of adventure, another progovernment pamphlet warned, "Oh! How difficult it must be for young men brought up on the delicacies of courtly life to imagine the evils of civil wars and the enterprises against royalty!"[31]

In Condé's manifesto of 1615, we find passages specifically directed at other interest groups on his list. The Parisian bourgeoisie, the magistrates of the Parlement of Paris, and the Huguenots were the most frequently and directly targeted. The principal technique used here was to to elicit doubt and fear concerning the policies of the queen mother's administration. A passage aimed at the Parisians accuses the faction in control of the government of having decided "to disarm the Parisians, to change the captains of the *quartiers*, to prohibit the placement of chains across the streets in order to weaken the forces of the city, and to garrison the Swiss [mercenaries] and other troops there."[32] In an effort to appeal to the magistrates of the Parlement, Condé's manifesto included a long account of the Crown's abuse of the "great and wise Company." The pamphlet takes the magistrates' side in an account of the struggle between the Parlement and the Crown after the closing of the Estates General, charging that the queen mother's ministers had declared "the Parlement incompetent to represent to the King the evils and disorder that every day increase the afflictions of his subjects and the dissipation of his state."[33] Passages such as the following one were designed to win support from the Huguenots.

> Those of the protestant religion, who only desire their peace under the guarantees of the edicts of pacification, proclaim loudly that the marriages are being advanced during the youth of the King . . . . before he would be able to understand that the protestants are useful members of his state. And in the mean time, those who desire the protestant's ruin completely control the King's power and authority, a victory that has been celebrated in Spain and proclaimed by a Jesuit in Paris a few days ago.[34]

30. Ibid., 17.
31. *Remonstrance aux mal contens* (1614), 14.
32. *Manifeste* (1615), 15.
33. Ibid., 17.
34. Ibid., 25.

The queen mother's supporters countered by defending her policies and by characterizing the princes' use of such issues as "pretexts" for their revolt. The authors of proadministration pamphlets also tried to frighten (or placate) the same audience groups. They sought to undermine any appeals to the Parisians with reminders of the hardships they had suffered during the League, "which forced them to taste delicious morsels of horses, dogs, and rats, . . . the price one pays for sedition."[35]

Because some of the queen mother's advisers (particularly Villeroy) were eager to calm the Huguenots, their official propaganda did not try to stir up Catholic antagonism. The administration's most militant supporters had no such scruples, however. They accused Condé of stirring up the "party chiefs" of both religions, men who wanted nothing more than to lead France down the road to civil war.[36] Cardinal Du Perron published a letter addressed to Condé in which he warned the prince "to be on guard against spirits that are volatile and anxious for innovations, and who will only abuse the occasion of your departure from the Court to light a fire that will be easier to prevent than to extinguish."[37] This was a diplomatic way of saying the Protestants would try to use Condé's revolt to start a civil war.

Just as Condé and his associates hoped to arouse the indignation of magistrates and financiers by complaining about the administration's fiscal mismanagement, the queen mother's supporters worked to placate these groups. In the spring of 1615 one of Condé's wavering supporters, the duc de Bouillon, published a pamphlet with detailed criticisms of the Crown's policies, especially its financial policies. Within a few days, Pierre Jeannin, the chief minister of finance, published a long and surprisingly detailed rebuttal.[38]

Propaganda also focused on concerns that transcended particular groups. For example, both sides invoked the "public good" in a general

35. *Manifeste et Declaration de la France* (1615), 6–7.

36. *Response pour la royne* (1614); and *Libre harangue faicte par Mathault* (1614).

37. *Lettre de monseigneur le cardinal du Perron* (1614), 7. The Protestant-Catholic polemics of this period closely resemble the arguments between the *dévot* and *bon françois* parties that became more clearly defined in the 1620s, as documented in Geley, *Fancan et la politique de Richelieu*, 5–24, and Church, *Richelieu and Reason of State*, 117–126. For a discussion of the Catholic church's favorable attitude toward the queen generally, see Tapié, *France de Louis XIII et de Richelieu*, 96–134. Protestant support for Condé was much less energetic, despite the long service of his family in the Protestant cause. As a child, Condé had officially abjured (along with Henry IV), but, more important, his actions in 1614 suggested to key Protestant leaders such as Sully, Rohan, and Lesdiguières that the prince was not genuinely interested in their causes nor likely to accomplish much. Cf. Clarke, *Huguenot Warrior*, 48–69.

38. The exchange was reproduced at length in *Mercure françois* 4:98–112 (see chap. 1, n.1). Bouillon, a Protestant, was trying to use Condé's revolt to strengthen both his own position within the king's councils and his leadership in the Protestant community.

and abstract way. Pamphleteers argued that the leaders of their faction were sincerely interested in this public good, and that the leaders of the opposing faction were acting contrary to it. These appeals were aimed at anyone who had feelings about what was good for himself, the welfare of his own family and community, and possibly his country. After religious propaganda, Villeroy saw this rhetorical battle over who represented the "public interest" and the "good of the state" as the second most dangerous aspect of the 1614–1617 pamphlet campaigns. Only the appeal to the Protestants was riskier. After Condé's first pamphlet was published, he warned the queen mother that it was essential to counteract the "pretexts" of religion and of the "public good" that Condé had "put into play."[39]

The accusation that under the direction of the queen mother the government was acting against the country's general interests was in fact a key element in the princes' rhetoric. We have already seen some of this in Condé pamphlets. His 1615 *Manifeste* contains the most explicit charge, accusing Marie and her advisers of using public office for personal aggrandizement and of caring nothing about France or her people. In the king's council, they deliberated "every day in the name of His Majesty, on all kinds of propositions tending to the oppression of the people and the dissipation of the State."[40]

Pamphleteers supporting the challengers also claimed the abuses of the administration were not simply a matter of selfishness, graft, and corruption but, rather, represented the perversion of the entire governmental process. *Le Protecteur des Princes. Dédie à la Royne*—one of the most skillful anonymous pieces supporting Condé in the 1615 phase of the conflict—contains a long list of these "perversions."[41] The author was able to capitalize on the failure of Marie and her advisers to enact a single reform following the Estates General of 1614–1615. The queen mother and her advisers had "committed treason against public society" and "dissolved the fabric of public order" with their dishonest and criminal activities. They corrupted the deputies of the Estates General, violated

---

39. "[To oppose Condé with military force] could greatly endanger sovereign authority, and the means and property of all the King's subjects. It could give reason to the Protestants to join their forces as a group to those of my Lord the Prince and his adherents, or, indeed, move the Prince to join their party in order to fortify with the pretext of religion the cause of the public good which he has put into play; the consequences of this would be much more dangerous than the present situation." Letter, 10 March 1614 (see n. 9 above), f. 125.

40. *Manifeste* (1615), 18.

41. *Protecteur des Princes* (1615).

the sanctity of Condé's household (by recruiting one of his gentleman clients as a spy), and allowed France to become the prey of foreigners. The reestablishment of the *droit annuel* in violation of an alleged promise to the deputies of the Estates, the author argued, was a flagrant example of this perfidy: "Ha! how well the public's trust is preserved."[42]

To combat such rhetorical appeals to the "public good," the queen mother's administration defended its integrity, motives, and policies. As Cardinal Du Perron put it nicely in one of his pamphlets: "there is no government so perfect that one cannot find in it something to complain about."[43] Du Perron and other pamphleteers emphasized that the queen mother had the interests of France and her people at heart, that she had tried very hard to satisfy everyone, that she kept the country at peace during the minority of the king (always a dangerous situation) while maintaining the king's authority and his state intact.[44] The purpose of the Spanish marriages was not to give Spain any power over France, but to keep the two kingdoms from going to war again, an occurrence that would cause much misery among the king's subjects. By way of a counter-attack, Marie's pamphleteers blamed the major disorders in the kingdom on the recklessness and ambition of the princes, who had brought confusion rather than relief to the people. What did this say about their concern for the public good? these authors asked pointedly.

The queen mother's supporters also sought to emphasize her legitimate right to act as sovereign, or at least as head of state. She had been legally selected as regent of France, they noted, which gave her the right to exercise the sovereign authority of her son. She, and not the princes or the Estates General, decided what was in the best interests of France. "Since the Queen was legitimately and solemnly declared Regent, we need no other touchstone for the public good than her will and authority."[45]

The queen mother's harsh treatment of the rebels and her extraordinary military expenditures were characterized as judicious, restrained, dignified, reasonable, just, and more than necessary in view of the military maneuvers of the princes. These rebels, not the administration, were tearing apart the fabric of society by teaching the general population disrespect for and disobedience to legitimate sovereign power.[46]

The Crown's most intense and apparently successful rhetorical tactic was to undermine in every possible way the princes' claims to be acting in

42. Ibid., 21.
43. *Lettre de monseigneur le cardinal du Perron* (1614), 4.
44. In addition to *Le vieux Gaulois*, cited above, *Response pour la royne à monsieur le prince* (1614) was one of the best-argued pamphlets in this vein.
45. *Resolution à la paix* (1614), 8.
46. *Discours sur le traité de Soissons* (1614).

the public good. And if reform were not their motive, the pamphleteers speculated, what was? Obviously, Marie's authors suggested, their own private ambitions. Thus, in addition to explaining away Condé's accusations of abuses within the government, the queen mother's pamphleteers professed to be outraged that the princes were willing to provoke a civil war for essentially selfish reasons. Condé was charged with wanting to control rather than to reform the state.[47] This allegation was intended to convince people how little the princes cared for the public interest and also to frighten people into supporting the administration.

As part of this strategy, pamphleteers supporting the queen mother made a concerted effort to keep the unpleasant consequences of war fresh in the minds, not only of the Parisians, but also of their provincial readers as well. Lurid descriptions of the treatment that provincial people received at the hands of rebel armies were common:

> The people ought not to hope for any relief from your enterprise. . . .
> During peacetime the arms and noses of women are not cut off after they
> have been violated, as recently happened around Soissons; . . . [tax collec-
> tors] have never beaten with batons those who, having nothing of value,
> could not pay what they owed; in peacetime, the cruelest judges do not
> banish peasants from their houses, as is now being done in Champagne.
> The peasants choose the company of wolves and serpents in the woods and
> caves, rather than your soldiers in the villages.[48]

PROPAGANDA AND POLITICAL COALITIONS

The struggle for power between the administration of the queen mother and the faction led by the prince de Condé involved a form of party politics. Success in the struggle was predicated on successful coalition building. The coalitions were more nebulous than those of the sixteenth century because the Protestant-Catholic and Guise-Bourbon rivalries did not always fall along the same axis. Condé attracted some Protestant militants because of his famous Huguenot ancestors. But he did not at first intend to become, and never succeeded in becoming, a leader of the Protestant community. The Guise family maintained close ties to militant Catholic leaders, although a younger member, the duc de Mayenne, joined the opposition at several points. Religious issues and family ties were important, but more specific concerns motivated many of those who took part in the conflict. Ties between specific localities and great patrons within the government or church were of particular importance.

47. *Le vieux Gaulois* and, even more vehemently, *Le Franc taupin* (Paris, 1614), Bibliothèque Mazarine 37279, piece 31.
48. *Le vieux Gaulois*, 18.

This change in national politics shifted the emphasis away from dynastic and religious issues toward factionalism and the struggle for royal patronage. Religious discord remained a vital part of the political scene, but the points at issue were more narrow and specific. The new pattern of national struggle could still result in civil war, but in the seventeenth century such wars were remarkably limited in duration.

Printed propaganda took on a more definite role in this context. From 1614 on, both sides tried to reinforce and to build their political coalitions by involving the most important individuals and political interest groups. Pamphlet authors and political leaders strategically aligned their causes with the concerns of key groups—the nobility, religious militants, officers of the sovereign courts, and municipal officials. They worked hard to influence the general public's perception of the conflict as well. Experienced tacticians such as Villeroy realized that the confrontation would actually be won in the sphere of public opinion before it was won on the battlefield.

Pamphlets had to circulate among the right audience, not just in Paris, but throughout France, in order to be influential. For this to happen, reliable networks responsible for the publication and dissemination of pamphlets had to be in place. If opposition literature were to be effective, then government censorship had to remain ineffective. We turn to these considerations next, but they are only preliminary. What actually happened when a partisan pamphlet arrived in a provincial community? How accurately can we reconstruct the psychology of politicization and determine the issues that really motivated partisan political action?

◆ ◆ ◆

THREE

The Production and Distribution of Pamphlets

Madam,
We received on the 21st of March your letters of the 6th of March along with the printed copies of the letter from Monsieur the Prince and the response by Your Majesty that you have been pleased to send us. Even though this was a holy Friday . . . your above mentioned letter [the queen's published response to Condé] was turned over to the printer so that everyone could more easily gain an understanding of this communication. We [the Chambre de l'Edit of Castres] also handed down a decision prohibiting the dissemination of any false rumors, or the publication of any writings tending to alter the public tranquility.
—ANTOINE DE LESTANG, PREMIER PRESIDENT DE LA CHAMBRE DE L' EDIT,
1 APRIL 1614

Our investigation of propaganda strategies and tactics in early seventeenth-century France demonstrates that politicians believed strongly that pamphlets affected a broad and important audience. How widely did pamphlets actually circulate? Although severe in its punishments and stifling in many ways, censorship was evaded with relative ease. But because pamphleteering was generally a clandestine activity, direct evidence concerning authorship, production, and dissemination is scarce. A reliable picture of pamphlet production and distribution can therefore be pieced together only by drawing on several different sources. Pamphlet title pages often reveal information about the city or locale of publication. Information on the circulation of pamphlets can be found in the diplomatic correspondence of the period or the city council deliberations of some provincial towns. Censorship proceedings in the Parisian courts also provide useful data on the distribution networks. The criminal archives of the Châtelet and the Parlement of Paris are relatively unexploited sources in this regard.

PAMPHLET PRODUCTION

The twelve hundred or so pamphlets published during the four-year period under study were not produced in a steady, uniform flow.[1] Dur-

---

1. See Figure 1, in chap. 1.

ing periods of intense publicity, such as the winter of 1614–1615 or the fall of 1615, production was much heavier, with an average of more than a dozen pamphlets per week being published in France. Even at a modest press run of several hundred for each title, this was a considerable amount of printed propaganda for an early modern political culture to consume. The most popular pamphlets might have reached the hands of 1 percent of France's urban population.[2] The great variety as well as the sheer quantity of pamphlets are striking. The style, content, length, quality of production, and purposes of the pamphlets were extremely diverse. This very diversity demonstrates that the pamphlets served many and complex functions.

Pamphlets were usually made out of a single sheet of inexpensive printing stock. Printed on both sides and folded three times, the typical pamphlet ran about sixteen pages and was approximately four by six inches. Pamphlets of eight pages were common, and pamphlets of more than sixty-four pages were not rare. The content and style ranged from satiric or panegyric verses to the most serious political and theological debate. Few engraved images or wood-block prints have survived, and those with an explicitly partisan purpose must have been fairly rare. At least a dozen such items, however, were produced during the 1614–1617 campaigns.

The most common types of pamphlets were (1) official documents, (2) letters, (3) argumentative discourses, and (4) literary pieces—usually dramatic dialogues. Official documents consisted of publications emanating from some organ of the royal government—an official printing of a royal edict or of an *arrêt* from the Parlement of Paris. Such items were usually published first by the royal printers; the prestigious firm of Morel and Mettayer did a booming business in Paris.[3] Although they did not always function as partisan propaganda, such publications were often polemical and could even be inflammatory under certain circum-

2. This estimate is based on calculations of the margin of profit a printer could expect from a given press run and is necessarily speculative. A good worker could print from sixty to seventy sheets an hour, and a shop with two presses could print both sides of thirteen hundred sheets a day, according to Clouzot, "Notes," 25. Such a workshop could turn out thirteen hundred pamphlets of sixteen octavo pages in a day's work. This suggests that an economical run of pamphlets was probably somewhere between five hundred and twelve hundred. Thus, a particularly popular pamphlet, printed in ten editions or more, might have existed in ten thousand copies. If the urban population of France was approximately one million people in 1614, then one can estimate very roughly that the contents of the most popular pamphlets could have reached 1 percent of the urban population—a small but strategically vital audience.

3. Cf. Martin, *Livres*, 1:48.

stances.[4] If published *lettres patentes* or an *arrêt* contained a judgment against a great noble in opposition to the government, it became in effect a pamphlet and worked as part of a partisan campaign.[5] The Crown also published a good deal in the way of announcements and descriptive accounts of royal ceremonies, including parades and royal "entries" into Paris. These also functioned as propaganda. The ceremonies and celebrations accompanying Louis XIII's marriage to Anne of Austria in 1615 were heavily rhetorical, seeking to distract attention from the rebellion of the prince de Condé and his allies and to glorify the queen mother's administration.[6]

Many of the leading political figures in the 1614–1617 struggles had portions of their official diplomatic correspondence printed as pamphlets. These letters were often written in such a way that they easily doubled as propaganda, as was a "letter" by Marie, referred to in the epigraph for this chapter. Functioning much like a twentieth-century news leak, such letters revealed to the public the normally confidential communications of persons in power. As I note earlier, such an exchange of pamphlet-letters between the prince de Condé and Marie de Médicis in February 1614 initiated the ensuing three years of pamphlet warfare.[7]

As a genre, the argumentative pamphlets are distinguished by their frank self-portrayal as political commentary, opinion, or advice. The discourse was almost always anonymous and was frequently characterized by very high quality argumentation and factual accuracy. The *advis,* or letter of advice, was a stylistic variation of the argumentative pamphlet. Here, the anonymous "councillor" consults political leaders in the style of an official adviser. The advice could vary from a banal rehearsal of platitudes to the most serious discussions of political strategy.[8] Argumentative pamphlets were generally written in high-quality, polite prose, even when they sought to expose the scandalous posturing of their adversaries. Their stylistic features emphasized the knowledge, wisdom,

4. It should be noted that many such publications are catalogued separately as *Actes royaux* (F series) in the Bibliothèque Nationale, and, therefore, those that are neither catalogued as pamphlets (Lb series) nor appear in Lindsay and Neu are missing from the "progovernment" production figures cited in this book.

5. Among other examples are *Declaration du roy contre le prince de Condé* (1615) and *Arrest de la Cour de Parlement* (1615).

6. As discussed below, Simon Millanges of Bordeaux printed more than a dozen pamphlets covering the events surrounding the double marriages; Desgraves, " 'Bulletins d'information' imprimés à Bordeaux," 30–34.

7. *Copie de la lettre envoyee à la tres-chrestiene royne regente* (Mézières, 1614); and *Double de la responce de la royne regente* (Paris, 1614).

8. For the banal, see *Advis à monseigneur le prince* (1614). For a work of political science, see *Conseiller fidele a son roy* (1614).

experience, and good intentions of the authors, anonymous or not. The arguments were usually genuine attempts at persuasion—addressing the policy, financial, or legalistic issues of concern to the ministers advising the queen mother and other informed elites.[9] Many of these pamphlets contain relatively learned historical references to France's past.[10]

Literary pamphlets departed from these conventions and were more closely related to the literary genres of the time—verse, drama, and epideictic oratory. Many were dramatic dialogues, almost like one-act plays, or pieces of short narrative fiction featuring stock characters such as "Jacques Bon-Homme." More likely to be openly inflammatory, slanderous, and seditious, such pamphlets generally accused particular nobles or the queen mother and her ministers of having evil and selfish designs, of being belligerent, dishonest, incompetent, or worse. They were more likely to drag religious emotions into the conflict. Some were written in a lower-quality, more "popular" style and were designed explicitly to frighten people by raising the specter of civil war, increased taxation, Spanish domination, or the general ruin of France. Others in this genre were among the most creative pamphlets. Dialogues and monologues spoken by fictitious characters provided an entertaining (and remarkably subtle) variety of satire, banter, demagoguery, slander, and political discussion.[11] One pamphleteer complained bitterly about these stylistic devices and chided his fellow pamphleteers for using the voices of "unreasonable beasts" and "persons of low condition" to defame princes.[12]

In every category of pamphlet a variety of styles, points of view, and rhetorical devices was evident. Many were authored by men with a deep

9. Cf. Walker, *Typologische und Terminologische Untersuchungen*, 12–42. Walker argues that exposing scandal and the hidden truth was a basic rhetorical device in many of these pamphlets. He suggests a further typology of argumentative pamphlets based on the rhetorical distinctions in Angenot's work (see Introduction, n. 56), i.e., "pamphlets," "polemics," and "satires." Pamphlet authors sought to dilute or destroy the already existing influence of their opponents over the audience. The author of a polemic sought to win over an uncommitted audience also being wooed by the opposition. The author of a satire intended either to mobilize a public partially sympathetic to his side, or to gain influence over an already hostile audience. Although I did not adopt these categories in my own analysis, I find them helpful.

10. Richet, "Autour des Etats-Généraux."

11. *Burlesque* was actually used in the titles of several of these pieces, many of which are closely related to the literary world of satire and parody described in Bakhtin, *Rabelais and His World*. Farce was still the mainstay of popular Parisian theater in the early seventeenth century, according to Mongrédien, *Grands Comédiens du XVIIe siècle*, and some pamphlet authors probably tried to imitate the stage dialogue of these performances. This subject is explored further in chap. 5 and in my article, "Jacques Bon-Homme," 23–32, but the literary devices used in pamphlets remain a largely unexplored mine of information about popular political culture.

12. *Discours sur les calomnies* (1614), 9.

understanding of France's political system who also had considerable rhetorical or literary talent. Pamphlets also presented, intentionally or otherwise, a distorted vision of politics, composed in a vague or exaggerated oratorical prose. Some pamphlets addressed political issues far removed from the immediate struggle for control of the state. And there were campaigns within campaigns. The Jesuits exchanged pamphlet barrages with their Huguenot and Gallican enemies. The financiers and their enemies traded broadsides. The Parlement's partisans tried to assert its allegedly traditional role in political affairs. Once a particular campaign was under way, pamphleteers addressed the arguments published by their opponents, and the result was a highly complex dialogue. Responses were often composed in the same genre—letter was met with letter, discourse with discourse, slander with slander, and burlesque with burlesque.

Despite the great variety of pamphlet literature, one is struck by the extent to which argumentative pamphlets addressing the central political issues of the period dominated production as a whole. Some very significant trends can be seen in J. M. Hayden's survey of 858 pamphlets published (in 1,425 editions) during 1614 and 1615.[13] Hayden found that of the 858 titles, approximately 523 focused on the struggle between Marie de Médicis and the prince de Condé. Of these, 116 were in letter form, and another 187 were discourses. An additional 40 were copies or discussions of edicts and political agreements. The meeting of the Estates General was the central focus of 180 pamphlets, while about 96 titles can be classified as descriptions of ceremonies. The remaining pamphlets, some of which were pieces of religious propaganda, were also mostly polemical. Hélène Duccini's analysis of a corpus of 806 pamphlets published from 1614 through 1617 produced similar results; about two-thirds of these consisted of serious discussions of political events and issues.[14] In other words, partisan polemic dominated the 1614–1617 campaigns.

Although the number of pamphlets that directly discussed the Estates General of 1614 was relatively small, the meeting of the Estates clearly had a significant impact on the tone and content of pamphlets. The assembly offered the perfect opportunity for publishing general discussions about France's political situation. The meeting of the Estates was seen as an occasion for the deputies to pressure the Crown to adopt reform legislation. Accordingly, a significant number of pamphlets proposed such reforms in the fall of 1614 and winter of 1615. The proposals often included lengthy and informed discussions of various abuses in the financial and judicial systems and of problems in society generally. The

13. Hayden, "Political Pamphlets."
14. Duccini, "Littérature pamphlétaire," 1:116–117.

deputies from each *bailliage* and *sénéchaussée*, who came to Paris to represent their constituents, were likely readers of these pamphlets and,
moreover, would take them back to the provinces.

Hayden and Duccini point to another crucial feature of the 1614–
1617 pamphlet campaigns. The supporters of Marie de Médicis and her
political coalition dramatically outpublished the prince de Condé and his
allies. Among the nonpolemical genres, Duccini calculates that only
slightly more than 17 percent of the pamphlets favor the princes.[15]
Among the polemical pamphlets, the princes fared a little better, but still
were favored in only 26 percent. Hayden's analysis points to the same
disparity. He calculated that for the 1614–1615 period alone, 46 percent
of the pamphlets favored the government, 23 percent favored the
princes, and 3 percent took a middle ground.[16] The sheer volume of
progovernment propaganda was probably a key factor in the ability of
Marie de Médicis's administration to fend off the challenge of Condé
and his faction for three and a half years, although quality and distribution must also be taken into account.

AUTHORS

The authors of these hundreds of pamphlets are as difficult to identify
as the readers. The vast majority intentionally concealed their identity,
and for good reason. Many printers and book dealers received harsh
sentences in 1614 and 1615, and in 1618 two pamphleteers were executed.[17] Even authors with powerful patrons were unsafe, as the unfortunate Fancan was to discover. After using him in his climb to power in
the 1620s, Richelieu sacrificed the talented pamphleteer to his political
enemies as part of a political deal with the militant wing of the Catholic
party.[18]

---

15. Ibid. These figures would be still smaller if the *Actes Royaux* were fully included (see
n. 4 above).

16. Hayden, "Political Pamphlets" (the rest of the pamphlets were concerned with other
matters).

17. Bibliothèque de l'Institute de France, Ms. Godefrey, 114, f. 76. Cf. Martin, *Livres*,
1:463.

18. There have been differing views of this complicated and fascinating episode, which
is also discussed in the concluding chapter of this book. François Langlois de Fancan contributed heavily to a pro-Richelieu propaganda campaign in the early 1620s but was thrown
in prison by the cardinal in 1627 and later died there. Geley's view that Fancan was a victim
of Richelieu's shifting political strategy in the late 1620s is most likely correct. However,
Deloche argues convincingly that Fancan was uncontrollable and at odds with the political
climate of the later part of the decade. Cf. Geley, *Fancan et la politique de Richelieu*, 293ff.;
and Deloche, *Autour de la plume du Cardinal de Richelieu*, 430–435.

Duccini's analysis of pamphlets conserved in the Bibliothèque Nationale informs us that about 10 percent of these pieces are signed.[19] The pattern of anonymity is not totally consistent from year to year, however. In 1614 the coming of age and the marriage of Louis XIII gave authors an opportunity to express their poetic talents in the production of harmless panegyric. There was little danger in this, and so the percentage of signed pieces in 1614 rose to just under nineteen.[20] In contrast, the years 1615 and 1616 were rife with armed conflict and civil war. Consequently, the percentage of signed pamphlets dropped dramatically during these years to just under eight and about five and one half respectively. Overtly factional pamphleteering was clearly dangerous, and this encouraged anonymity.

Reconstructing the identity of pamphleteers is extremely difficult. The literary milieu of the early seventeenth century (especially before 1620) is obscure, and the authorship even of some famous works produced by Richelieu's stable of writers is difficult to determine.[21] In any event, "authorship" was then a more ambiguous matter. Jouhaud has shown for the period of the Fronde that a pamphlet could be written by more than one individual.[22] A great noble could dictate to his secretary the general substance of a pamphlet he wished to see appear, and the secretary would polish it up for publication. This appears to have happened in the 1614–1615 campaigns as well. Authorship in such cases was a collective effort.

Relatively few pamphlets appear to have been written by hired professionals merely selling their persuasive skills to the highest bidders. Most of the known authors of pamphlets were not playwrights or poets but, rather, clergymen or legal professionals of some kind who were clients or allies of the principals in the political struggle. Bishops, secular priests, and men in the teaching orders of the regular clergy were heavy contributors. They supported the queen's politics, and their professional skills were easily bent in the direction of political polemic.

Clues can be found here and there concerning individual pamphleteers. Secretary of State Villeroy was offended by a pamphlet written by a *secrétaire* of the duc de Bouillon and printed in Sedan.[23] Thomas Pelletier, an old Holy Leaguer, published a retraction addressed to the prince de Condé, admitting that he had indeed published some things in

19. Duccini, "Littérature pamphlétaire," 1:77–98.
20. Ibid.
21. Church, *Richelieu and Reason of State*, 461–504.
22. Jouhaud, "Ecriture et action," 45, 49.
23. In a letter to J. A. de Thou, 26 April 1615, Jeannin describes Villeroy as "fort offencé" by the publication of this pamphlet in Sedan by "un secrétaire de Monsieur le Maréshal de Bouillon," B.N. Ms. Colbert 12, f. 232.

the past but was not the author of a particular piece that had greatly annoyed the prince.[24] Such information is not especially useful, however, for the present analysis. The value of knowing the exact identity of a particular author is small when both his general and partisan points of view are evident enough from his work. It would be interesting to compare a list of the prolific, militantly Catholic pamphleteers with the Holy League's stable of propagandists. How much of the League's propaganda machinery was still intact? A valuable project, certainly, but our interest in the political function of pamphlets has turned the present analysis in different directions. The authors' identity reveals less about the political function of pamphlets and the propaganda process as a whole than the matter of dissemination. What were the primary targets? How effectively were they hit?

THE DISSEMINATION OF PAMPHLET PROPAGANDA

Pamphlets appear to have been particularly important in struggles over political control of provincial towns. Both the prince de Condé and the queen regent worked hard to distribute their pamphlets in areas where the loyalty of the inhabitants was questionable. The west and the southwest were thus key targets in part because of local tensions between Catholics and Protestants. But other provincial areas were involved.

Much can be learned about the dissemination of pamphlets through an analysis of the title pages. About 40 percent of the pamphlets published from 1614 to 1617 contain on their title pages the name of a printer or publisher, and around 60 percent name the town where the pamphlet was allegedly printed.[25] As one might expect, the vast majority of identifiable printers and publishers worked out of Paris. At least sixty-one Parisian publishers printed a pamphlet of one kind or another at some point during the 1614–1617 campaigns. The production of pamphlets in smaller provincial towns, although not equal to that of Paris, was surprisingly large and well organized strategically. Forty-three printers in provincial towns are known to have engaged in such activity.[26]

Of the twenty-four most active producers of political pamphlets in 1614 and 1615, only four were located outside the capital city.[27] These figures reflect the general dominance of the Parisian printers in the industry as a whole but do not correspond exactly to the geographical

---

24. Pelletier, *Lettre à monseigneur le prince de Condé* (1614).

25. Duccini, "Littérature pamphlétaire," 1:72, based only on the holdings of the B.N., and excluding the *Actes Royaux*.

26. My figures for printers active in the pamphlet wars are based on the sources cited below, n. 28.

27. Hayden, "Political Pamphlets," app. I.

distribution of printers in France. From 1610 to 1620 approximately 270 printing establishments were active in France, 141 of which had Parisian addresses and 129 of which operated in provincial towns.[28] Only slightly more numerous than their provincial counterparts, the Parisian printers were decidedly more active in the production of propaganda.

In Paris pamphlets were sold in printers' shops and by colporteurs congregated in the same areas dominated by their predecessors in the sixteenth century—along the rue St. Jacques and other streets of the University quarter, around the Palais de Justice (where the Parlement met), and around the city gates.[29] Colporteurs working in and around the city constituted a major retail outlet in Paris and probably in provincial towns as well.[30] Trial records indicate that in Paris these ambulatory street merchants sometimes worked for a particular printer and sometimes worked independently. When arrested, they tried to avoid taking responsibility for clandestine material, claiming they obtained it from

28. These figures are taken from Lindsay and Neu, *Catalogue de l'histoire de France,* and a number of other sources, including *Répertoire bibliographique des livres imprimés en France du seizième siècle,* and *Répertoire bibliographique des livres imprimés en France au XVIIe siècle;* Delalain, *Inventaire des marques d'imprimeurs;* Renouard, *Imprimeurs parisiens, libraires;* and the odd book by Poche, *Quelques adresses de libraires.* In addition, several histories of printing in specific localities were consulted, notably those of Desgraves for southwestern France. At the time this inventory was made, Desgraves's reference work for the seventeenth century was unfinished and more printers will certainly have been identified by now. See also Aquilon's "Les Réalités provinciales," 1:351–363 (for printers active in the sixteenth century); and Lanette-Claverie, "Librairie française en 1700," 3–44 (for printers active at the end of the seventeenth century). For the early seventeenth century, Chartier gives the figure of approximately 130 identifiable "éditeurs" in "Pamphlets et gazettes," 1:408.

29. Renouard, *Imprimeurs parisiens,* provides a street map of sixteenth-century Paris with the addresses of printers marked on it, and these are the same addresses one finds noted on the title pages of many pamphlets published in 1614, e.g., Fleury Bourriquant, "en l'Isle du Palais, rue traversant, aux Fleurs Royales"; Pierre Buray, "au mont S. Hilaire à la court d'Albert"; Toussainct du Bray, "rue S. Jacques, aux epics meurs, et en sa botique au Palais en la gallerie des prisonniers"; Antoine du Brueil, "rue S. Jacques, au dessus de S. Benoist, à la Courrone"; Melchoir Mondiere, "rue S. Jacques, devant S. Benoist, aux deux cochets."

30. B.N. Ms. fr. 22115 contains a great deal of information about the history of colporteurs in seventeenth-century Paris, notably copies of legislation regulating their number, places of business, and activities. The "legal" number of colporteurs in 1614 was twelve, but there were clearly dozens more, as demonstrated by the frequent efforts to control them. Legislation in 1634 mentions the legal number of colporteurs as fifty, but cites illegal colporteurs as a serious problem and a principal cause of the frequent exposition of "libeles diffamatoires et autres ouvrages deffendus" (B.N. Ms. fr. 22115, f. 31).

As for the provinces, see below. The Parlement of Bordeaux issued an *arrêt* prohibiting within its jurisdiction "touts imprimeurs, libraires, merciers, revandeurs, et crieurs de livres, [d']imprimer, ne exposer en vente aulcuns livres, letres, et aultres discourses tendans a revolts des subjects du Roy, divisions, et partiallites" (cited below, n. 59). The *merciers* were peddlers who must have functioned as colporteurs of a kind, and the *crieurs* probably did as well.

men whom they didn't know, that they bought it without reading it, or that they were forced by their employer to sell the material.[31] They often hawked their pamphlets in the courtyard of the Palais de Justice, as mentioned above, around the Louvre, and on the Pont-Neuf. At least one Protestant colporteur of Paris probably traveled regularly to Charenton on Sundays to sell pamphlets at the door of the church there where many Parisian Protestants worshiped.[32]

The number of colporteurs active in Paris is hard to determine with accuracy. Certainly the twelve colporteurs officially recognized by the University of Paris and the "community" of printers, binders, and book dealers had no effective means of enforcing their legal monopoly. The very nature of their business made it extremely difficult to police. In March 1616 the official colporteurs brought suit against three unofficial colporteurs in the civil chamber of the Châtelet, but the malefactors were released with a warning.[33] Because all manner of persons were selling pamphlets, even unknown vagabonds (it was alleged by the court), it was inappropriate to arbitrarily punish a few who had been caught. Subsequent legislation designed to cut back on the number of colporteurs suggests that their numbers were quite large in the early seventeenth century; perhaps from fifty to one hundred full-time, well-established book peddlers roamed the streets of Paris during the 1614–1617 conflicts. If one includes *all* the hawkers of books and booklets in Paris— even those perched on the pont Neuf—the number according to contemporary sources may have been near a thousand.[34]

The place of colporteurs in the distribution network suggests that pamphlets were relatively inexpensive. The small, cheaply printed, un-

---

31. Bernard Picard's father claimed that Georges Bellier, for whom Bernard worked as an apprentice, had ordered his son to sell illegal pamphlets on the affair of Poitiers, A. N. X^{2A} 189, *arrêt* of the Parlement, 29 July 1614. Jacques Couette, a colporteur, said that "Varin" had given him the "wicked book" and that he had not read it before he took a dozen on consignment; as is gathered from an interrogation of Couette by a judge of the Parlement, A. N. X^{2A} 977. The interrogation took place shortly before judgment of 5 October 1615, A. N. X^{2A} 193. I am grateful to Alfred Soman for providing me with the reference to Couatte's interrogation and for showing me how to locate these cases in the registers.

32. *Arrêt* of the Parlement against Jehan Anthoine Jonallin, 20 August 1615. Jonallin, whom Alfred Soman informs me was arrested repeatedly, appears to have been a Protestant and may have specialized in printed contraband. Desgraves, in *Haultin, 1571–1623*, notes that Jonallin commissioned the Protestant printing house of the Haultins to produce the anti-Jesuit pamphlet *Trente deux demandes proposées par le Père Coton.*

33. B.N. Ms. fr. 22115, f. 23 (sentence of 3 March 1616). The judicial decisions of the Parlement were called "*arrêts*"; the judicial decisions of the Châtelet were called "sentences."

34. Barbiche, "Régime de l'édition," 1:374.

bound (or cheaply bound) booklets sold by colporteurs usually cost less than a livre.[35] The well-known connoisseur of political propaganda, Pierre L'Estoile, kept records of his purchases only a few years prior to these pamphlet wars—a few deniers for a sheet of verse to ten sous for a particularly significant or infamous pamphlet. For a more or less typical pamphlet—such as the anti-Jesuit tract, *Trente deux demandes proposées par le Père Coton*—L'Estoile paid four sous, or one fifth of a *livre tournois*.[36] Nominal prices probably had not changed much by 1614. At midcentury (before the Fronde) a Grenoblois book dealer—whose account books have been analyzed by Martin and his collaborators—sold cheaply produced books in the same price range.[37] The prices of pamphlets must have hovered between three to fifteen sous, depending on the size, reputation, place of publication, and legality of each title. This made pamphlets easily affordable to the urban elite, but a bit expensive for the artisan classes. It cost two and a half sous to see the *farceurs* play at the Hôtel de Bourgone during this period.[38]

Of the 129 provincial firms known to be in operation between 1610 and 1620, only forty-three printers affixed their names to political pamphlets during the 1614–1617 campaigns, and nearly half of them operated out of important commercial and administrative centers. More than anything else, these figures indicate that provincial printers were more vulnerable to reprisal, less well protected by their political patrons, and therefore more wary of becoming involved in a partisan pamphlet campaign. Among the twenty-four most active printers in 1614–1615 were Mesgissier of Rouen (possibly protected by the Guise family), Jean Janon of Sedan (clearly under the protection of the duc de Bouillon), Simon Millanges of Bordeaux (clearly under the protection of the Cardinal de Sourdis), and Nicolas Jullieron of Lyon (probably under the protection of Villeroy).[39] Although Millanges had a virtual monopoly in Bordeaux, Jullieron and Mesgissier were only two of several established printers who published pamphlets out of Rouen and Lyon. Other well-established printers worked out of Rennes, Toulouse, Grenoble, Avignon,

---

35. It is impossible to say what, exactly, counted as a book (*livre*) and what counted as a pamphlet (*livret* or *libel*) in the minds of contemporaries, but the binding and type of publication were probably more significant than the number of pages. There was an important hierarchy of quality in binding—(1) unbound, but sewn with string, (2) bound with wooden covers, and (3) bound with leather covers. Missals and breviaries, the two fundamental texts of Catholic piety, could be purchased in octavo, bound in wooden covers for about half a livre.

36. L'Estoile, *Mémoires-journaux*, ed. Brunet et al., 8:237, 239, 242, 251, 254–55, 257 (mentioning pamphlets L'Estoile bought in 1607).

37. Martin, *Registres du libraire Nicolas*, 67–73.

38. Mongrédien, *Grands comédiens*, 1.

39. Hayden, "Political Pamphlets," app. I.

Aix, Nîmes, La Rochelle, Châlons-sur-Marne, Caen, Orléans, and so forth, but few acknowledged printing more than one or two pamphlets. The largest group of printers in a single provincial town worked in Lyon, a traditional publishing center. At least six Lyonais printers actively participated in the 1614–1617 campaigns.[40]

In addition to the well-established printing firms in large towns, a multitude of smaller presses contributed to the pamphlet campaigns. A large number of such presses operated in southwestern towns—Niort, Fontenay, Saumur, Bergerac, Xaintes, and Poitiers. Obviously it was no accident that some of these towns were Protestant strongholds protected under the Edict of Nantes; several of these printers were habitually in the service of the Protestant cause.[41] Printing a pamphlet was not a particularly difficult operation, and many otherwise minor presses must have been able to turn out a pamphlet. Secret presses were known to exist in France, in colleges, in the basements of churches, in abbeys, and the like.[42] Some powerful nobles and bishops had their own private presses. The duc de Sully and Agrippa d'Aubigné had presses transported to their chateaux in order to supervise more closely the printing of their works. Cardinal Du Perron also had a press at his château.[43]

Given these conditions, the potential for the production of pamphlet literature was tremendous. The output of a major printer like Simon Millanges in Bordeaux is instructive. Special circumstances in Millanges's case allowed him to publish more openly. Under the protection of the powerful archbishop of Bordeaux, Cardinal de Sourdis, he was heavily committed to the cause of the Catholic church. Moreover, as the site of the ceremonies celebrating the marriage of Louis XIII to Anne of Austria, the City of Bordeaux held a special place in the 1614–1617 conflict. Millanges thus had both cause and a safe environment for producing progovernment propaganda. He published at least eight political broadsides in 1614, sixteen in 1615, seven in 1616, and eight in 1617—excluding pamphlets on the marriage and on theological matters.[44] His entire "progovernment" repertoire for these years amounted to double or triple such figures. Although this level of production may have been excep-

40. Biteaud and del Socorro, "Brochures politiques editées à Lyon," 125–130, list more than twenty printers of political pamphlets active in Lyon from 1601 to 1610.

41. Far from eliminating the trade in pamphlets pertaining to religious controversy, the Edict of Nantes and the later reign of Henry IV initiated in some ways a period of renewed vigor; see Desgraves, "Aspects des controverses," 153–187; and *Etude sur l'imprimerie dans le Sud-Ouest de la France.*

42. Such presses are outlawed in article 4 of a *règlement* issued in 1610 by the Chambre de la Police of the Châtelet of Paris, B.N. Ms. fr. 22087, item #47.

43. Duccini, "Littérature pamphlétaire," 1:76.

44. Desgraves, *Livres imprimés à Bordeaux,* 38–58; " 'Bulletins d'information' imprimés à Bordeaux," 30–34; "Supplément à la Bibliographie," 10–11.

tional, it gives us an idea of the extent of pamphlet production in major cities other than Paris.

The publication of progovernment pamphlets in provincial towns was, in at least one instance, directly solicited by the Crown. In February 1614, right after the appearance of Condé's first pamphlet, the queen appealed to Cardinal de Sourdis for help in ending the "mauvaises impressions" that Condé's challenge might create "in the minds of the subjects of the King." The letter reveals the strenuous efforts of the queen and her advisers to disseminate propaganda in the provinces.

> You will have been informed of the news to this point by my previous letters. But now I will tell you that two days ago a gentleman sent by my nephew, the Prince de Condé, presented me with a letter from him which is in effect a document confected expressly to denigrate the conduct and administration of affairs. I have also been informed that those who are leading this conspiracy have had copies of it printed which they are circulating throughout all the provinces of the Kingdom. I will have a response made to it, and will send you a copy so that for your part you will better be able to put a stop to the harmful impressions that such artifices might place in the minds of the subjects of the King, my Lord and son. Meanwhile, I pray you to work on this matter constantly and make known to everyone the sincerity of my actions and my good intentions concerning the welfare, peace and relief of our said subjects.[45]

This letter was written early in the struggle, yet the queen and her advisers were already soliciting the production of progovernment propaganda. The administration clearly viewed the publication and dissemination of Condé's letter as a serious escalation of the conflict and was intent on counteracting its effects in the provinces. The queen mother's letter says that a copy of her response to the prince's letter would be sent to de Sourdis so he could construct the proper arguments for his own propaganda initiatives. After some preliminary bargaining over what favors he would obtain in return for his services, the cardinal honored the queen mother's request. De Sourdis wrote from Bordeaux in April 1614 that he hoped the Crown would help him obtain an additional bishopric and an abbey, and that he was doing his part on the propaganda front.

> Your loyal allies work to have leaflets [*billets*] spread about in the towns of this province, so afflicted with the same bad treatment and aggressions that . . . [other regions have received because of] the disgraceful behavior of the malcontents. This is to render their actions hateful to the people here, and in this way to recommit them, in these stormy times, to the continuation of the obedience they owe the King.[46]

45. Marie de Médicis to Cardinal de Sourdis, 24 February 1614, B.N. Ms. fr. 6379, f. 181.
46. B.N. Ms. Clair. 364, f. 99.

Many pamphlets published by Millanges under the archbishop's protection fit this description.

The process whereby local political leaders orchestrated provincial publicity for Marie de Médicis at the behest of the Crown worked elsewhere. In a letter dated 1 April 1614 from Castres (near Toulouse), the local magistrate, de Lestang, informed the queen mother of regional efforts to control political publications on her behalf.[47] His remarks, reproduced in the epigraph for this chapter, are especially revealing in that they name a particular pamphlet that was to be reproduced and disseminated locally. De Lestang's letter also alludes to unusually vigilant censorship efforts. The queen mother could not have asked for a clearer indication of cooperation with her efforts to control the flow of public discourse in the provinces through the use of pamphlets and censorship.

CENSORSHIP AND CONTROL OF THE PUBLIC SPHERE

Fear of the printed word also led Marie de Médicis and her advisers to initiate extraordinary censorship proceedings in Paris. From the publication of Condé's first pamphlet in February 1614, the queen mother and her advisers feared that opposition propaganda might spin out of control. Special measures were therefore needed to stop this from happening because the ordinary mechanisms of censorship were ineffective.

In Paris the original responsibility for policing the community of printers, booksellers, binders, and colporteurs lay with the University of Paris and the poorly organized printer's guild.[48] Both the university and the guild depended on the royal courts for enforcement. The Châtelet (the *bailliage*-level sovereign court in Paris) heard both criminal cases involving illegal printed matter and civil suits involving the violation of local laws. The Parlement of Paris heard such cases as well, usually on appeal.

Royal edicts repeatedly insisted that printers and authors obtain royal permission for any published *livre* or *écrit*, and include an extract of the *privilège*, or permission, somewhere in the work. The king's chancellor had jurisdiction over the granting of such permission, but the power was often delegated to lesser officials.[49] The Châtelet exercised a lesser jurisdiction over *privilèges* in Paris. A royal *privilège* functioned basically as a copyright; it was not a guarantee against future prosecution if the publication were later found to be defamatory, seditious, or heretical. The words *avec permission* were frequently printed on pamphlets sponsored by or sympathetic to the royal government. So legal mechanisms

47. Antoine de Lestang to Marie de Médicis, B.N. Ms. Clair. 364, f. 54.
48. See also chap. 1, "Pamphlets in the Public Sphere."
49. Barbiche, "Régime de l'édition," 1:368–375.

for obtaining permission were in operation during the 1614–1617 conflict. But many pamphlets escaped such regulation.

Although most of the records of the Châtelet from the early seventeenth century have been destroyed, we can still reconstruct the efforts of this court to suppress illegal pamphlets in Paris. A number of appeals to the Parlement further reveal the operations of the system. On the whole, this judicial evidence suggests the double standard that affected the attitudes of politicians also characterized the views of magistrates. Printing and selling pamphlets without permission was generally illegal, but certain pamphlets were perceived as much more dangerous than others.

The first major case against a group of printers involved in the 1614 campaigns appears to have been the one decided in the civil chamber of the Châtelet on 14 May 1614. Thomas Ménard, Antoine du Brueil, Gillet le Veau, Antoine Champenois, and Claude des Periers had their books and papers confiscated for having printed or sold material without permission. Each defendant, save Ménard, was fined eighty *livres parisis*. The court ordered Ménard to assist in further investigations. Because he denied having printed the stack of illegal pamphlets found in his room during a raid by the sergeant of the Châtelet, Ménard was ordered to produce the individual from whom he bought them.[50]

A short time after this civil trial, the Châtelet proceeded against several other printers in its criminal chamber.[51] On 12 July Philippes Lenrillon, François D'Aufroy, Bernard Picard, and their accomplices were condemned to be beaten and whipped while stripped to the waist at the entrance to the Pont Neuf, or near Sainte Inez in the University quarter. The legal record does not provide all the details, but one can ascertain that in the course of official investigations, raids were made on various printing establishments at least three times. François du Souhait and Antoine du Brueil had been imprisoned and interrogated. Lenrillon, D'Aufroy, and Picard had also spent some time in the jail cells of the Conciergerie du Palais, the place of detention for criminal defendants on trial before the sovereign courts of Paris.

The Parlement of Paris overturned the sentence of the Châtelet, and the printers were probably happy with the much more lenient judgment of the higher court. Lenrillon, Picard, and D'Aufroy were "reprimanded while on their knees" and warned not to deal in illegal material in the future, otherwise they would be subject to corporal punishment. Du Sou-

50. B.N. Ms. fr. 22087, item #44, *Sentence* of the Châtelet.
51. *Arrêt* of the Parlement of Paris, 29 July 1614, A. N. X[2A] 189, the first portion of which (known as the *veu*) reviews the evidence considered by the court. Such a record can be used to reconstruct part of the history of the case, including actions taken by a lower court, if any. Unfortunately, this form of reporting decisions gives little or no evidence as to the particular law that has been violated.

hait was banished from the City of Paris and its environs for nine years and warned to keep his ban or be subject to death by hanging. Du Brueil—who had powerful political connections or may somehow have been less culpable—was fined twenty *livres parisis*.[52]

As the political climate heated up in 1615, the officials of the Châtelet were increasingly pressured to step up their antipropaganda efforts. In September two letters in the name of the king were written to Henri de Mesmes, the *lieutenant civil* and the Châtelet's most powerful magistrate, urging him to "institute criminal proceedings against the authors, printers, and colporteurs of [illegal] books."[53] De Mesmes responded that he had been working continuously to discover the authors and printers of *ces libelles* but his efforts had produced few results. He claimed to have arrested several colporteurs in an effort to gain information and to have learned that many of the pamphlets were printed outside of Paris. The colporteurs "bought the pamphlets from people they did not know who brought them right to their houses and sold them almost for nothing." Notwithstanding these excuses, de Mesmes protested that he had prosecuted several of the vendors and "condemned them to endure every pain that a mortal body could suffer without dying." He complained, however, in clear but polite language that his tough sentences were mitigated upon appeal to the Parlement. De Mesmes added that he hoped a new ordinance mandating the death penalty for the selling of illicit pamphlets and books would help stem the tide.

De Mesmes was evidently frustrated that his prosecutions of pamphlet dealers produced no useful information about authorship. He appears to have regarded the pamphlet authors as the real source of evil; others held the same belief. In a meeting with representatives of the Parlement of Paris on 23 May 1615 on another matter, the queen mother complained to the first president of the Parlement, Nicolas de Verdun, "You allow to be produced and sold libelous pamphlets against the honor of the King and myself without bringing anyone to justice."[54] Giving a pamphlet to a secretary, she asked him to read some of it aloud. After hearing

52. Ibid. Curiously, du Brueil was one of the twenty-four most active publishers of pamphlets from 1614 to 1617.

53. B.N. Ms. Dupuy 91, ff. 212–212 verso, is a copy of De Mesmes's letter to Louis XIII, dated 18 September 1615, in which he repsonds to Louis's letters of the 4th and 10th of the same month.

54. Register of the Parlement of Paris for 23 May 1615, recounting the meeting of that day between deputies from the sovereign court and the queen mother and her advisers, A. N. X[1A] 1870. The *procureur général* in the Parlement, Mathieu de Molé, tried to follow through by initiating an investigation into the publication of the pamphlet, probably *Cassandre François*. His efforts were frustrated by the *avocat général*, Louis Servin, who suggested an investigation also be opened into the publication of *Harangue faite de la part de la chambre ecclesiastique, en celle du Tiers-Etat,* a piece of militant Catholic polemic; Mathieu de Molé, *Mémoires,* 1:104–106.

a few scandalous pages, the first president responded that only three days previously he had investigated the matter but could discover nothing. To which the duc d'Epernon responded that the idea was, not to persecute the printers, who were only looking to earn a living, but to find the authors.[55] The first president evidently had better things to do, however, and no such general inquiry was launched.

Certainly, if an author wished, he could conceal his identity fairly successfully. This was true during the years of the Holy League, and it was true in 1614. At the same time, the magistrates appear less than wholeheartedly intent on tracking down authors. Their treatment of printers and colporteurs seems lenient given that the death penalty was frequently proposed for traffickers in seditious libel. As nearly as I can determine, every sentence of the Châtelet that was appealed to the Parlement was overturned. Banishment from Paris or France was usually substituted for the severe corporal punishment handed down by the lower court. The actions of the Parlement in mitigating the sentences of Lenrillon, D'Aufroy, Picard, du Souhait, and du Breuil in 1614 are mentioned above. In the summer of 1615 the magistrates were equally lenient in several cases involving sellers of illegal pamphlets. Jean Millot had been sentenced to death by hanging in the Châtelet while Jehan Jonallin was sentenced to watch the execution before undergoing his own sentence of being beaten and whipped while stripped to the waist with a cord around his neck, after which he was to be banished for life from Paris.[56] Bellièvre, the principal judge in charge of the case on appeal before the Parlement, decided that Millot should be banished from Paris for a period of three years and Jonallin should be publicly reprimanded while on his knees. In another case, the stiff sentence against Jacques Couette was similarly set aside.[57]

The case that came before the Parlement in July 1614 is also of interest because the sentence against Lenrillon and others gives us the titles of sixteen pamphlets that are expressly outlawed. From this list one can draw some conclusions as to what kinds of pamphlets were regarded as particularly potent or offensive by the magistrates. Several pieces are satirical, others are slanderous, and still others contain particularly violent religious polemics. Unfortunately, an ideological analysis cannot be pushed too far because of the unusual circumstances surrounding the case. It was tried in the Chambre de l'Edit, and one of the chief judges was an ally of the prince de Condé's, President Le Jay.[58] Le Jay clearly

55. A. N. X[1A] 1870. *Mercure françois* (1617), 4:80, also relates some of this.

56. *Arrêt* of the Parlement of Paris, 20 August 1615, A. N. X[2A] 193. I owe this reference to Alfred Soman.

57. Ibid.; *arrêt* of 5 October 1615, also courtesy of Soman.

58. The *arrêt* mentions sixteen pamphlets, not all of which can be identified exactly because of the abbreviated titles. (See chap. 5, n. 13, for a partial list.)

used the case as an opportunity to stem the tide of pamphlets being published about the Poitiers affair, a pivotal event in the 1614–1617 struggle for power, which will be examined in the following chapter.

Magistrates in the provinces as well as in Paris were equally concerned about pamphlets and inflammatory rumors. Particularly dramatic actions were taken in Bordeaux, Agen, and Poitiers. On the morning of 24 March 1614 the consuls of Agen convoked a general assembly in the town hall.[59] The clerical, judicial, and municipal leaders, in addition to a great crowd of ordinary citizens, attended. The purpose of the meeting was to read aloud a communication recently received from Bordeaux. It included a printed copy of a recent *arrêt* by the Parlement of Bordeaux, issued at the instigation of the *procureur du roi*, which explicitly prohibited the writing, printing, distribution, and reading of "printed letters and discourses," that might (in the words of the court) lead "the people" to believe in the "vain imaginings and promises" of some "grandees" who were searching to form a "league" allegedly "in the service of the King."[60] The operative clauses read as follows:

> The court forbids and prohibits any subject of the King to compose or publish any book, letter, or discourse tending to disturb said subjects or lead them away from the obedience that they owe his Majesty. [The court also forbids and prohibits] any printer, book dealer, or other retail merchant to print or offer for sale such material. All persons of whatever quality, condition, or religion are forbidden to purchase or to read, publicly or in secret, any such material. [Anyone found guilty of the abovementioned offenses] will be liable to corporal punishment, and prosecution as a disturber of the peace.[61]

After the *arrêt* had been read in its entirety to the full assembly, the city fathers retired to their private chambers. Each of them signed the printed copy sent from Bordeaux (by way of acknowledgment), and the document was solemnly and "instantaneously placed in the great chest of the archives of the city of Agen."[62]

The communication from Bordeaux must have gone to other towns known to have printers within the jurisdiction of the Parlement of Bordeaux. Agen was not a great center for printing; it appears that Antoine Pomaret owned and operated the only viable printing establishment.[63] The magistrates hoped mainly to discourage Protestant and Catholic

---

59. Archives Communales d'Agen, A.D. Lot-et-Garonne (Agen), Register of the Hôtel de Ville, BB 42, ff. 130 verso and following.

60. Ibid., f. 135.

61. Ibid., f. 135 verso.

62. Ibid., f. 136.

63. Desgraves, "L'imprimerie à Agen au XVIIe siècle," 233–254.

writers from starting up their propaganda machinery, as demonstrated by the many references to "both religions" and to "living in peace together."

It is unlikely that such measures were enforced evenhandedly either in Agen or Bordeaux. Millanges of Bordeaux was one of the most active printers, as we have seen, during the 1614–1617 campaigns. Although in general he printed only mildly propagandistic pieces celebrating the king's marriage, he also published a version of *Le vieux Gaulois*, a militantly Catholic pamphlet viciously condemning the revolt of Condé and his allies. Both Agen and Bordeaux remained loyal to the queen's government throughout the struggle. Officials probably looked the other way when Millanges and others published inflammatory, illegal works tending to "the service of the king."

Paris dominated the pamphlet production, as we have seen, of the 1614–1617 years, consistent with its traditional role as the political, financial and cultural center of France. Parisians, however, were not the only important audience. Provincial cities and towns may have been more significant propaganda targets even if the relative volume of propaganda circulating in the provinces was smaller. Indeed, the elites of provincial cities may have been a more strategically important audience. The court and its politics were more visible to the Parisians, so they learned of the news more directly. Moreover, the Parisians' heavily Catholic orientation predisposed them to favor the queen mother's policies and to reject Condé's bid for popularity. Provincial cities were strategically important because they provided vital economic and military support for the administration as well as its challengers. Besides, urban elites were hard to control directly, and their political loyalties were uncertain. Provincial towns often had powerful political ties to local military governors and provincial governors. Most of the great nobles in the prince de Condé's faction were military governors of provinces and important fortified towns. When confronted with their military governor at the head of a band of soldiers, provincial towns and cities could not deny aid and shelter without considerable political risk. Cardinal de Sourdis understood this and, so, began in the spring of 1614 to disseminate leaflets among the towns of Guyenne designed to frighten their inhabitants away from joining the rebels. Playing a pivotal role in the conflict, this kind of political and rhetorical struggle for control of the towns will be investigated in the next chapter.

◆　◆　◆

FOUR

Pamphlet Readers and the Public

To the people of Poitou, greetings. Let it be known that it is today more than ever necessary to oppose with arms in hand the secret intrigues of the Prince and his confederates, traitors to the King and to their country, who are working for the return of those we have banished. . . . It is widely known that M. de Saluert, Councillor in the court of Parlement, since his return from Paris, has loudly and publicly spoken against the King and his town, and in favor of the banished, and that he tried to suborn several good men. . . . He tried to have a pamphlet against the King printed, and spoke to the printer Mesnier to this end.
—FROM A PLACARD POSTED ABOUT THE TOWN OF POITIERS, DECEMBER 1614

What kind of readership did political pamphlets enjoy in the early seventeenth century? Except for references to pamphlets here and there in the correspondence of political elites, there is little direct evidence about the reading public. Readers undoubtedly existed: our analysis of production and distribution shows that both Parisians and provincial towndwellers were an important audience for the several hundred thousand pamphlets circulating in France during the 1614–1616 crisis. But is it possible to develop a more precise picture of the reading public? Does it make sense to begin by trying to group readers into their respective "orders"— clergy, nobility, and the Third Estate? How important were regional affiliations? What other variables helped to define specific groups of readers?

Some preliminary remarks about seventeenth-century French literacy are in order. The earliest useful data on literacy for France as a whole are for 1690. A survey of signatures on marriage documents suggests that at that time fewer than 25 percent of French males and about 10 percent of French females had benefited from some basic schooling.[1] It is reasonable to assume that literacy rates were about the same for the early dec-

---

1. Furet and Ozouf, *Lire et écrire*, 1:8. The French language has no synonym for *literacy*. The nearest equivalent is *alphabétisation*, i.e., the most basic level of skill in reading and writing. The 1690 figures are based on a study by a nineteenth-century inspector of public education, Maggiolo, who found that just under 25 percent of French males and about 10 percent of French females could sign their names, indicating at least a rudimentary knowledge of reading and writing. There is much that is problematic about such data, and the many subsequent studies that have been done in France. See Graff, *Legacies of Literacy*, 108–221.

ades of the seventeenth century.[2] Although low compared with present-day standards, a male literacy rate of around 20 percent would be substantial in an overwhelmingly agrarian and peasant society. If we accept Pierre Goubert's generalization that France was more than 95 percent rural and about 80 percent of its population was made up of peasants at this time, then these figures suggest not only that literacy rates among urban dwellers were quite high but also that a sizable percentage of the rural population was basically literate.[3] The most basic reading skills, however, did not provide a person with access to the world of print. A reader of simple religious or practical texts might well be incapable of reading learned theological or political debate. Such a conclusion is consistent with what we know about the levels of literacy and the function of books and printing in the French Reformation.[4]

There can be little doubt that in the seventeenth century the primary reading public consisted of educated urban elites.[5] This is confirmed by the account books of Nicolas, the Grenoblois book dealer whose business Martin and his collaborators have analyzed.[6] Among the 504 identifiable purchasers of books in mid-seventeenth-century Grenoble, more than half were government officials, and the town's legal professionals were the most numerous book buyers of all. The next largest group, about one-fifth of the reading public, consisted of ecclesiastics. Another tenth were lesser provincial nobles, and yet another tenth were simple bourgeois.[7]

Information about the social status of pamphlet readers is also available from Nicolas's account books. During the years of the Fronde, Nicolas sold a fair number of *mazarinades*.[8] When he sold these pamphlets on

2. For an overview of the general pattern of education in the seventeenth century see Chartier, Compère, and Julia, *L'Education en France*. Catholic reformers placed considerable emphasis on primary education in the seventeenth century, just as the Protestant reformers had in the sixteenth, but this probably did not effect a dramatic increase in the level of education. As Huppert has emphasized, the municipal *collège* was an extremely popular institution in the sixteenth century; see his *Public Schools in Renaissance France*.

3. Goubert, *Ancien Regime,* 43–44, for population figures.

4. Cf. Chartier, "Publishing Strategies," in *Cultural Uses of Print,* 163–178. See also Davis, "Printing and the People," 189–226; and Kingdon, *Geneva and the Coming of the Wars of Religion.*

5. Remarkably few Latin-language pamphlets were published during the 1614–1617 conflicts—perhaps 1 percent of the total—even though in 1600 as many as one-fourth of all major publications coming from Paris were still in Latin (mostly religious books or scholarly works in fields such as law), Martin, *Livres,* 1:76.

6. Martin et al., *Registres du libraire Nicolas.*

7. Ibid., 1:137–265.

8. Ibid., 1:96–97.

credit, he noted the name of the purchaser. Although an analysis of these names does not provide a totally accurate portrait of the purchasers of *mazarindes* (since Nicolas presumably sold to other clients in cash transactions as well), it is nevertheless enlightening. About two-thirds of the purchasers were legal professionals, and more than half were officials in the sovereign courts.[9] Nobles account for 12 percent of Nicolas's list, clergymen for 7, while merchants and artisans for 5 percent. The upper and upper-middle classes, apparently, were important consumers of pamphlet literature. The high percentage of officials from the sovereign courts among purchasers of pamphlets is particularly noteworthy because these men accounted for less than a third of Nicolas's clientele.[10]

Looking at the public from a different angle, we can ascertain the popularity of certain pamphlets by the number of editions that were reprinted. Some pamphlets were printed in more than fifteen editions.[11] The printing of five or six editions, three or four of which came from Paris, was not at all unusual. Multiple printings were, at least in part, the result of popular demand. Original and official editions may have been paid for by sponsors, but a large proportion of subsequent editions (especially pirated ones) must have been printed to be sold at a profit to customers. Moreover, L'Estoile tells us that pamphlets were often purchased, read, and resold.[12] In this way, an edition of one thousand pamphlets could easily find its way into the hands of many more than a thousand readers.

Although clearly the primary audience, the literate public was not the sole consumer of pamphlet literature. The content of printed material was passed along second- and thirdhand, through sermons, town meetings, and everyday conversations in the marketplace. Rather than thinking of print as a novelty that replaced the traditional oral channels of communication, we should think of it as interwoven with everyday discourse. Official publications were read aloud by town criers, and the content of pamphlets must have also been passed along in oral readings. In a politically charged urban atmosphere, the contents of a newly arrived, sensational pamphlet probably reached a broad cross-section of the population very quickly. The contents of pamphlets certainly reached a larger and socially more diverse audience than the book-buying public.

9. See Chartier's analysis of these data in "Pamphlets et gazettes," 1:413–423.
10. Ibid. The officers constituted 30 percent of Nicolas's known clientele (138 out of 460 persons) and 58 percent of the known purchasers of *mazarinades* (48 out of 83).
11. Duccini, "Regard sur la littérature pamphlétaire," 328.
12. L'Estoile, *Journal*, ed. Lefevre and Martin, 1:331–332.

LOCAL POLITICIZATION AND THE ISSUES

The combination of oral and written dissemination of propaganda is illustrated by the transmission of important political news early in the 1614–1617 campaigns. In the case of most major urban centers outside Paris, the first suggestions of political trouble were contained in handwritten royal letters from the capital, delivered by courier. The court's first set of letters to the provinces went out in mid-February, a few weeks after the forces of the rebels had gathered in Mézières. The letters arrived, for example, on 13 February in Poitiers, on 17 February in Angers, on 22 February in Dijon, and on 20 February in Bordeaux.[13] The Crown appears to have been able to circulate prejudicial information about Condé's enterprise several weeks before pamphlets from either side began to appear. The earliest mention of Condé's first pamphlet in such correspondence is in a letter from the queen mother dated 24 February to Cardinal de Sourdis.[14] The first bit of evidence that Condé's pamphlet was in general circulation is the mention of its appearance in Poitiers on 8 March.[15]

When letters from the Crown arrived in a provincial city, a number of things happened. Most important, they were generally read aloud at a special meeting of the town council or, in some cases, a much larger assembly. The town council then proceeded to order the posting of guards (or additional guards) at the city gates.[16] Prelates who were strong allies of the queen mother took it upon themselves to give or order spe-

13. See the references to municipal deliberations below and for Bordaux in *Inventaire Sommaire* (see sec. II of the Bibliography), 4:221–22. In Bordeaux the lieutenant governor was a close ally of the administration and had already ordered special guards on 13 February "en vue d'une surprise du prince de Condé," well before the order arrived from Paris in the official correspondence.

14. Ms. fr. 6379, f. 181.

15. Délibérations de l'Hôtel de Ville of Poitiers, 8 March 1614.

16. The deliberations of the Chambre de la Ville of Dijon and the Hostel et Maison de la Ville of Angers are instructive. When the municipal governments received the queen mother's letter (characterizing Condé's departure from the court and requesting political assistance), a special meeting of the city council was convoked in Dijon on 22 February, first to hear Marie's letter of 13 February read by the clerk, then to give the bearer of the letter a chance to make more detailed explanations, and finally to hear the advice of local notables, including a representative of the governor; Archives Municipales du Dijon, B 251, ff. 178–181. Similar meetings took place in Angers on 17 February, Archives Municipales d'Angers, BB 60, ff. 97–100; in Bordeaux on 20 and 22 February (see n. 13 above); and in Agen on 24 February, Archives Communales conserved in the Archives Departementales, Lot-et-Garonne (Agen), BB 42, ff. 129–130. At the Angers meeting, the baron de Sainte-Suzanne, governor of the town, presented a letter from his father, governor of the province, saying that all the towns on the Loire River had posted guards and that it would be appropriate to do so in Angers as well "for the service of the King and the preservation of the town."

cial services dedicated to the health and safety of the king and his mother. The initiatives of Cardinal de Sourdis, archbishop of Bordeaux, were probably typical. De Sourdis appended political speeches to his sermons that were greeted with cheers of "Vive le Roi, Vive la Reine, vive le Cardinal."[17] The queen mother and her advisers were grateful for these orations; a letter from Secretary of State Pontchartrain thanked the cardinal on behalf of the queen mother for "the public exhortations" and for the "handbills urging prayers to God for the health of their Majesties."[18] No doubt many other clergymen engaged in the same kind of activity.[19]

Many local officials clearly saw it as their duty to publicize the news of Condé's "movements" and the potential for trouble in their own localities. Publicity was a major purpose of the larger town council meetings convoked to hear the February 1614 letters from the queen mother. The propagandistic function of these ad hoc municipal meetings is underscored by the attendance of local military governors, community representatives, and other persons not usually present at such gatherings. In Angers, for example, six Protestants were specially invited to the reading of the regent's letter on 17 February so that the Protestants would not misconstrue any military preparations by the town's militia.[20]

Both the letter and the oral messages delivered by courier were aimed at consolidating support for the queen mother's administration, even though Condé was not yet characterized in official propaganda as the leader of a "revolt." Villeroy's letters are measured, yet clearly partisan, calls for political discipline and support. The oral messages were more direct and polemical, even provocative. The sieur of Fondrière, who delivered the queen mother's letters to Dijon, spoke at some length about her political intentions.[21] He said she had done everything in her power to keep Condé and the other princes content but was prepared to proceed with the Spanish marriages and had raised an army of twenty thousand foot soldiers and three thousand horsemen for security. Fondrière denied the "false rumor" that the queen mother wanted her regency to continue for two additional years and defended the administration's foreign policy. The sieur of Fourcquevoller, who delivered the same

17. A limited description of de Sourdis's orations can be found in Ravenez, *Histoire du Cardinal Sourdis,* 284ff.

18. Letter of 29 February 1614, B.N. Ms. fr. 6379, f. 189.

19. Bishops writing to Pontchartrain also appear to have been one of the Crown's primary sources of intelligence about developments in the southwest. See, in addition to the bishop of Poitiers's correspondence mentioned below, other letters to Paris from Sourdis and from the bishop of Luçon (Richelieu), B.N. Ms. Clair. 364, ff. 229, 275.

20. Archives Municipales d'Angers, BB 60, f. 97.

21. Archives Municipales du Dijon, B 251, ff. 179–179 verso.

letter to Angers, added "some words of confidence with which he was charged," in addition to the contents of the queen mother's letter, but the record provides no further details.[22]

Such emissaries provoked widespread discussion in taverns, at market, and in the normal conversations of business and daily life. Through immediate measures such as the increased security at a city's gates, inhabitants of the suburbs as well as the towns were alerted to the likelihood that something politically important was about to happen. Organizing the town militia to keep watch at the city gates must have been especially significant. Participation in the watch was often demanded of every citizen of the town, and sometimes even of women. Keeping watch, especially at night, was considered a burdensome obligation that people often tried to avoid. City fathers were reluctant to order a watch unless it was absolutely necessary, in part because it caused additional expenses such as purchasing wood to keep fires going at night. The need for the watch at the city gates and the assignment of guard duty provoked discussions among neighbors and arguments with city authorities.

These were the first steps, in early 1614, toward a broad politicization of the French public. Through the actions of local magistrates or through news carried by messengers, the possible revolt of the prince de Condé rapidly entered the consciousness of the public. Even at this early state of the 1614–1617 conflict, political participation was both local and national. People were defending their towns, and defending the town was identical (for many) to supporting the administration of the queen mother against troublemakers—the princes, their henchmen, or others who might try to take advantage of the situation. Preservation of the town "for the service of the king" was a kind of patriotic duty, ultimately linked to maintaining law and order both in the realm and in one's own community.[23]

Further escalation of the conflict and the identification of national and local issues occurred as pamphlets and local leaders elaborated on the basic issues and introduced new ones. In the context of 1614–1617, further politicization was especially intense in towns that were already deeply divided along politico-religious lines, or towns that had some special relationship with one of the rebel leaders. In these cases, the act of preserving the status quo exposed and exacerbated existing political divisions in the town and sometimes led to a violent struggle for control. In Poitiers, for instance, a very broad cross-section of the public participated in these contests, and printed propaganda was an important source of agitation.

22. Archives Municipales d'Angers, BB 60, f. 98 verso.

23. De Lestang used the following language in his letter to Paris: "For all that is represented in the letter of my said Lord the Prince [i.e., Condé's manifesto], there are no disturbances in this area, although certain people continue to spread rumors detrimental to the service of the King and the authority of your majesties," B.N. Ms. Clair. 364, f. 54.

THE AFFAIR OF POITIERS

In most of France the political behavior of the public was characterized throughout 1614–1617 by cooperation with Marie de Médicis's administration. Urban elites generally and royal officials in particular rallied early and decisively in support of the government. The most important exceptions to this rule were towns with strong ties to Condé or one of his confederates through a governorship, and towns under the control of Protestants. Poitiers was one of the former.[24] The loyalties of the military governor of Poitiers, the duc de Roannes, vacillated. Two of Condé's partisans, the marquis de Bonnivet and the marquis de Rochefort, were among the more prominent nobles of the region. The struggle for control of Poitiers began as soon as Condé launched his challenge in February 1614. The queen mother and her advisers watched events very closely and wrote several letters to the town warning the citizens not to involve themselves in political conspiracies and intrigues (*pratiques et menées*), to live harmoniously together (*vous maintenir tous ensemble en bonne union et amitié*), and to guard the city gates carefully in order that "no one enter whoever he be, if followed by anyone other than his usual companions, on whatever pretext, unless he carries a passport or an express order from the King."[25]

The struggle for control of Poitiers is of particular interest here for three reasons. First, there is considerable evidence about the involvement of ordinary citizens in the struggle. Second, it displays interesting ideological configurations that appear closely tied to the printed propaganda then in circulation. Finally, it is a microcosm of the much broader struggle for control of France. Poitiers, like any major town, would be a major asset to either political coalition. This was particularly true because the region was heavily populated by Protestants, and many local antagonisms remained from the religious wars. Early in the 1614 struggle, the militancy of the bishop of Poitiers became a central issue. He was accused of practicing Holy League politics and of trying to build his own "royal throne" in Poitiers.[26] Like other prelates in the region, the bishop was a strong partisan of Marie de Médicis's administration, and he worked

24. The story about to unfold was reconstructed from printed pamphlets, documents in B.N. Ms. Clair. 364, and the Délibérations de l'Hôtel de Ville of Poitiers, Bibliothèque Municipales (Register) 68. See also the careful study by Ouvré, "Essay sur l'histoire de la ville de Poitiers," 365–528, based largely on sources available in the Bibliothèque Municipale of Poitiers.

25. Délibérations de l'Hôtel de Ville of Poitiers, Bibliothèque Municipales (Register) 68, f. 201, 206–207, and 213–215 (several such letters were copied into the register).

26. The phrase *Throsne de la Roiauté qu'il imagine de former à Poitiers* appears in Condé's letter to the queen of 11 July, B.N. Ms. Clair. 364, 223. This was one of several letters that Condé sent to Paris, the first of which are dated 26 and 27 July. The letter of 25 June (e.g., to Jeannin, B.N. Ms. fr. 3799) is reproduced almost word for word in the pamphlet entitled *Lettre de Monsieur le Prince envoyée à La Royne* (1614).

very hard to ensure that Condé's faction, tinged with Protestantism, did not gain a foothold in the province or the town.[27]

Politicization occurred along lines of a traditional Poitevin rivalry—the militant Catholics on one side, the moderates (or *politiques*) on the other. The existing rivalry between bishop and other local notables—particularly the mayor and the town's royal (military) governor—helped to consolidate these divisions. The bishop, Henri-Louis Chasteigner de la Rocheposay, was an intelligent, energetic, and well-educated prelate from an ancient and wealthy family among the local nobility. He liked and understood political power. He was also a Catholic reformer and an ardent papist. The governor, Louis Gouffier, duc de Roannes, was the ambitious and quarrelsome head of another important local family.[28] A political pragmatist, he was tolerated by the municipal government and local Protestants. The mayor, Nicolas de Sainte-Marthe, and his family were decidedly *politique*. They had also been members of the municipal oligarchy for years and resented the bishop's intrusive power.

These tensions were aggravated by the broader military and religious situation in the Province of Poitou. The duc de Sully, Henry IV's famous Protestant minister of finance (now retired), was still the royal governor of the province. The lieutenant-governor, the marquis de Rochefort, was a favorite of the prince de Condé and an officer in his household.[29] Sully never openly supported Condé nor raised any troops for the rebels in the 1614–1617 conflict. At the same time, he was critical of the queen mother's administration and encouraged the Protestants to remain independent of either coalition, while quietly agitating behind the scenes and urging military preparedness.[30] In such circumstances, all sides could legitimately fear a change in the balance of power in the City of Poitiers and the surrounding province.

These rivalries were transformed overnight into an overt struggle for control of Poitiers by the arrival in March of Condé's pamphlet. On 8 March a messenger arrived from Rochefort on behalf of Condé carrying a printed copy of Condé's February manifesto and a handwritten letter addressed to the mayor and the city council.[31] In an effort to dissociate himself from any conspiracy, the mayor immediately convoked a special meeting of the municipal leadership in order to receive and interrogate

27. Formon, "Henri-Louis Chasteigner de la Rocheposay," 165–231.

28. Beauchet-Filleau et al., *Dictionnaire Historique et Généalogique des Familles de Poitou,* 4:255–257.

29. Aumale, *Histoire des Princes de Condé,* 1:21 (see sec. II of Bibliography).

30. Sully's position is evident from his letters to Villeroy, Bibliothèque de l'Institute de France, Ms. Godefroy 268, ff. 44 and 57.

31. Délibérations de l'Hôtel de Ville, Poitiers, Bibliothèque Municipales (Register) 68, f. 220.

the courier. When the blatantly partisan content of the message became apparent, the mayor quickly tried to sever all ties to the pamphlet and to Condé. He made a public show of sending the letter and the pamphlet to the queen mother and her advisers in an effort or demonstrate his loyalty.

Condé's pamphlet was probably not immediately reprinted and disseminated about the city, but it nonetheless played a crucial role in the ensuing political struggle. The pamphlet's very existence may have been as politically important as its content. It was a clear indication of Condé's hostile political stance and his probable tactics. To the progovernment faction it meant that Condé was a rebel and was trying to win over the town. The contents of the pamphlet, like the contents of the queen mother's letters, were made known first to the political elite of the town and then to the general public. It had passed through a number of hands on its way to Poitiers, including those of Condé's noble allies in the region. Moreover, Marie's partisans were not necessarily trying to keep the pamphlet secret; some saw it as incriminating evidence of the rebels' real intentions.

The appearance of the pamphlet did a great deal to undermine the political position of the moderate party. The bishop began publicly to portray the mayor and his friends as agents of Condé, intent on opening the town gates to the prince and his unruly soldiers. The bishop's interpretation of events was convincing, and his credibility among the townspeople grew. Within a few weeks of the arrival of Condé's pamphlet-carrying messenger, the inhabitants of Poitiers had split decisively into two opposing camps, one hostile toward the prince de Condé and loyal to the bishop, the other antagonistic toward the bishop, but not necessarily supporters of Condé. Eager to break the bishop's hold over the town, however, they were probably willing to use Condé toward this end.

The bishop's effort to politicize Poitiers gained strength in April and May. By early May at the latest, it became clear that Condé's party had gained a foothold in the province. The bishop wrote to Paris on 3 and 17 May claiming the marquis de Bonnivet had raised several hundred troops in the countryside around Poitiers, strongly recommending that the court try to purchase the marquis's loyalty with a military commission.[32] The bishop claimed that Bonnivet's company had gained such strength and caused such destruction in the countryside around Poitiers that food was becoming expensive and the citizens of Poitiers were up in arms. Bonnivet's actions were clearly allied with Condé's enterprise, he asserted, which further polarized the city.

The conflict was also escalating at the national level. Both sides raised

32. The bishop's letters of 3 and 17 May 1614, B.N. Ms. Clair. 364, ff. 102, 131.

armies but then agreed to a treaty signed on 15 May at Sainte-Mé-nehould. This agreement called for the cessation of hostilities and disarmament on both sides. As many supporters of the administration feared, however, Condé used the peace as a chance to further undermine the government and to build his political faction. Condé moved his headquarters to Amboise (just east of Tours), where he occupied a fortified château the queen mother had given him as a sign of her good faith. In return, Condé tried to use his friends' influence in the region to strengthen his party and to enlist Protestant support for his cause. The timing of this move was very important because deputies to the Estates General (scheduled to meet in the fall) would be elected in the late summer and fall; of course, Condé hoped to secure the election of deputies favorable to his cause. The queen mother's supporters in the region, including the bishop of Poitiers, were aware of this strategy and worked hard to defeat it.

By mid-June the people of Poitiers were intensely involved in the struggle over their town. At least one citizen was killed; another was wounded. The bishop took control from the governor and the mayor, and the queen mother sent a special commissioner to restore order. But later in the year the militant Catholics defiantly banished several leaders of the opposition.

One of the Crown's political tactics, orchestrated by the bishop, was to sponsor a loyal mayoral candidate in the municipal elections on 27 June. Removing the incumbent mayor (Sainte-Marthe) would weaken the position of his party of moderate notables—a party consisting of Saint Clair (*procureur du roi* in the local sovereign court), the mayor's uncle (a local *tresorier*), Roannes (the governor), and La Charoulière (second in command of the municipal guard after the mayor). Condé learned of the plan, and on 19 June, just a few days before the mayoral election, he sent two of "his gentlemen" and their lackeys to Poitiers with a letter addressed to the city fathers, informing them of his "sincere intentions" to serve the queen mother, to which he added "some complaints about the Bishop" who had spoken of him "in an undignified manner."[33] This delegation (including a local gentleman named La Trye) was attacked in the streets of Poitiers by henchmen of the bishop's party. According to Condé, the attackers cried to La Trye, "You are carrying letters from your Prince against our reverend Bishop. You die."[34] At this signal armed men attacked the two messengers. La Trye was wounded by several bullets and his lackey was killed on the spot. La Trye was taken to the mayor's house to recuperate from his wounds, and Blanchardière (the

33. Condé's letter to the queen on 25 June, B.N. Ms. Clair. 364, f. 163.
34. Ibid.

other gentleman) was allowed to return to Condé with news of the attack. The lackey's body was left in the street until the next day—a powerful symbol about who controlled the town.

The people of Poitiers reacted sharply to news of the violence. Some were outraged, but many more celebrated a "victory" on behalf of the town and the bishop. The mayor had been powerless to impose his authority. The level of political activity reached an even higher pitch when news reached the town days later of Condé's decision to personally rescue La Trye.[35] Lookouts were put in the church steeple, chains were stretched across the streets (to stop horses), and barricades were erected. Although the mayor was legally captain of the bourgeois militia, the members of the militia were more responsive to the bishop. When Condé arrived (23 June), the city's militia and the gates were in the hands of the bishop's followers.

According to his own account, Condé had separated himself from the greater part of his armed followers and headed for Poitiers with "only fifteen horsemen" after learning of the "assassination" of his men. Condé was determined to enter the town to inform himself more fully of the incident and, no doubt, to try to loosen the bishop's hold over the inhabitants. Five hundred yards from the gate, he met a messenger, Beaulieu de Persac, who claimed to have direct orders from the queen mother that the inhabitants of Poitiers had been commanded by their majesties to obey the bishop. Condé was not to enter the town unless the bishop saw fit. Ignoring this, Condé approached the closed and fortified gate and asked to be admitted. He was refused. He then asked to speak to someone in authority and was addressed from the ramparts with great insolence by an excitable fellow named Berland. Berland replied that the refusal was the decision of ten thousand armed men within the town who would die rather than allow him entry and that if the prince would not leave peacefully, he would be shot at.[36] Condé retired from the city gates deeply humiliated and lodged himself and his troops nearby at Chatellerault in order to plan his revenge.

Two days later, on 25 June, the military governor, Roannes, arrived from Paris. Concerned about both his authority generally and the municipal elections, he tried to impose his own control over the town with miserable results. Again, the bishop's ability to control the bourgeois militia was crucial, although he caused a scandal by wearing battle armor

35. Report of Special Commissioner Le Masuyer to the court, 28 June 1614, B.N. Ms. Clair. 364, ff. 193–194.

36. Berland's words are characterized by Condé as "infinies insolences." Cf. Richelieu, *Mémoires*, 1:292.

and carrying a pike around town.[37] By the end of the day, the inhabitants of the town had more or less imprisoned Roannes in the bishop's residence, where he spent the night. According to Roannes, a sergeant in the militia came to see him that night as a spokesman for some of the townspeople and addressed him in the following fashion. "My Lord, I come on behalf of 2000 men of this town who are very disturbed by what has happened to you. They offer you their protection, knowing well that you are a good servant of the King, and their governor. Nevertheless, they desire that you submit to the authority of the Bishop."[38]

The next morning Roannes was escorted outside the city gates by a deputation of the bishop's supporters. And on the following day, 27 June, Brilhac de Nouzieres, a supporter of the bishop and a *lieutenant criminel,* was elected mayor. Poitiers was now completely in the hands of the bishop and his party. Condé's allies had lost the election and were soon afterward driven from the city.

The prince was furious, and he wrote several letters to the queen mother complaining of the grave offenses that the bishop and the town had committed against him. It was, after all, peacetime, yet the bishop had tried to have one of his messengers assassinated, had armed a town against him, sounded the tocsin at his approach, and engineered his public humiliation at the gates of the city. Condé demanded that the bishop be punished and his henchmen turned over to the courts. He also demanded he be allowed personally to take revenge on the sieur de Saint George (a relative of the bishop). He would "die a thousand deaths before enduring such an affront" to his dignity without taking revenge.[39] The Crown responded by explaining that before deciding how to handle the affair, the queen mother wanted to hear the report of a special commissioner, M. Masuyer, a *maître des requêtes* who was immediately dispatched to Poitiers and who would begin sending the results of his investigations to Paris on 28 June.

The role of the political propaganda and of the common citizens of Poitiers in all of this is visible at numerous points in the record. Particularly telling is the evidence in the letters to the Crown from Roannes and from Masuyer, although one must take account of the latter's wish to smooth over some difficulties by exonerating the bishop on the one hand, and Roannes's wish to stress the "insubordination" of the bishop

37. *Apologie pour messire Henry-Louys Chastaigner de La Rochepozay* (1615) is a 267-page polemic attributed to the young Jean Du Vergier de Hauranne, a protégé and admirer of the bishop with a famous career ahead of him as the abbé de St.-Cyran.

38. *Proces Verbal de la revolte faicte* (1614), 14. Roannes wrote letters to Pontchartrain and the queen on 29 June, B.N. Ms. Clair. 364, ff. 165–167 verso, complaining of the bishop's activities. Later he wrote a long *proces verbal* describing the events of 25 June; B.N. Ms. Colbert, 12, ff. 256–26 verso, published almost word for word in pamphlet just cited.

39. Condé's letter of 25 June to Jeannin, cited in n. 26.

on the other. The governor and the commissioner depicted the involvement of the townspeople in different fashions, but both attested to the
intensity of this involvement.

Masuyer's letters contain a plausible interpretation of the towndwellers' fear of Condé and his agents.[40] Masuyer reported that before the
refusal at the gate, the people of Poitiers had been greatly disturbed by
the prince's meeting since the peace had been formalized with the duc de
Vendôme (who had recently taken over the fortified town of Vannes in
defiance of the Crown) and the duc de Rohan, a leading Protestant. Few
in Poitiers believed the political maneuvering had really subsided, and
many feared there was a conspiracy to place the town under Condé's
command. If the mayor and his friends were not part of the conspiracy,
they were, at least, rather lax in opposing it. In contrast, the bishop was
seen to be a valiant defender of Poitiers's interests, and the people had
great confidence in him. They interpreted Condé's attempt to enter Poitiers as an effort to take it over, especially in view of the injury to La Trye
and Condé's entourage of Bonnivet and others. Much of this thinking
was undoubtedly shaped by the bishop and his agents, but it was nevertheless authentic public opinion.

In the course of his investigation, Masuyer found some disturbing
evidence of popular political attitudes. Many citizens of Poitiers had
clearly felt the Crown had not supported them strongly enough in their
stand against Condé. One individual confessed to having had dreams of
assassinating the king. Masuyer tried to mitigate the implications of this
utterance by stressing that the man was mentally disturbed and the son
of an epileptic.[41] He was obviously worried, though, and took especial
note of one man who professed, during the excitement surrounding
Condé's attempted entry into Poitiers, that "there are still a dozen in
Poitiers who would happily do what Ravaillac [assassin of Henry IV]
did."[42] These accounts demonstrate a certain political consciousness. It
may have been a distorted and highly emotional version of the elites'

40. Masuyer sent at least twenty-one dispatches to the court (extant in B.N. Ms. Clair.
364) from the time of his arrival in late June 1614 until he was thrown out of the town in
December.

41. Masuyer's accounts of these particular investigations are in B.N. Ms. Clair. 364, ff.
319–319 verso. In his letter to the queen mother, Masuyer observed that "he was of a
melancholy humor, a hypochondriac, and the son of a father who was epileptic. He had a
habit of swearing and blaspheming, and his usual oath was to give himself to the devil."
And this was only a partial list of the young man's problems. In the letter to Secretary of
State Pontchartrain, Masuyer explains that the fellow was a lackey to one of the gentlemen
in the service of the bishop of Poitiers and his relative, the sieur de La Rocheposay.

42. Ibid., 321–321 verso. In the postscript, Masuyer reports to Pontchartrain on the
progress of two cases, one concerning an individual "qui durant ces esmotions de Poictiers
dict ces mots parlant de contentions des grands, qu'il y avoit encores une douzaine dans
Poictiers qui feroint bien Ravaillac. Il est funest que ce siècle produise tant de monstres."

political consciousness, but it was a vision of "national" politics that clearly helped the bishop to take control of Poitiers.

The role of pamphlets in spreading political consciousness and in influencing specific events is difficult to determine. Following the brief appearance of Condé's pamphlet in early March, diplomatic sources do not mention any pamphlets circulating in Poitiers. A printing establishment was active in the town, but nothing can be attributed to it with much certainty until late in the summer.[43] Without question, pamphlets and placards eventually played a role. Following Condé's attempt to enter the town, there was an explosion of pamphlet literature dealing with the affair of Poitiers. Letters from Condé and Roannes to the Crown about the affair were reproduced as pamphlets.[44] Proadministration responses quickly followed. Supporters of the regent published several of her letters, including one describing the affair of Poitiers to Monsieur de Roquelaure, lieutenant-governor of Guyenne.[45] One of Masuyer's dispatches to Paris was also published.[46] In addition, a more polemical literature soon surrounded the affair, most of which favored the queen mother.[47] Some of this literature was intended for local audiences and printed by local printers.[48]

One pamphlet clearly aimed at a popular audience was *La Carabinade du mangeur de bonnes gens: A messieurs de Poictiers.*[49] References to the lives of simple people abound in this satirical piece, poorly printed on cheap paper. It scolds the citizens of Poitiers for having selfishly tried to protect their chickens from the ravages of the rebels and for not having allowed themselves to be led about by the nose like animals. Then, in a shift from satire to invective, Condé is the real monster (the "mangeur de bonnes gens") and Berland, the rabble-rouser who insulted Condé, is a

43. There were probably two printers working in Poitiers—Julian Thoreau and Antoine Mesnier. The first piece concerning this affair attributable to either of them was probably published later in the summer of 1614, when the royal family arrived—*La rejouissance de Poitiers*.

44. Condé, *Lettre de Monsieur le Prince envoyée à La Royne* (1614, exists in four editions) and *Justice que monseigneur le prince demande* (1614). *Proces Verbal* (1614, exists in two editions).

45. *Lettre de la Royne à monsieur de Roquelaure* (1614).

46. *Lettres du sieur de Mazuyer* (1614).

47. *Remerciment au roy par les habitans de la ville de Poictiers* (1614); *Libre Discours sur les mouvemens derniers de la France et particulièrement de Poictou* (1614).

48. In addition to *Carabinade*, local printers also published *Accueil au roy par Gabriel Bien-Venue* (1614), a less-creative piece in the same popular genre. Later, when the king and queen actually arrived in Poitiers, many pamphlets were produced celebrating their visit. Several pieces of official correspondence cited in this chapter were later published as pamphlets in Bordeaux by Millanges. For the generally high level of printing activity in this region at this time, see Desgraves, "Aspects des controverses," 153–187.

49. B.N. Lb36.316.

"valiant champion" who helped Poitiers escape from a terrible siege. The bishop's probity is praised through an insinuation that he might have given up a cardinal's hat by having been such an uncompromising defender of the town. The principal purpose of the pamphlet was to reinforce people's fear of the rebel princes and to encourage disdain for their politics in the precarious months following Condé's humiliation. Comparing the discipline of the king's forces with the disorder of Condé's, the pamphleteer exclaimed that "a single regiment of the King's guards" would "destroy like plaster everything" that the rebels "could put in the field in ten years."

An even more direct appeal to the citizens of Poitiers was printed later in the year (December) and posted on doors throughout the city. This placard (from which the epigraph for this chapter was taken) was so vehement and so reminiscent of Holy League politics that some Catholics accused their enemies of having printed it in an effort to discredit them.[50] The partisan rhetoric surely echoes the vicious language flung about the streets of Poitiers. The placard even named several citizens still present in the town who could not be trusted and against whom the loyal citizens had to protect themselves. It spoke in nearly hysterical tones of their efforts to render the prince master of the town and, in so doing, to place it under Huguenot rule. For this reason, the citizens were urged to enforce the banishments and to endorse further banishments, if necessary, in order to preserve a town "on which depends the health of the Pope and of the King, and the conservation of the state religion, for which to die would be an honor to the faithful Catholic servants of the king."[51]

Pamphlets and pamphlet-inspired rhetoric surrounded the struggle for control of Poitiers. The appearance of Condé's February manifesto was especially important and greatly aggravated political tensions. These pamphlets confirm the view that mobilization of support in the struggle for control of the town involved concrete choices. These were both issue-motivated, e.g., religion, and pragmatically motivated, e.g., local political power. The personality of the bishop and his general support for the queen mother and her policies were also clearly issues on which such

50. Two handwritten copies of the text of this placard exist, both described as "affiche seditieuse des habitans de Poitiers mise aux principalles portes lors que le Roy y envoya M. Mangot pour restablir les principaux de la ville qu'ilz avoient chassez, le mois de decembre 1614"; B.N. Ms. fr. 3653, ff. 44–55, and B.N. Ms. Colbert 17, ff. 188–188 verso. The placard was entitled "De l'Ordonnance et arrets de quatorze cens fidelles de cette ville hardiment resolue de mourir pour la manutantion de la foy catholique, apostholique et Romaine et service du Roy Louis XIII."
51. Ibid.

choices were based. The bishop represented a militantly proadministration stance, to which the mayor and his friends were opposed. Many of the townspeople, however, clearly approved. Moreover, as the "seditious" placard makes particularly evident, the loyalty of Poitiers was seen by many as an important factor in the broader struggle for control of France's destiny.

The Poitiers affair also shows how many of the inhabitants of Poitiers and the surrounding countryside participated in the defense of their town against Condé. Popular anxiety ran high, and the bishop was not reluctant to exploit it for his own purposes. He contributed a great deal to this intense politicization by providing knowledge about Condé's activities in the area, by challenging the mayor and the governor, and by emphasizing the military danger to the town. It also seems likely that the bishop encouraged the townspeople to interpret the conflict in religious terms.

The bishop tried to represent himself to the Crown as keeping the town out of Condé's hands and maintaining law and order in a difficult situation. In July, when news arrived from Paris that the bishop would be forced to remove himself from the town, he wrote back saying that people were so disturbed and "carried to such extremities" that he would have "feared a revolution" if M. Frazelière's arrival with some reassuring news from court had not calmed them down.[52] The bishop explained, in as diplomatic a way as possible, that people felt "abandoned" by the royal government in their efforts to protect themselves from the rebel prince and had expected more help from the Crown.

In spite of the somewhat different gloss he would impose on these events, Roannes's letter confirms this picture of general agitation in Poitiers.[53] Although Roannes tried to portray a law-abiding townspeople being excited to "sedition" against him by their bishop, he could not conceal the extent of public involvement in the preparations against Condé. At several points he encountered great crowds of the bishop's supporters. Although he saw it as "disobedience," he confirmed that the people were mobilized to protect themselves. The streets of the town were barricaded and chained, and bands of armed citizens roamed the streets. There was an intense struggle for control of the militia, in which all levels of command, from sergeant to captain, were involved. He also confirmed the extensive polarization of the elite.

Despite the heavy influence of religious rhetoric, the structure of the

52. Poitiers to Pontchartrain, 7 and 10 July 1614, B.N. Ms. Clair. 364, ff. 211 and 220.

53. Roannes's letters to Pontchartrain and the queen on 29 June, B.N. Ms. Clair. 364, ff. 165–167 verso, complaining of the activities of the bishop, and B.N. Ms. Colbert, 12, ff. 256–260 verso. These letters provide abundant evidence of religious zealotry and popular sedition, which Roannes is eager to attribute to the bishop's fanaticism.

struggle and the composition of the two factions suggest that neither religion nor socioeconomic interests alone were enough to determine the political choices of Poitivins in 1614. Both factions were composed of an assortment of municipal officials, royal officials, and local gentlemen, all Catholic, with the possible exception of Bonnivet and some of his gang. Local political ties, more than anything else, appear to have been the decisive factor, but those bonds were impregnated with ideology. The bishop's close relations with Paris and his militant Catholicism went hand in hand. The sympathy of the mayor, Sainte-Marthe, and his group for Condé reflected a desire to be more independent of both the bishop and the Crown. Within this general framework, there was also a great deal of room for local issues to be related to the national political struggle.

In Paris, the "conservation" of Poitiers was interpreted by Villeroy as an important but narrow victory. He argued long and hard in the regency councils that the king and his mother should follow through with a visit to the region in an extended tour that would consolidate support for the administration on the eve of the elections for the Estates General.[54] Over the objections of the chancellor and Concini, who thought such a trip too dangerous, the king and queen mother made the journey in July and August. The court visited Orléans, Blois, Tours, Poitiers, Angers, and Nantes. Royal entries and elaborate ceremonies were staged in each of these places with great success.[55] By the end of the tour, the king and queen regent were able to return confidently to Paris to prepare for the celebration of the king's majority and the opening of the Estates General.

The queen mother and her supporters thus won a decisive victory in the public arena early in the 1614–1617 struggles. The following chapter will explore some reasons for this. Not only was the Crown able to produce more pamphlets than the opposition during these years, but it also produced better pamphlets that skillfully blended popular ways of looking at politics with a more convincing interpretation of the facts. Much more so than the rebels, the government was able to link its program with a broadly appealing rhetoric of law and order.

54. Richelieu reports that Villeroy and Jeannin had to argue strenuously against Concini and Chancellor Brûlart de Sillery to convince the queen mother to take this trip; see his *Mémoires*, 1:293. Hayden, "Deputies and *Qualités*," 507–524, discusses briefly the regency's considerable effort (of which this tour was a part) to secure the election of loyal deputies to the Estates, see esp. pp. 517–519.

55. The registers of the hôtel de ville of Angers show the town going to great trouble and expense to welcome the court appropriately. A mock naval battle was staged on the Loire; see Archives Municipales, Anger, BB 61, ff. 22 ff. By all accounts the tour was a great success, and people turned out in great numbers to cheer the young Louis XIII. A series of pamphlets described the ceremonies in several towns; see Bourgeois and André, *Sources de l'histoire de France*, 4:21–22.

FIVE

◆ ◆ ◆

Ethos and Audience

Alexander the Blacksmith having thus spoken, everyone in the crowd stared at one another [speechless], and it seemed as if a log from Jupiter had fallen into a pond of Frogs who were hoping to change the state of their Republic.
—*LA HARANGUE D'ACHIOR L'AMMONITE SUR UN ADVIS DONNE À MONSEIGNEUR LE PRINCE* (1614), 2

The broad distribution of pamphlets and the events in Poitiers (analyzed in Chapter 4) point to a large and important public in the 1614–1617 political conflict. Further evidence about the public and its responses to pamphlet literature can be gathered from the texts themselves.[1] The strategic importance of particular segments of society has already been pointed out. Recall Villeroy's description of the groups to which the Crown should pay particular attention—"great nobles, officers of the Crown, governors of provinces, gentlemen and lords of all conditions, as well as the Parlements, the other sovereign courts and royal officials, along with the magistrates and corporate organizations of the towns . . . [as well as the] Protestants as a body."[2] This concept of the public is reflected in the persuasive strategies employed by pamphleteers. The ways in which authors addressed a particular audience through the use of a stylized ethos or a dramatized persona are especially instructive, as is the use of humor and satire. The frequent resort to commonplaces also helps to identify the audience. Such rhetorical choices made by authors provide useful evidence about *how* pamphlets were intended to be read, and they confirm, from yet another angle, the richness of this middlebrow political discourse.

We know that "audience" was a category very much on authors' minds in 1614 because rhetorical theory occupied a central position in the intellectual life of the age. Seventeenth-century rhetoricians understood persuasion as the art of "moving" the "will" of the audience.[3] This meant

---

1. Parts of this chapter first appeared in my "Jacques Bon-Homme and National Politics," 23–32.
2. B.N. Ms. fr. n. a. 7260, 123 verso.
3. Dompnier, "Missionaire et son Public," 105–122.

correctly gauging the "passions" of the audience and creating vivid images with words that would stick in the minds of the audience, thus inclining them to act in particular ways. Complex and often bizarre rhetorical theories were formulated to help authors accomplish these ends.[4] The rhetorical paradigm was built into the traditions and conventions of pamphlet discourse, and authors automatically relied on it when selecting, inventing, and arranging their arguments. In constructing his rhetoric, the pamphleteer made a range of choices about genre, stance, diction, emotional appeal, argumentative strategies, and so forth. Such choices can be reconstructed in an effort to reveal the attitudes and emotional commitments an author expected to encounter and even the specific kinds of political activity he hoped to encourage.[5]

The analysis of pamphleteers' rhetorical techniques helps to open up the world of seventeenth-century French public opinion and the system of cultural references within which it was formed. Denis Richet's study of a corpus of the more serious, argumentative pamphlets published between 1612 and 1615 illustrates the value of this approach.[6] Noting the emphasis in certain pamphlets on historical texts and examples, Richet demonstrates how deeply pamphlet discourse was embedded in a system of historical references. His analysis shows that pamphleteers worked hard to relate their partisan arguments to a basic fund of historical memories, which, it appears, were acknowledged by the audience as paradigmatic. Pamphlet rhetoric thus tells us much about the cultural level of pamphlet readers and the active manner in which they read.

An analysis of all pamphlet types and persuasive devices would be impossible here. To begin with, the types of pamphlets form a vast spectrum. Then there is a language barrier, even for scholars familiar with idiosyncracies of seventeenth-century French. Pamphlet prose is sometimes intentionally vague, often colloquial, and frequently twisted into baroque idioms that cannot always be distilled into grammatical clarity. Pamphlets make oblique references to other pamphlets. Especially when attempting to imitate popular speech, pamphlets employed a welter of allusions and references that is difficult to decode. Pamphlets addressed to specific local audiences pose particularly knotty problems of translation.

---

4. See France, *Rhetoric and Truth,* and *Racine's Rhetoric;* Ong, *Ramus, Method, and the Decay of Dialogue,* 3–16, 171–214; Yates, *Art of Memory,* 231–242; Fumaroli, *L'Age de l'éloquence,* 257–279 (on Jesuit rhetoricians and the "passions"); Du Vair, *De l'Eloquence,* 54–57; and an anonymous, unfinished treatise on rhetoric, B.N. Ms. fr. 4044, ff. 131–186.

5. Fish, *Self-Consuming Artifacts,* 78–155; Marin's *Récit est un piège;* and Bowen, *Age of Bluff.*

6. Richet, "Polémique politique en France."

The present chapter focuses on an intentionally literary corpus of pamphlets. Although long recognized as distinct from straightforward polemic, these pamphlets have been assigned no convenient rubric.[7] Many are satires; others are best described as dramatic dialogues. One rhetorical and literary device that often characterizes these texts is the use of a fictional persona. Instead of overtly revealing their political views by writing in the first person, pamphlet authors argued through fictional characters. The use of personae opened up a range of possibilities for humor, dramatization, and emotional appeals not offered by conventional prose.

Satires and dramatic dialogues were used in France during the second half of the sixteenth century in the service of Protestant and Catholic pamphlet warfare.[8] They were widely used in the last phases of the religious wars to attack Henry III and his "minions," and the leading members of the Guise and Bourbon families. *Satire Ménippée*, *Réveille-Matin*, and *Dialogue d'entre le Maheustre et le Manant* are among the more famous works that use satire and dramatic dialogue in order to make a serious argument.[9] It has already been noted that Henry IV explicitly commissioned Guillaume Du Vair to write a pamphlet in this style, and other clues point to the effectiveness of the genre.[10] In 1593 the duc de Mayenne reacted sharply to the publication of the *Dialogue d'entre le Maheustre et le Manant*, arresting several of the possible printers and offering the enormous sum of one thousand écus to anyone who would reveal the author's identity.[11]

Pamphleteers skillfully exploited these styles and a wide variety of other literary forms in the 1614–1617 pamphlet campaigns. Pieces in verse were relatively rare, but satire was common and apparently popular. Duccini calculates that the popular satirical form accounts for nearly

7. Pamphlets of this type were often bound together by collectors; see for example the collection of fifteen dramatic dialogues in the Bibliothèque Mazarine, 37279.

8. Salmon, "French Satire in the Late Sixteenth Century," 57–88; and Winandy, "Satire comme instrument politique," 269–291. The relationship of pamphlet discourse to *belles-lettres* in the seventeenth century needs to be explored further. There appears to be little if any direct borrowing from well-known plays or novels, but some of the *persona* pamphlets bear a close resemblance to Des Lauriers's *Facecieuses paradoxes de Bruscambille* (1615) and to d'Aubigné's *Aventures du baron de Foeneste* (1617), which in turn owe much to the Rabelaisian comic style as described by Bakhtin, *Rabelais and His World*. A more complete investigation (if possible) of the links between satirical pamphlets and the comic theater of the times would probably turn up some interesting relationships.

9. See Cazauy, "Essai de bibliographie des éditions de *La Satyre Ménippée*," 3–40; and Ascoli's intro., Cromé, *Dialogue d'entre le Maheustre et le Manant*.

10. (See chap. 1, "Rhetoric as Political Action.") Du Vair's pamphlet was *Response d'un bourgeois de Paris* (1594).

11. L'Estoile, *Journal*, ed. Lefevre and Martin, 1:331–332.

10 percent of the total pamphlet production during these years.[12] Such pamphlets provoked the anger and ridicule of contemporaries. One author noted the personae of "a Parakeet, an Alexander the Blacksmith, a Garment maker from Paris, a Peasant from Beauvaise, [and] a Master William" and commented that the use of unreasonable beasts and persons of low condition as mouthpieces proved the bad faith of pamphleteers and the weakness of their arguments.[13]

This author was reacting to a corpus of pamphlets that appeared in the spring of 1614. In some cases such personae were only slight modulations of the authors' own voices, as in "the Old French Warrior," "the Good Frenchman," or "the French Cato."[14] In other pamphlets the speakers were highly developed fictional characters, such as "Master William" (a fictional version of the well-known fool who entertained the court of Henry IV), "the Wandering Dullard," "the Servant of the State," and "the Faithful Client."[15] In several pamphlets, these personae are situated in dramatic settings, as when, for example, "the Blunt Roughneck" encounters some talk of rebellion in the streets of Paris.[16] In a few particularly interesting cases, the persona of one pamphlet responded directly to the persona of another pamphlet, as when an experienced "Captain" refuted the arguments of an agitated (Protestant) Blacksmith speaking before a village assembly, or when a peasant and an artisan offered conflicting interpretations of the princes' enterprise.[17]

12. Duccini, "Littérature pamphlétaire," 1:116, counts 77 "burlesques" in a corpus of 806 pamphlets.

13. *Discours sur les calomnies* (1614), 9. The pamphlets to which the author refers are: *Harangue d'Alexandre Le Fo[r]geron* (1614), *Lettre de Jacques Bon-Homme* (1614), and *Reponse du Crocheteur de la samaritaine* (1614), *Lettre de Perroquet* (1614), *Le reveil de maistre Guillaume* (1614), *Remonstrance de Pierre du Puis* (1614), and other "Maître Guillaume" pieces. Some of these are explicitly condemned in the *arrêt* of the Parlement of Paris on 29 July 1614 (see chap. 3, "Censorship and Control of the Public Sphere"), including *Remonstrance de Pierre du Puis, Alexandre Forgeron, Lettre de Jacques Bon-homme, Reponse du Crocheteur de la samaritaine a Jacques Bonhomme, Le reveil de maistre Guillaume, Le Franc taupin* (1614), and *Reponse du Crocheteur de la samaritaine.*

14. *Vieux Gaulois* (1614); *Bon François* (1614); and *Caton François au roy* (1614) (attributed to Jacques Gillot, one of the authors of the *Satire Ménippée*).

15. The Master Guillaume pieces have just been cited above. *Lourdaut vagabond*, Lindsay and Neu 2884–2885, was a creation of Pierre Beaunis de Chanterain. The other characters are from *Le Serviteur fidelle* (1614), which discusses the revolt between a noble "client" of the prince de Condé and a high-ranking adviser to the government. Chanterain is one of the few identifiable authors of this type of pamphlet and was certainly in the pay of the queen's administration as an official "historian"; see Fossier, "Charge d'historiograph," 79; cf. Ranum, *Artisans of Glory*, 96–147.

16. "The Blunt Roughneck" for the nearly untranslatable *Le Franc taupin* (1614). The character is a swaggering Catholic soldier walking the streets of Paris.

17. *Lettre de Jacques Bon-Homme* (1614); *Reponse du Crocheteur.* Other important pieces in this series are *Harangue d'Alexandre Le Fo[r]geron* (1614) and *Libre harangue faicte par Mathault* (1614).

PERSONA AND PERSUASION

An initial and obvious reason for using a persona was concealment. Anonymity, we will recall, was central to pamphlet discourse; almost three-quarters of the pamphlets published between January 1614 and June of 1617 were anonymous.[18] In addition to the obvious practical reasons for concealing one's identity, pamphlet authors had rhetorical reasons for maintaining their anonymity. Pamphleteers who wanted to be genuinely persuasive did not always want to state their point of view on the very first page. One had only to read the title *Letter from my Lord the Cardinal Du Perron: To my Lord the Prince de Condé* to know that one had a proadministration pamphlet in hand.[19] Indeed, the speaker's authority and his well-known reputation as militant defender of Catholicism were primary elements in the pamphlet's appeal. Such a pamphlet was intended less to persuade anyone of the prince's evil intentions than to declare support for the queen's administration on behalf of the ultramontane leaders. Yet *Letter from Jacques Bon-Homme* was not a title that immediately suggested a proadministration stance. Thus, the author had a chance to present his case against the prince before the reader could fully recognize the lines of argument. This technique of initially concealing one's ultimate position was used in argumentative pamphlets as well, as in the case of *Apology for my Lord the Prince de Condé*, which was in fact a bitter attack on the prince.[20]

Concealment was useful, but the power of the persona as a persuasive device went much deeper. The fictional voice in a dramatic setting freed the author to create a more simplified and vivid political world. Fiction often posed as a more objective rendering of political reality. For example, everyone knew that the language used in an exchange of letters between the prince de Condé and the queen mother was artificially restrained by the need to keep within the conventions of polite, diplomatic discourse. The persona "Mathault" did not suffer any such restraints; he could say "civil war" instead of employing a euphemism, and he could directly insult the prince.[21] This appearance of cutting through the ritual of politeness, or of unmasking hypocrisy, extended to the very issues that could be discussed. "Jacques Bon-Homme" expressed the widespread fear of troops on the march—an issue that had not been addressed in the official political pamphlets. Mathault addressed religious partisanship in a straightforward way. A responsible clergyman speaking in his own voice (such as the Cardinal Du Perron) would not care, in print, to be so

18. Duccini, "Littérature pamphlétaire," 1:77–98.
19. *Lettre de monseigneur le cardinal du Perron* (1614).
20. *Apologie pour monsieur le prince* (1614).
21. *Libre harangue faicte par Mathault* is one of the most caustic pamphlets of the entire campaign; see the discussion later on in this chapter.

direct. Until war actually broke out in 1615, Condé and the queen mother were careful in their official pamphlets to avoid associating themselves with religious militancy.

Freedom to enhance or dramatize the political issues also provided subtle ways to deceive the public. This was especially true in the satirical pieces. Slanders, exaggerations, and distortions flowed copiously from the mouths of personae. The personae speaking in favor of the queen mother did their best to imply that the prince de Condé was stupid, ambitious, reckless, uneducated, inexperienced, hotheaded, and so forth. Mathault suggested, for example, that the prince de Condé was really trying to take over the government completely and make himself king of France. One should not underestimate the power of this kind of ridicule and falsification. Later in the campaign, the vicious ad hominem attacks against Concini were in large part responsible for creating the environment in which he was assassinated and the queen mother driven from power. The celebration that followed his assassination and the bizarre, ritualistic mutilation of his corpse suggest that Concini may have been one of the most widely hated ministers of the era.[22] Concini was a scapegoat, though, and blaming him for France's problems was a way to avoid many difficult issues. Although less dramatic, the earlier ad hominem attacks on Condé functioned in the same way. The persona pamphlets critical of him generally avoided addressing the substantive criticisms of the government Condé had raised in his own propaganda.

In order to appreciate the ways in which personae created a more vivid and simplified political world, one can begin with *Letter from Jacques Bon-Homme,* one of the more creative pieces in the literary genre.[23] Jacques explains that he is a ninety-seven-year-old peasant with the temerity to write a letter advising Condé and his supporters. His age and station in life give him license, he says, to speak of important affairs with objectivity and wisdom. He is careful, however, to establish his authenticity as a peasant, and, so, explains that he and his wife farm their twenty-five acres and their two small enclosures with their own hands and that he has two sons and three daughters, all married happily "without having tried to change social condition."

More to the point, though, Jacques is proud of his reputation as a political savant. This he earned by having once resolved a potentially dangerous dispute between his village and some local lords. The problem arose when the mongrel watchdog of one of the villagers took a bite

---

22. Ranum, "French Ritual of Tyrannicide," 63–82, and "Guises, Henry III, Henry IV, Concini," 36–44.

23. *Lettre de Jacques Bon-Homme* (1614); this pamphlet and two others in the same genre have been published with useful annotations by Charlier, *Revue du seizième siècle,* 1–20 and 191–218. Further page references will be to these critical editions.

out of the tail of a gentleman's hound. As Jacques explains it, after he persuaded the seigneurs not to take revenge on the villagers by devastating their fields, he became known as one of the more persuasive men of the region. Jacques thinks it is conceivable, then, that his ability to "reason" with people, not to mention his rhetorical and diplomatic skills, may help to bring the discontented princes back to their senses and, ultimately, back to court.

Interestingly, Jacques has formed his opinion of Condé's enterprise largely through his familiarity with the contents of the "letter sent from Mézières"—Condé's pamphlet of February 1614—and from the queen mother's published response. He does not claim to have read these pamphlets, but he does mention having talked to a secretary (*greffier*) who had. In the course of a village assembly gathered under an elm tree, this secretary had explained some of the specifics of Condé's political complaints and of the queen's responses. Even though he will admit his information is secondhand, Jacques can see clearly enough from their rhetoric and actions that the princes have not been well counseled in this affair.

This pamphlet thus presented the seventeenth-century reader with an obviously fictional character, who is at the same time conventional (he is a peasant), exceptional (he is wise), uneducated, and yet fully informed. The author made no attempt to conceal these contradictions. In fact, he played with them. In an obvious joke, Jacques explains that he is named after his great-great-great-grandfather, the Jacques for whom the Jacquerie (an insurrection of the French peasantry in 1358) was named. At the same time, Jacques describes many of his life experiences in an authentic fashion and with enough consistency that he emerges in the end as a plausible character with an identifiable personality and point of view. No reader would be fooled into thinking that a peasant named Jacques actually wrote this pamphlet, but this implausibility hardly destroyed the author's claim to be representing accurately the views of some of "the people." Jacques lived in a world of literary *vraisemblances*.[24] If the audience could not recognize the fictional aspects of the persona nor sense the author's persuasive intentions, the pamphlet simply would have seemed absurd. Instead, the author used the ambiguities of plausible and entertaining fiction to force his readers to look at politics from a certain point of view.[25]

24. Genette, "Vraisemblance et motivation," in *Figures II*, 71–99. The tension between reality and its "imitation" in literture and art was a common theme in the aesthetic theory of the age; see Harth, *Ideology and Culture*, 23–33.

25. A version of Marin's *piège;* he, Fish, Bowen, and others (see n. 5) have called attention to various ways that other kinds of seventeenth-century discourse worked to overcome the reader's resistance to the author's point of view.

A significant part of the appeal of Jacques Bon-Homme is his ethos of good-natured friendliness and his evenhanded discussion of political affairs—qualities associated with *politesse* and *honnêteté*.[26] He is not concerned with other people's business, only his own; he is not interested in power, but in keeping his chickens and maintaining order in the community. Above all, he is not an ideologue. His analysis of current events was not presented as the result of partisan affection for the queen mother, the Catholic church, or any other locus of authority. His frame of references for interpreting the prince de Condé's enterprise is his own everyday experiences and the practical wisdom these have brought him. Jacques's condemnation of Condé's revolt was intended to appear "objective" because it was a frank, nonpartisan, levelheaded assessment based on common sense.

Purportedly disinterested, objective discourse in the mouth of an ordinary person also appears in a pamphlet featuring an old army captain, entitled *La harangue d'Achior l'Ammonite* (a passage from this work appears as this chapter's epigraph).[27] Achior happens to wander into town at the moment when Alexander the Blacksmith (a character from another pamphlet) is haranguing an assembly of villagers. The blacksmith's speech is not reproduced, but the reader is made to understand that it was a call to join Condé's cause based on a Huguenot interpretation of still another pamphlet.[28] Achior is a *chevalier* and veteran of the civil wars, a man whose presence commands immediate respect. Despite the rudeness and uncouth behavior of the villagers (someone dares to spit in his presence), Achior agrees at their insistence to offer his political opinions about the excitable blacksmith's speech. Achior then launches into a long, detailed, and well-reasoned analysis of French foreign policy. The main point of his discourse is that those who are anxious for war against Spain in the Low Countries and who may be urging Condé to start such a war (i.e., Protestants) have forgotten the difficulties that always attend French involvement there. Although a warm supporter of the queen mother and of the obedience that subjects owe their sovereign, Achior is a moderate who favors religious toleration and respect for Protestants who are good citizens.

Both Jacques and Achior, despite their different social status, present an ethos of the honest, plain-speaking man who possesses all of the moral

26. Magendie, *Politesse mondaine et les théories de l'honnêteté*, 1:31–87, 306–401; see also Grente, ed., *Dictionnaire*, 2:501.

27. *La harangue d'Achior l'Ammonite* (1614).

28. The implication is that the Blacksmith was reading *Advis a monseigneur le prince* (1614), a pamphlet, urging Condé to take up Henry IV's anti-Spanish foreign policy, especially with regard to Flanders.

qualities valued in the seventeenth century—good manners, integrity, openness, reliability, and a sense of justice and proportion.[29] It was hoped, of course, that these virtues would also be associated with the political faction supported by the personae, that is, the queen mother's administration.

A very different rhetoric is found in *Libre Harangue faicte par Mathault.* Unlike the good-natured Jacques, Mathault is decidedly vicious, and this viciousness is an important part of his ethos. He addresses Condé in a mocking and insulting fashion, using the familiar *tu* and *toi.* The scene for Mathault's address is the Chateau d'Amboise, recently given to Condé by the Crown.

> Now, my nephew, as I call you to your face, now the principal cause of your revolt has evaporated into nothing, and your ugly disposition, sufficient to scare men and beasts, has finally been calmed. Now, thanks to God, the good order preserved in the towns and the vigilance of town militia, in addition to the affection of our Parisians toward my little Master, Louis XIII, we have a signed contract of peace. . . . Now I ask you, as the King would his Sergeant or the Queen her beloved, tell me frankly my little reformer . . . what was the purpose of leaving the court, and clouding the horizon of my young master, and troubling the public peace? . . . You must not really want to be King, for if one judges events by their results, you seem rather to be aiming for the position of concierge than ruler, not unlike the English who are happy with fleurs-de-lys of paint, and to be Kings of France according to the inscriptions on their coins.[30]

Mathault does nothing to disguise his militant Catholicism. He mentions by name two leaders of the Catholic party close to the queen mother (Cardinal Du Perron and the duc de Ventadour) as people to whom the reader should pay attention. He says no one wants war, but he threatens that the Parisian working people will give every last cent they have to wage war on the Huguenots if they start something. Mathault's rudeness toward his social superiors is supposed to be excusable because of the righteousness of his cause and the depth of his commitment. Condé's enterprise, in contrast, should inspire only indignation and ridicule. Although the strongly Catholic views expressed in many of the progovernment pamphlets are not unusual, the open invitation in *Libre harangue* to

---

29. Cf. Magendie, *Politesse,* 1:305–409. The notion of men of integrity, often covered by the term *gens de bien,* was a pivotal notion in early seventeenth-century French culture. Interestingly, one of the characteristics of *gens de bien* was that they didn't speak out of turn or publicly say bad things about others. A number of pamphlets begin with the author's humble apologies for publicly criticizing others. "Le bon François" suggests that "Le vieux Gaulois" (mentioned below) could hardly be a person of integrity in view of his public criticisms of the prince de Condé.

30. *Libre harangue faicte par Mathault* (1614), 3.

associate a rejection of Condé with the politics of the Holy League is a bit surprising. Such an appeal suggests that militant Catholic authors anticipated a substantial, equally militant Catholic readership.

Many of the 1614–1617 pamphlets exploited a fundamental ideological division in French political life, often referred to as the opposition between the *dévôt* and *bon François*. The two positions were first clearly articulated in the very early 1600s in the course of a debate over Henry IV's foreign policy, and continued to influence the debate over Richelieu's foreign policy.[31] The *bon François* held a more secular and nationalistic view of politics, while the *dévôt* felt an overriding concern for the welfare of Catholicism. The two positions are seen clearly in the 1614–1617 campaigns, especially in the early stages. Two pamphlets that exemplify the conflict are *Le vieux Gaulois* and *Le Bon François,* both published in 1614. The Old French Warrior violently condemned Condé's revolt and fully supported the administration of the queen mother. In addition, he was committed to the completion of Louis XIII's marriage to Anne of Austria and to the accommodation with Spain that it implied. Conversely, the Good Frenchman saw in the marriage an effort to exploit the minority of the king in order to advance the causes of Spain and the pope at the expense of France. How ironic, the Good Frenchman observed, to find these militants preaching "obedience" and "sovereignty" in 1614 when just a few years earlier they were all screaming for sedition, murder, and an uprising against the king.[32] This was, of course, a reference to the "resistance" rhetoric used by the militant Catholics against Henry III and Henry IV, who were perceived as enemies of the church of Rome.

Personae such as the Old French Warrior and the Good Frenchman display a certain predictability that must have undermined their persuasiveness. Their intentions were completely obvious: associate the queen mother's administration with good old-fashioned Catholicism in the case of the former, or with fanatic, ultramontane Catholicism in the case of the latter. One senses that few political conversions were brought about by these efforts and that such pamphlets simply confirmed the readers' existing political convictions—although a pamphlet like *L'Harangue de Mathault* may have heightened the powerful religious emotions.

Pamphlets such as *Lettre de Jacques Bon-Homme* appear to have functioned differently. Jacques's response to Condé's enterprise was not automatic, and his elaborate effort to convey his ideas implies that his audience's response would not be automatic either. This pamphlet had a genuinely persuasive purpose. It provided a plausible interpretation,

31. Geley, *Fancan et la politique de Richelieu,* 5–24; Church, *Richelieu and Reason of State,* 117–126; Bailey, "Writers against the Cardinal"; and Babelon, *Henri IV,* 933.
32. *Bon François* (1614), 10.

and then a reasoned rejection, of Condé's revolt. The anticipated audience was not necessarily neutral, but neither was it completely close-minded by partisanship. What kinds of rhetorical devices did the author use to reach such an audience?

POLITICS AND COMMON SENSE

In order to make their propaganda as effective as possible, pamphleteers worked ingeniously to associate their arguments with their readers' everyday lives and with "self-evident" truths that their daily experiences confirmed. One widely used technique was the deployment of "commonplaces," whose function in the persuasive process, according to seventeenth-century rhetorical theory, is actually very elaborate.[33] Basically, a commonplace provided some point of agreement between speaker and audience related to the issue at hand.[34] The proper commonplace, or truism, could function as the major premise for political or moral argument because it immediately invited the reader's agreement. The scholarly rhetoricians of the early seventeenth century, such as Antoine Arnauld, systematically collected commonplaces, and their political pamphlets often contained elaborate amplifications of these stock devices.[35]

A number of commonplaces appear repeatedly in the 1614–1617 campaigns. Sometimes expressed simply in aphorisms or *sententia,* they more frequently provided a skeleton for more elaborate persuasive devices. By using a fictional speaker in a dramatic setting an author could elaborate on these commonplaces in a more vivid or entertaining way. The following anecdote addressed to the princes by Jacques Bon-Homme is an excellent example of the technique.

> I remember what happened in Beauvais once in 1533, when I took some pigeons there to sell at the market. Some young men, having agreed as one learned later, to a meeting at precisely three o'clock, found themselves late for their appointment. So they went to the keeper of the town clock and explained to him that the clock was an hour fast, and that he should turn it back. When he refused to do this, they became abusive. Things passed from words to blows, and in the scuffle the mechanism was damaged. As a result, the damaged clock functioned erratically for the next eight days.

33. See the commentary by Radouant on commonplaces in Du Vair's *L'Eloquence françoise,* appendix, 169–181 (cited in sec. II of Bibliography).

34. For modern theories of the role of commonplaces in argument, see Angenot, *Parole pamphlétaire,* 24–25, 145–210; Perelman and Olbrechts-Tyteca, *New Rhetoric,* 83–110; Toulmin, *Uses of Argument,* 94–145; and Dupriez, "Ou sont les arguments?" 35–51.

35. Arnauld's collection is mentioned by Radouant in Du Vair's *L'Eloquence françoise,* 169–181. For a revealing example of the technique, see Arnauld's 1614 pamphlet, *Utile et salutaire advis au roy, pour bien regner.*

> This shows that violence is the enemy of order and the right way to do things. The gentle and gracious means are always the most desirable and often the most convenient.[36]

This tale is not simply entertaining; it is a clever elaboration of a master commonplace about law and order and an obvious analogy for the political situation in 1614. The prince de Condé and his supporters are behaving like impulsive adolescents. Things have not turned out exactly the way they wanted, so in an effort to get their own way, they are going to ruin things for everyone else. Their behavior is at least reckless, and probably stupid and malicious. Not only do they want the ridiculous, but they are also willing to use violence to get it.

The persuasive elements in this analogy are complex. It is designed less to illustrate the validity of the author's point of view than to expose the positions of his opponents to ridicule.[37] The anecdote trivializes the revolt of the princes by comparing it to youthful vandalism, reinforcing in a vivid way the image of irresponsibility and political recklessness. But beyond that, to refuse to accept the march of time is to reject the natural, God-given order of things. The suggestion here is that the revolt of the princes has been based on some fundamental misunderstanding about how the world works and might lead to more serious violence and deeper disorder than the reader had imagined.

The author concluded the clock anecdote with two truisms. "This shows that violence is the enemy of order and the right way to do things. The gentle and gracious means are always the most desirable and often the most convenient." In a general way, the anecdote might have imposed such a conclusion on the reader without having been explicitly stated, but the actual statement of the commonplaces helped to reinforce both the logic and the partisan meaning of the anecdote. Common sense tells us that reckless behavior leading to violence and disorder should be repudiated (a major premise). The analogy between Condé's behavior and that of an ill-mannered adolescent tells us that the princes' demands will lead to violence and disorder (a minor premise). Therefore, (conclusion) the behavior of Condé and his confederates should be repudiated.

The anecdotal and universal qualities of this kind of argumentation are part of its appeal. The commonplace that "the gentle and gracious means are always the most desirable . . ." is made to seem part of the basic structure of reality—something so fundamental that even a peasant can see its significance. The attempt to turn the clock back reinforces this idea. Nothing is more self-evidently ridiculous than trying to go back-

36. *Lettre de Jacques Bon-Homme,* 14–15.
37. Cf. Walker, *Typologische . . . Untersuchungen zur französischen Pamphletliteratur,* 82–84.

wards in time.[38] Thus, the revolt of the princes, who may be trying to go backwards in time politically, would appear to be a contradiction of the basic structure of reality. Much of *Letter from Jacques Bon-Homme* is an elaboration of this theme—an effort to make the reader wonder why Condé and his associates do not have a better understanding of how things "really work."

The notion that violence is the enemy of order and that the gentle way of doing things constitutes political wisdom dominated the proadminis-tration campaign as a whole. Moreover, the recent civil wars made it easy for pamphleteers to invoke the horrors of violence and disorder. The logic behind much of the government's rhetoric was simple. Anything that brings about the pain and suffering of civil war must be avoided. Condé's revolt will lead to civil war. Therefore the revolt must be stopped.

As long as the queen mother's administration appeared to represent legitimate "sovereign authority," the strategy worked well. The adminis-tration was able to call for a politics of orderliness, graciousness, and peace because it represented the status quo; it was legally (and by public consent) in a position of authority. The queen mother's pamphleteers were therefore able to mobilize many of the conventional moral appeals associated with obedience to authority. Jacques was a spokesman for this position. He claimed that "all those who have risen up against sovereign authority have only brought about confusion, shame and reproach, re-gardless of the pretexts they have used to camouflage their intentions." It was an old political trick, observed Jacques, to profess to be acting for the public good—he had heard his father mention hundreds of times how some discontented princes tried the same ploy under Louis XI.[39]

This kind of logic is graphically illustrated in one of the few surviving engravings from these years, an elaborate picture (Figure 2) published sometime in 1614.[40] "Dezanville's Illustrated Aphorisms" represents the pleasures of law and order on the one hand, and suffering caused by the breakdown of law and order on the other. It is, on one level, a meditation on the metaphysics of royal power. Justice, order, and piety form the

38. Elizabeth Marvick brought to my attention that the implicit connection here between politics and a mechanical clock is also revealing—perhaps of the desire to link political order to a depersonalized regularity.

39. *Lettre de Jacques Bon-Homme*, 13.

40. Except for engravings celebrating Louis XIII's marriage, or return to Paris follow-ing the tour of the west in the summer of 1614, there are very few pieces of visual propa-ganda from this period extant in the Bibliothèque Nationale. Those conserved in the Cabinet des Estampes are for the most part in series Qb1, as is the piece reproduced here.

Figure 2. "Dezanville's Illustrated Aphorisms." Reproduced with the permission of the Bibliothèque Nationale de Paris.

essential base for royal authority. If any of the three are undermined, royal authority (and hence royal power) will also be undermined. Civil war tramples on justice, order, and piety. Thus, anyone truly concerned for the authority of the king will do all he can to avoid civil war.

The political message is reinforced by making the partisan decision of 1614 a simple choice between good and evil. The picture presents the viewer with two alternatives—the good, well-ordered society or the society of evil and chaos. In the society of disorder (on the right half of the page for the viewer) people "murder each other and leave the Realm as prey" while "foreigners delight to see the bloody tragedy of the French." In this society, people are hypocrites, thieves, murderers, and atheists. Houses are burnt, babies are stabbed by soldiers, women are violated, and in the end the corrupted souls make the journey to the underworld. In the society of order (on the left side of the page) people play music and dance, soldiers engage in sporting contests, fishermen fish peacefully, and *amours pastorales* transpire under the curious eyes of sheep in the countryside. The child king Louis XIII, standing on a pedestal placed between these two societies, looks to his right, indicating his rejection of the politics of violence. Good Frenchmen should work toward a society in which order, "fidelity, justice, and peace" govern human relationships. Not only will this strengthen royal authority, but everyone will have more fun!

The pleasure/pain calculation was an important part of the message. But, again, another important message was the reinforcement of general truths about the structure of reality. The political world, just like the world in general, had a certain God-given order. There were rules to be followed, hierarchies of authority to be acknowledged, and moral imperatives. To challenge them was, almost by definition, to abandon virtue for vice. At best it was foolish. At worst it was downright evil, because it challenged God's plan for mankind.

How could Condé's demands possibly work for the good? The ad hominem attacks on Condé were designed partly to reinforce this theme. The whole enterprise could only be the result of an unruly and sinful appetite for personal power and aggrandizement. In *Mathault,* Condé's reckless behavior was said to result from his political "ambition" and "quarrelsome personality," partly to show that the prince's very identity was associated with immorality, breaking the rules, violence, disorder, and suffering.

A technique closely related to the rhetoric of law and order was the exploitation of fear. Dezanville's picture contains some rather gruesome scenes. Fear, or, rather, knowing when to be afraid, was an important part of Jacques Bon-Homme's common-sense wisdom as well. The actions of Condé and his friends could lead to war. War meant soldiers, and soldiers meant devastation. Jacques has several amusing stories to relate about soldiers stealing chickens—a ubiquitous theme in this literature.[41] As in the anecdote about the clock, chickens were more than poultry. They were symbols of the loss and devastation wrought by soldiers in the everyday lives of ordinary French citizens.

Condé's supporters capitalized on fear with a curious lack of sensitivity. In two of their persona pamphlets, the image of a hotheaded lackey was evoked. His fanatical devotion to the prince makes him dangerous to those who are not equally committed; at a mere suggestion from his lord, he will be more than happy to unsheathe his sword. The character was used awkwardly in a piece entitled *Response of the Garment Maker of Paris to Jacques Bon-Homme,* in which the author apparently could not decide whether his main intention was to destroy the credibility of the opposing pamphlet by lifting the mask of Jacques's persona, or to humiliate Jacques in his own world of discourse.[42] The result was a confused combination of jokes, threats, and innuendos about the opposing author that could not have been very effective, except perhaps to expose the cleverness of the earlier pamphlet. The garment maker was familiar with Jacques's letter because he himself had delivered it to Condé's household. He would not have thought it written by a peasant, he said, except that Jacques had carefully filled in one of the corner margins in order not to waste any of the paper. Condé, with the nonchalance of a great nobleman, happens to have remembered seeing Jacques once, with his quaint peasant dress and hair. The learned prince doubted that Jacques was really a descendant of the leader of the Jacquerie.[43] In the pamphlet the company around Condé is generally amused by Jacques and his discourse, but Condé's followers are affected rather differently, especially one of his Gascon captains who is transported into a rage.

> We will have a war without him [Jacques], conjurer that he is! . . . How scandalous that people might rather believe a flatfoot like him than two thousand soldiers ready, at the first word of their leader, to take the Bastille, if one would only let them! Can one not see that he only speaks for his interest, out of fear of losing a few chickens or lambs? . . . God damn me if the peasant doesn't pay for this![44]

Such passages seem designed less to defend the legitimacy of Condé's enterprise than to frighten or awe people into supporting it. Perhaps the

41. A satirical account of the chickens defending themselves against the rebel troops is the main idea behind *Remerciement des poules* (1614).

42. *Reponse du Crocheteur de la samaritaine a Jacques Bonhomme* (ed. Charlier). As Charlier notes (p. 193), the author of the *Reponse* suggests that the original *Bon-Homme* is a replay of a 1607 pamphlet.

43. Ibid., 194.

44. Ibid., 195–196.

author felt that such language would inspire some readers with the kind of devotion that the prince could inspire in his servants. But the main message was that noblemen take revenge on those who cross them. Revenge against commoners was beneath the dignity of a great prince, of course, but certainly not beneath that of his lackeys. The pamphlet does not urge people to rebel against the royal government; Condé is "too wise a prince" to encourage sedition. But, at the same time, the respect and obedience that peasants and bourgeois owe a great lord are also a part of the natural order, and those who do not acknowledge this reality had better beware. Such punitive sentiments could not have been terribly appealing; they promised nothing but pain and suffering. The queen mother's supporters were far cleverer about undermining Condé's position. They simply appealed to the self-interest of the ordinary person.

Still, the administration had to defend itself against Condé's appeals regarding the public welfare and his legitimate, or at least plausible, attacks on the government—corruption, taxes, and the like. Pamphlets in the *Bon-Homme* vein also handled this task well by downplaying Condé's grievances against the government. Several of the persona pieces suggested that the complaints were simply not worth taking seriously. Jacques was willing to acknowledge some problems, but questioned whether Condé had any solutions.

> You demand, the clerk tells us, that the people be provided with some relief. In truth, we are obliged to you for the concern you show for us, because, indeed, we are a bit overburdened. But we are not at the point, thank God, that we have not endured worse, and we would one hundred times rather endure our present condition for thirty more years than live through three months of civil war.[45]

Other pamphlets amplified this theme; that is, the abuses might exist, but Condé's efforts to redress them were surely wrongheaded. Were there injustices perpetrated under the queen's administration? What kind of justice would one find in civil war? Were taxes heavy? How much of one's crop would one keep with soldiers around? Were the Protestants insecure? How would their cause fare if civil war prevented the government from guaranteeing their civil liberties? Along these lines, Plato was invoked as a man of immense wisdom, who believed it was better to suffer the worst kinds of disorder in a state than to try to reform it through violence.[46]

45. *Lettre de Jacques Bon-Homme*, 18.

46. "Plato is said to have always abstained from the public affairs of Athens . . . [because on the one hand] the people of his time were so badly constituted that he could not govern by reason and by persuasion, and [on the other hand] reason and piety would in no way permit him to force them through violent means to do their duty." *Remonstrance faicte sur les esmotions de ce temps* (1614), 4.

Pamphleteers tried to affiliate their political factions with common sense, with the realities of everyday life, and with the natural order of things. They tried to relate their positions to the experience of the reader, his fears, hopes, and religious allegiance. The persona was useful in such a campaign in part because it provided a way to dress up some very simple ideas and to exploit the popular political lore of the age. The elaborate ways in which these personae are developed, however, suggest that the intended audience was far from simpleminded. The peasant from Beauvais is not speaking to other peasants. He speaks elegant French, and his discourse is punctuated with Renaissance learning. How, in a more concrete political sense, was the public expected to respond to such pamphlets? What can these intended responses tell us about the social and ideological characteristics of the audience?

WHOSE ACTION OR INACTION?

Condé's *Manifeste* of 1615 and other pamphlets openly called on readers to arm themselves and join the conflict with military support. The queen mother's allies published similar pieces. Most of the pamphlets, however, conveyed more complex messages. This is true of most of the personae pieces, and is especially so with pieces from 1614 that we are considering here in part because many were published when it was not yet clear there would be a military dimension to the struggle.

The most militant pamphlets advocated joining the political conflict by directly supporting one side or the other with military and financial aid. This rhetoric was generally aimed at two groups, militant Protestants and militant Catholics. Among the latter, Parisians were of particular importance. Pamphlets such as *Mathault* combined appeals to the popular Parisian classes with the militant Catholic rhetoric. Such pamphlets, without exception, were on the side of the queen mother. Again, the specter of the Catholic League played a very important part in the rhetoric, although the League itself was rarely mentioned.

On Condé's side, militant language was largely aimed at the nobility. No other social group could have responded very positively to *Le Crocheteur,* for example, and an emphasis on recruiting the nobility was, in any event, consistent with Condé's strategy. Later in the struggle, in the summer of 1615, Condé openly called on Protestants to arm and come to his aid, but this was done with less emotion than the administration's appeals to militant Catholics.

Most pamphlets did not advocate active, armed involvement. The vast majority were published by supporters of the administration and advocated inaction and noninvolvement. Jacques Bon-Homme and the Vieux Gaulois were above all advocates of law and order, not political engagement. They tried to discourage the notion that military action would help solve any of France's political problems. Even after the military dimension of the conflict became obvious and central, the proadministration pamphleteers sought to undermine support for Condé rather than to elicit highly emotional support for the government. They preached obedience to those normally "in command," not popular political engagement. The more experienced members of the queen's council knew better than to encourage a general militarization of the kingdom.

Rhetorical evidence corroborates our analysis of political strategy; the primary audience for most of these pamphlets was the traditional urban elite—the key political interest group in the 1614–1617 struggle. *Jacques Bon-Homme* is a complex pamphlet, and it anticipated a serious and skilled reader. When *Jacques* appeared, the king and the queen mother were about to take a tour of western France in an effort to stall any political momentum that Condé might be developing there. The elections for the Estates General were imminent, and the Crown wanted loyal delegates selected. One of Jacques's main points is that people should not be tempted to support Condé's "protest" with the naive view that he will bring about genuine political reforms, a thinly veiled reference to the coming Estates General.

Many of the humorous aspects of *Jacques Bon-Homme* are clearly aimed at this public. In the following passage (ostensibly addressed to the princes, as was the whole of Jacques's discourse) Jacques reminds the princes of the pleasures they will forgo if war breaks out.

> Let us consider the question of pleasure, my honorable seigneurs! One gains a good deal more satisfaction from a walk in the gardens of the Louvre, hunting deer at Fontainebleau, practicing martial arts in the Place Royale, and eating Portuguese omelets at a chic cabaret . . . than from eating the dust of the countryside, feeling the midday heat on your back, sleeping under the barrel of a cannon, and getting up at three in the morning for a raid against some stronghold. . . . Such inconveniences would seem all the more insupportable in view of your delicate upbringing and your experience in every sort of pleasure and pastime.[47]

Ostensibly addressed to great nobles, this passage clearly mocks their pastimes and even ridicules the military ethos they cultivated. This pamphlet would have amused the urban elite, who knew that "princes" were fond of such diversions. In a more serious vein, the pamphlet insinuates that the revolt of 1614 might be just another frivolous diversion. If so, it would be dangerous, the pamphlet cautioned, to take it too seriously because when the princes grew tired of playing, their less-privileged supporters would be left to face the full wrath of the government.

47. *Lettre de Jacques Bon-Homme*, 12.

A few of Condé's supporters also tried to reach the audience of urban elites through persona pamphlets. *The Good Frenchman* and *The French Cato*, both published in 1614, were among the most skillful productions of this kind. Indeed, the latter work was one of the most serious and analytical pieces published by the opposition. In a lengthy legal and historical discussion, the stern and moral Cato speaks in favor of rehabilitating the power of local magistrates and makes other points that would have appealed to provincial urban elites. Cato, however, did not openly advocate involvement in Condé's faction but suggested instead that the best chance for reform would be at the coming Estates General—an ambiguous position given the factional struggle. The pamphlets published by Condé and the opposition in this genre did not project a coherent political vision. Often they were weak and derivative responses to the initiatives of the proadministration pamphleteers.

The pamphleteers supporting the queen mother's administration were more skillful as well as more numerous than those supporting Condé. This is particularly evident from the quality and number of the persona pieces. Condé's faction was outpublished in this genre by at least three to one. Those pamphlets supporting the queen are more accomplished stylistically, more inventive argumentatively, and above all more consistent and coherent in the political positions they advocated. They mobilized a rhetoric of piety, law, and order well suited to the social and political interest groups they addressed.

Condé's campaign, in contrast, was relatively clumsy. He tried to mobilize a defamatory rhetoric of government corruption, injustice, and tyranny, but it was not well sustained. Poignant examples from everyday life were lacking, and the range of literary invention was limited. Condé's supporters were stylistically and argumentatively on the defensive. The prince did not emerge, even in his own propaganda, as a convincing alternative to the status quo or as a political leader with a coherent, attractive political platform.

The queen mother's rhetorical victories were a vital contribution to the effort by her administration to defeat the challenge of Condé and his faction. Not until Concini defiantly arrested and imprisoned Condé in 1616 did public opinion begin to turn against the queen mother's administration. As one pamphleteer put it, even though the revolt of the princes would attract many people, the credit and authority of the government "would retain four times as many on the side of their majesties."[48] Certainly the queen mother started out with a significant advan-

48. *Discours sur les conferences faites* (1615), 15.

tage because of her legitimate claim to direct the government and her support among royal officials and militant Catholics. But her administration's pamphleteers did well to maintain the loyalty of this core group of supporters. They successfully identified and then won over (or at least obtained the neutrality of) important interest groups that might otherwise have joined the princes.

SIX

The Rhetoric of Absolutism

Monarchy, which is by an individual, is manifest in the person of our French kings—monarchs who are sovereign, absolute, loved and revered, feared and obeyed—whose grandeur and power is such that there never was a Monarchy in which the kings were so amply endowed. And so it is that by this sovereignty and supreme grandeur, French kings are rendered entirely absolute, and have always commanded according to their own wishes, along with their piety and zeal for the good of their people—thus the fact that for the good and relief of their State, they have on their own made laws and appointed officials. . . .

—L'ASSEMBLEE DES NOTABLES DE FRANCE, FAITES PAR LE ROY EN SA VILLE DE ROUEN, AVEC LES NOMS DESDICTES ESLEUS ET NOTABLES (ROUEN: I. LE CARTEL [1617]),4

This Universal Father [the pope] would never undertake any action that would prejudice the absolute authority of your Majesty. . . . They [the French clergy] know that you [Louis XIII] are a sovereign endowed with every kind of temporal sovereignty in your Realm, not being a feudatory either of the Pope or any other Prince. . . .

—LE PRINCE ABSOLU (PARIS, 1617),7

The practical purposes of pamphleteering have been the central focus of this study. But pamphlet authors had ideological purposes too, which they attempted to link to their pragmatic goals. The partisan arguments of 1614–1617 were therefore tied in certain ways to the great ideological struggles of the age. This was especially so with religious doctrine and political theory. For the reasons discussed in earlier chapters, pamphleteers tended to be cautious in these highly charged fields of discourse, especially with respect to religion. Nevertheless, authors were eager to exploit emotionally appealing ideas, even when they were troublesome and controversial.

In this vein, the pamphleteers of 1614–1617 mobilized a public discussion of several issues of political theory. Such discussions were rooted both in "popular" political discourse and in the most advanced political discourse of the age. At both levels, abstract argument had an immediately practical meaning in the context of 1614–1617, even when the language was highly conventional. In fact, the arguments of most pamphlets were constructed of well-worn ideas and themes.[1] But neither the con-

1. An interesting collection of formulaic words and phrases could be assembled to explore how much of the political discourse of the early 1600s had been recycled from the rhetorical battles of the sixteenth-century religious and dynastic wars.

ventionality of the language nor its abstractness conceals the specific (and short-term) persuasive intentions of pamphlet rhetoric.

The way in which the 1614–1617 campaigns exploited (or failed to exploit) certain traditional ideas is particularly noteworthy on three counts. First, the rhetoric used to defend the queen mother's authority against the challenge of the great nobles was surprisingly legalistic—not simply political, religious, moralistic, and pragmatic. Second, a major theme of this legalistic rhetoric was the idea of an "absolute" monarchical sovereignty. Third, the great nobles who were in revolt against the royal government (and presumably, therefore, against some elements of "absolute" royal authority) failed to provide in their pamphlets any alternative political vision.

In some respects it is surprising that a discourse emphasizing the "absoluteness" of royal authority played such an important role in the pamphlet rhetoric of 1614–1617. Political authority in general and *sovereignty* in particular were ambiguous notions in early seventeenth-century France.[2] The definition of France as a "monarchical" state was never significantly challenged, nor was the right of the king to exercise the powers of a sovereign. But according to the political theory of the age, monarchical states were often tempered with "aristocratic" and even "democratic" elements.[3] This meant that the king might be obliged in some circumstances to consult with others, such as the peers of the realm, the parlements, or local authorities. Moreover, the power of the monarch was widely understood to be circumscribed by "fundamental" laws (ancient custom) and moral laws (God's commands), which together constituted a kind of natural law that required the sovereign to act for the good of the kingdom and his subjects.[4]

More immediately, the minority of Louis XIII, who was just twelve years of age when the revolt against his mother's government broke out in February of 1614, posed a special set of issues. The queen mother's administration was clearly not the instrument of a fully competent adult monarch. Until 2 October 1614, at which time Louis XIII was declared legally sovereign, Marie's authority depended largely on her position as regent. A regent ruled in the name of the king as a kind of legal guardian over the person, the estate, and the authority of the monarch-to-be. The process of a regent's selection and the extent of his or her personal and political authority were surrounded by many unresolved legal questions.[5]

---

2. Sée, *Idées politiques;* and Parker, "Sovereignty," 42–50.
3. Mayerne, *Monarchie Aristo-democratique* (Lyon, 1610).
4. Giesey, "Medieval Jurisprudence," 172.
5. Cf. Hanley, *"Lit de Justice,"* 231–295; and Lightman, *Sons and Mothers,* 55–169.

With this background in mind, the political events of 1614–1617 were sure to stimulate an intense discussion of monarchical authority generally and sovereignty in particular. Condé's revolt raised the old and still very difficult issue of the great nobility's political authority. What was the proper role of "the peers of the realm" in the royal government? To what extent did the authority of the great nobles remain insulated from royal disfavor? Was it a "law of the realm" that princes of the blood had a right to be "admitted into the government and administration of the State?"[6]

From Condé's first acts of defiance in 1614 to Concini's assassination in 1617, Marie de Médicis's supporters defended her position as *the* head of state—first as regent, then as "head of the king's council" (*chef du conseil*). During the regency, the queen mother's propagandists insisted on her rights to enjoy "absolutely" the prerogatives of the king in whose name she ruled. They accused the rebels of sedition and treason for presuming to challenge her authority and trying to usurp the direction of affairs of state.

In France, as in England, the adjective *absolu* did not have an exclusively political, much less an anticonstitutional, connotation.[7] However, arguments about the unique, perfect, and supreme—in other words, the absolute—nature of sovereignty were readily available in the writings of jurists such as Jean Bodin and Charles Loyseau.[8] The propagandists supporting the queen mother's administration adapted this legalistic vocabulary to their immediate ends. They argued that the absolute supremacy of the royal government was self-evident, and that political opposition was not simply wrong, inappropriate, and contrary to public interest, but was contradictory to the fundamental and expressed laws of monarchical government. Possibly for the first time, a comprehensive rhetoric of absolutism (although not the term itself) was used systematically in the 1614–1617 campaigns to justify the policies of the royal government.[9] By 1617 the idea that the *pouvoir absolu* of the monarch was a fundamental legal principle underlying the French state had become a commonplace.

6. Such issues are raised, for example, in *Declaration et protestation des princes, ducs, pairs* (1617), 20–21.

7. Cf. Cotgrave, *Dictionaire*, s.v. *absolut;* and Huguet, *Dictionnaire de la langue française du sezième siècle*, s.v. *absolu*. The English use of the term *absolute* in a similar setting helps enormously to clarify French usage in the pamphlet literature from 1614 to 1617. See Daly, "Idea of Absolute Sovereignty," 227–250.

8. See especially J. U. Lewis, "Jean Bodin's 'Logic of Sovereignty'," 206–222; Parker, "Thought of Jean Bodin," 253–285; and Lloyd, "Political Thought of Charles Loyseau," 53–82.

9. On the invention of the term in the nineteenth century, see Rowen, "Louis XIV and Absolutism," 312.

It is clear from the argumentative strategies of pamphlet authors on both sides that they anticipated widespread acceptance for the queen mother's legal claim to absolute authority—first as regent, and then as head of her son's councils. The rebuttals of Condé and his propagandists were remarkably timid on this score. Condé did not characterize his challenge as a quest to reapportion the distribution of sovereign power within the state. Rarely did his pamphlets attack Marie's legal right to act in the capacity of an absolute ruler. Traditional metaphors of hierarchy, supported by allusions to noble virtues, social preeminence, and royal blood were the main reasons *les grands* offered to support their claims for a more active role in the king's councils.

From a long-term perspective, the absence of any substantive discourse on resistance to absolutism in the course of the 1614–1617 pamphlet wars may be the most consequential feature of the campaign. The prince de Condé and his associates, especially in their appeals to the delegates of the Estates General or to the members of the Parlement of Paris, had at their disposal several traditions of opposition rhetoric. Regional political authorities naturally objected to the incursions of royal agents in matters such as the collection of taxes, and they frequently used a rhetoric of "representation" and "consultation" to justify their resistance. The meeting of the Estates General in 1614–1615 presented the perfect opportunity for this rhetoric to manifest itself, either in general or in direct opposition to the queen mother's administration. The theory of France as something of a "mixed" monarchy—one incorporating democratic and representative principles into the operations of the royal government—was still current in some intellectual circles. One finds only timid references to these theories, however, in the 1614–1617 propaganda campaigns. A handful of pamphlets gave expression to "extreme" views, attesting to the existence of resistance rhetoric, but these views did not govern any major pamphlet initiatives.

Ironically, when the queen mother eventually lost the political battle for control of Louis XIII's government, it happened in such a way as to reinforce the principle that monarchical rule was necessarily absolute. After the arrest and imprisonment of Condé in the fall of 1616, it was widely alleged in the pamphlet literature that Concini, not the queen mother or the king, had been in control of the king's councils for some years. This claim seriously undermined the central defense of the queen mother's authority since 1614. However, the assassination of Concini in April 1617 was portrayed as having brought the real sovereign, Louis XIII, to power. This turn of events signaled the defeat of both Marie's coalition and what remained of Condé's confederation. The sixteen-year-old king was suddenly heralded as the authentic ruler of France, the "absolute" sovereign who would bring peace and unity to the faction-torn country. In a paradoxical twist, a coup d'état against the queen mother helped to affirm the very view of sovereignty that Marie and many of her supporters had been promulgating since 1610. A great rhetorical celebration of absolutism's victory over tyranny was launched by pamphleteers and much of the nation when Louis appeared willing to personally assume the direction of affairs of state and to exercise the absolute power that was his alone. The king had killed the monster plaguing his state and had taken power "into his own hands" (see Figure 3).[10]

THEOLOGIANS AND JURISCONSULTS VS. BIRTH, HONOR, AND TRADITION

One of Condé's propaganda tactics was to complain that the great nobles in general and the princes of the blood in particular had not been sufficiently honored by the queen mother. Their voices had not been heeded in the kings's councils, and their traditional role in the government of the kingdom had been undermined. (This claim was largely untrue; the rebels simply belonged to the less-influential faction at court.) The moderates among the queen mother's advisers adopted a tone of conciliation toward this claim. They protested that the princes held their accustomed place in the council, but that, at the same time, it was natural for the queen mother's most experienced ministers and officers of the Crown to handle much of the government's business.[11] It was emphasized that these ministers were, after all, the same advisers upon whom Henry IV had relied; their ability and integrity ought to have been above reproach.

The queen mother's more militant supporters were much more strident. Very early in the campaign an anonymous apology addressed to Condé in the voice of the queen suggested that the rebels "consult the theologians and jurisconsults" in order to see for themselves "what the divine and positive laws permit to be done to those who are found planning to assemble for the purpose of troubling the peace of their country."[12] This was an obvious reference to legal concepts of sovereignty and lese majesty, and an only slightly veiled reference to treason. Lese majesty was a capital offense and the charge had been used as recently as the reign of Henry IV against the great nobility. Henry had the duc de Biron executed for lese majesty, based (among other things) on the thin evi-

10. B.N. Cabinet des Estampes, Qb1 1617.

11. The queen stressed this point in her letters of February 1614 to dignitaries around the kingdom; e.g., her letter to the marquis de Mirabeau, acting governor (*lieutenant général*) of Burgundy, 13 February 1614, published in *Correspondence de la Mairie de Dijon*, 1:126–129.

12. *Response pour la royne a monsieur le prince* (1614), 19.

Figure 3. A placard celebrating the victory of young Louis XIII over the monster Concini. One of the banners reads, "He takes the power in his own arms." Reproduced with the permission of the Bibliothèque Nationale de Paris.

dence that the duke's troops may have once fired on Henry's royal entourage.[13] A quick glance at the relevant passages in Bodin and Loyseau reveals that the monarchy's leading theorists had decisively categorized armed rebellion and political organizing on the part of *les grands* as lese majesty.[14]

In practice, however, the opinion of the public was more significant than that of "jurisconsults." The pretensions of the great nobility were persistently tolerated, but how far could the "peers of the realm" and "princes of the blood" go before they violated the political norms in 1614?

The deputies to the Estates General in 1614 appear to have concurred with theorists such as Bodin and Loyseau on lese majesty. In the discussions of the assembly on the comportment of the nobility, the deputies were generally sympathetic to the plight of poor country gentlemen, but were quite unsympathetic toward insolent military officers. This view was particularly prevalent among the members of the Third Estate, most of whom were both judicial officials and members of the urban elite.[15] Several articles in the *cahier* of the Third Estate complained that the governors and lieutenant governors of provinces, in addition to military commanders, extorted money and produce from local populations, protected brigands, interfered with the administration of local justice, and the like.[16] Even more revealing was an article in the *cahier* of the Second Estate (the nobility), urging the king to curtail the political power of

13. The duc de Biron's alleged complicity in a Spanish conspiracy against Henry (which never materialized beyond the planning stages) seems also to have played a part in the duke's execution. The formal charge was "lese majesty," but many saw the punishment as far out of proportion to evidence against the duke. In order to get the Parlement to go along, it was apparently necessary to stress that Biron had not only conspired against the "authority" of the king but had also once tried to have Henry murdered. Biron protested violently against this charge all the way to the scaffold and was still fuming when the charges were read to him publicly just before his execution. See the account in the Bibliothèque de l'Institute de France, Ms. Godefroy 112, ff. 5–24.

14. Bodin's rejection of the great nobles' political authority, that is, of "feudal" political authority, is set forth in *Six Livres de la République*, book 3, chap. 5. He was nonetheless aware that, as a practical matter, the claims of the heads of great noble families to certain "offices" had to be handled respectfully: see book 4, chap. 3. Loyseau was even more hostile to the political pretensions of the great nobility; see *Cinq livres du droit des offices*, book 4, chaps. 4 and 6. Cf. Harding, *Provincial Governors*, 11.

15. For the occupations of the deputies of the Third Estate, see Hayden, *France and the Estates General*, app. 3, pp. 266–283. Of the 196 deputies, 111 were royal officers of some kind, mostly judges in *bailliage*-level jurisdictions; cf. my "Judicial Corruption and Legal Reform."

16. Lalourcé and Duval, eds., *Recueil des cahiers généraux*, 4:305–322 (see second section of the Bibliography). This collection has an account of the Third Estate's grievances in 1614, including those against the nobility.

les grands by suppressing their patronage networks. "Let no pensions, charges, estates, or other benefits be awarded through the intercession of the Princes and Lords of your Kingdom; in this way the obligation of those who receive [such benefits] will be entirely to Your Majesty, and not to [the said princes and lords.]"[17]

The deputies of the Third Estate were adamant on the issues; they used their *cahier* to explicitly repudiate the efforts of *les grands* to usurp the functions of the central government. In particular they repudiated the formation of political factions for the purpose of undermining sovereign authority. At the head of their *cahier* they placed a series of policy statements on this matter that they hoped the queen mother's government would ratify.

> Let it . . . be held as a fundamental law of the State that no subjects of Your Majesty, of any estate or condition whatsoever, be allowed to form leagues or associations among themselves, or with other princes and foreign lords, without written letters of permission [from the king.]
>
> Let all gentlemen and others receiving pensions from foreign princes be held as criminals guilty of lese majesty, and let none of your officers or domestics take any pensions from any princes, lords, or communities.
>
> Let all those who would raise troops and arms, [or convoke] assemblies and councils without Your permission be considered criminals guilty of lese majesty, and let no grace be extended to them. Let it be permitted to all persons to descend upon them, cut them to pieces, and attack them at the sound of the tocsin for this purpose.[18]

The deputies of the Third Estate were not upset that *les grands* were being excluded from positions of power, but that such men were already too powerful. They rejected the great nobility's use of organized violence as a political tactic and stated unequivocally that political authority emanated from the king alone and that the nobles could not usurp public functions without his explicit written permission. The determination of the Third Estate on this issue and their attachment to the discourse of sovereignty are underscored by their use of the legal term *lese majesty* to describe organized resistance against the central government. It would be hard to imagine a more explicit defense of absolutism and unequivocal condemnation of the tactics used by Condé and his confederates to challenge the administration of Marie de Médicis.

The deputies' rejection of the political pretensions of the great nobility was noteworthy in itself, but it was even more so when bound together with the "divine right" issue. The three articles that the Third Estate placed at the head of their *cahier* were originally to be preceded by an-

17. Ibid., 4:192.
18. Ibid., 4:273–74.

other article, the famous first article exalting the "divine right" sovereignty of the French king. This article (if it had been adopted) would have required all officials of France to take an oath of allegiance to the king, acknowledging him as the absolute monarch by divine right and explicitly repudiating ultramontanism. Roland Mousnier was certainly correct to emphasize that the first article was not simply about the events of 1614.[19] The oath was also part of an extended reaction to the assassination of Henry IV and yet another turn in the old quarrel about the French church—that of the Gallicans and *politiques* on the one hand, and of the militant Catholics (Jesuits and other ultramontanists) on the other; Denis Richet's discovery that the author of this article was Antoine Arnauld—the well-known lawyer with *politique* and anti-Jesuit views—reinforces this interpretation.[20]

Paradoxically, the first article was a tremendous embarrassment for the queen mother. Her ultramontane supporters, so crucial in her struggle to defeat Condé, were violently opposed to it. They viewed the article as an essentially Protestant proposal modeled after an oath that James I had drafted for English subjects.[21] For many militant Catholics, important theological and moral principles were at stake. What of an individual's religious convictions and conscience if he happened to be the subject of an absolute, divine right monarch who was an incompetent, a tyrant, or a heretic? The Gallican position, defended by members of the Parlement of Paris and most of the legally trained royal officials of the realm, exalted royal obedience and favored the adoption of such an article. The deputies of the Third Estate from every province of France, with the exception of Guyenne (whose delegation was under the watchful eyes of Cardinal de Sourdis), voted unanimously to adopt the first article into the general *cahier*. These local notables of the Third Estate, many of whom were royal officials, were also important members of the queen mother's political coalition.

19. Cf. Mousnier, *L'Assassinat d'Henri IV*. Hayden discusses parts of the confrontation in greater detail, in *Estates General*, 131–148. Cardinal Du Perron's pamphlet opposing the oath, allegedly a version of his speech delivered to the Estates, is *Harangue faicte de la part de la chambre ecclesiastique, en celle du Tiers Estat, sur l'article du serment.* . . .

20. Richet, "Paris et les Etats de 1614," 73. Cf. Salmon, "Gallicanism and Anglicanism," 166–173, 182–185.

21. Ibid., 184. Drawn up following the Gunpowder Plot in November 1605, King James I's "Oath of Allegiance" was also directed against the militant Catholics—the Jesuits in particular—and thus contained a clause denying the pope the kind of moral influence over political issues that the Catholics believed he should have. James and other English writers took a great interest in the French dimension to the debate. The Cardinal Du Perron's polemic (mentioned in n. 19) was the occasion for James's celebrated tract, "A Remonstrance for the Right of Kings," in *Political Works of James I* (see sec. II of the Bibliography). Similar responses to Du Perron were published by Frenchmen. Bignon's *Grandeur de nos roys* (Paris, 1615) was typical.

The queen mother was persuaded by her militant Catholic advisers, however, to request that the article be stricken from the *cahier*. The Third Estate eventually complied, but not very willingly. The final vote of 20 January 1615, on whether to withdraw the article from the *cahier* or to protest further to the queen mother, was a narrow victory for Marie. The delegations of two of the twelve provinces were split, and the delegations from four of the provinces voted to protest. Since six of the provinces voted to obey the queen mother, however, the article was withdrawn.[22] The deputies' attachment to the Gallican interpretation of divine right and royal authority, even in the face of intimidation from the Crown, was obviously powerful.

On the whole, Marie benefited greatly from these ideological confrontations, despite the short-term political awkwardness. The debate over the first article involved two factions of the best educated, most politically sophisticated, and rhetorically skilled people in the kingdom eager to disseminate their versions of absolute divine right in support of the queen mother's administration. The Protestants, *politiques,* and royal officials supported their interpretations of an absolute divine right for the French monarch. They were willing to associate this defense of divine right with a general defense of the queen mother's administration in part because a stronger royal government would be better able to resist the influence of the militant Catholics. Although the militant Catholics opposed the extreme statement of absolute divine right found in the article, they strongly favored the regent's religious and foreign policies. Thus, they were eager to keep the queen mother in power and were more than willing to emphasize the need for absolute obedience to the sovereign as part of a campaign to keep Condé out of power.

THE RHETORIC OF SOVEREIGNTY AND SEDITION

Marie de Médicis's most militant supporters thought Condé and his confederates should be confronted as seditious rebels and dealt with accordingly. They argued that if the queen reacted too timidly to their challenge, the authority and power of the royal government would be greatly damaged. For this reason, these supporters wrote and sponsored pamphlet literature stressing the inviolability of sovereignty, the absolute power of the Crown, and the absolute obedience owed by the great nobles to those in control of the government. These supporters frequently

22. The information on voting is from Mayer, ed., *Estats généraux*, vol. 16 (see sec. II of the Bibliography), which reproduces the eyewitness account of Rapin, entitled *Recueil très exact et curieux de tout ce qui s'est passé de singulier et mémorable en l'assemblée général des Etats à Paris en l'année 1614.*

emphasized the importance of having one "will" in charge of the state, and they spoke as if the queen mother's administration embodied this principle. An anonymous pamphleteer emphasized that Marie's legitimate selection and confirmation as regent gave her the privilege to run the government as she saw fit. "The Queen, being in her place, must enjoy her rights."[23] She was in effect the holder of sovereignty, and she alone should manage the affairs of state.

Two facts were very helpful in this rhetorical context—(1) Marie was formally pronounced queen shortly before the assassination of Henry IV, and (2) the government quickly rallied around her after Henry was killed. Apologists in 1614 were quick to recall the events of 1610.

> In such a situation as the Queen found herself [following the assassination of Henry IV], there was nothing that could have safeguarded the state from the pernicious divisions that menaced it but the absolute command of some person who would inspire confidence, whether by his or her quality or by public decree, . . . [so that his or her authority] could not be called into question.[24]

The meaning of this passage was clear. The queen mother had helped to preserve the royal government in a time of need precisely because she took over completely the sovereign authority of Henry IV.

The theoretical difficulty posed by Marie's ambiguous personal claim to royal authority was often sidestepped by treating sovereignty in abstract terms and then associating monarchy generally with the rule of a single individual, or "will." The author of *Le vieux Gaulois* was a militant Catholic and was therefore an enemy of absolutism in many ways. But he endorsed the principle of "one person" rule, and even argued that the principle was a foundation of political order in all states. "There is no state at all well policed where the sovereign decision does not belong to the monarch, and no republic which, in the anticipation of trouble, does not choose a single leader on which to confer the right of government."[25]

Arguments stressing the need for an individual person, or "will," to possess an unchallengeable right to command served two main purposes for the pamphleteers. One was to defend the regent's right to act as sovereign, and the other was to undermine any notion that Condé and the other great nobles might have inalienable rights to share in this authority. The author of *Remonstrance aux mal contens* made these points very clear, using both the "one will" principle and the idea of lese majesty.

23. *Vieux Gaulois* (1614), 11.
24. *Response pour la royne a monsieur le Prince* (1614), 8.
25. *Vieux Gaulois*, 12.

Now, it is very much the case that in any state where the head of it commands fully and absolutely, one usually rejects, even holds as a capital crime, anything which a private individual dare say . . . against the manner of governing it. This sanctuary ought not to be approached except by those whom it pleases the sovereign to call there.[26]

In addition to the legal concepts lurking behind this kind of argumentation, there was also a complex set of assumptions about how government worked. Some pamphleteers argued explicitly that the maintenance of royal authority depended on a smoothly operating network of loyalties and allegiances to the king *personally;* they were surprisingly frank in their explanations of how the system worked. Money and other benefits, they stated, accrued to those who served the king. The judicious dispensing of patronage by the king in person was believed to create bonds of sincere loyalty and allegiance. Loss of personal control over the patronage system was therefore seen as a particularly dangerous threat to the king's power.

There is nothing more prejudicial to a Monarch than to confer his favors through the recommendation of others, except in cases where he recognizes the merits of those who receive these favors. . . . It happens frequently that *les grands,* who acquire followers at the expense of their master, alienate the loyalty of those who receive these favors. Then, their willfulness makes them misbehave and gives them the boldness to intrigue, as was done against King Henry III, the most liberal Monarch in the world.[27]

The surest way for the king to prevent such intrigues, the author concluded, was for him to take control of the operations of government "with his own hand" so that those who occupied important positions felt directly dependent on the king for their privileges and power. This line of argumentation obviously implied that if great nobles like Condé were able to exercise the kind of patronage they wanted, then royal government would cease to function properly. Other historical examples besides Henry III were cited.[28]

The queen mother's supporters were willing to concede that Condé and his confederates had some role to play in advising the councils and even in administering the kingdom. But at the same time, they were quick to refute the notion that this role was a right conferred upon them because they represented the "people," "the king," or any form of public authority. Marie's propagandists argued that the princes had the privilege to advise the king, but they could do so only as simple subjects, not

26. *Remonstrance aux mal contens* (1614), 4.
27. *Conseiller fidele a son roy* (1614), 44.
28. Cf. *Discours sur les conferences faites* (1615), 11.

as public figures. One pamphleteer put it this way: "With regard to those who do not have the government in hand, who are thus without commission or legitimately conferred charge, they are not able to formalize the interests of the people nor the interests of the Monarch."[29] In other words, not even princes of the blood had any legal claim to public or state authority. Therefore, Condés claim to represent the public good and the king's true interests was not a legitimate basis upon which to challenge the administration of the queen mother.

Before the summer of 1615—at which point Condé publicly proclaimed an armed rebellion against the government—Villeroy's moderation guided much of the official propaganda against Condé. When hostilities broke out in July 1615, Villeroy lost influence over the direction of the Crown's policies. Chancellor Brûlart de Sillery, Concini, and a small circle of advisers that included several militant Catholics now controlled the queen mother's administration. They wanted the royal government to oppose Condé and his supporters more strenuously in both rhetoric and military action.

In September 1615 Marie's advisers drew up a "Declaration of the King" against the rebels that charged them with the capital offense of lese majesty. It is unlikely that the chancellor and the queen mother actually intended to prosecute Condé and his confederates further. The language of the declaration and its manner of publication suggest they were most interested in its propaganda value.[30] In fact, the first versions of the declaration were worded so that Condé and his associates were to be considered guilty of lese majesty only if they did not render their complete obedience to the Crown within thirty days. Failure to fulfill this condition, however, would make the first prince of the blood and all those following him guilty, immediately and without further trial.

The principal charges were that Condé had "begun to conspire and to form factions and conspiracies" among the subjects of the king, addressing himself to both Catholics and Protestants in order to persuade them to join with him in an uprising against the government. He had "openly

29. *Remonstrance faicte sur les esmotions de ce temps* (1614), 7.

30. *Declaration du roy contre le prince de Condé et ceux qui l'assistent.* The author of *Mercure françois,* who reproduced the text of the declaration, notes that the *arrêt* was disseminated and displayed in the principal squares of Paris, 4:226–237. Similar publication was apparently a common practice in provincial towns as well. Patte, a bourgeois of Amiens, noted in his journal the publication of several declarations against Condé; that of September 1615 "was proclaimed at the sound of a trumpet" at a great town meeting, *Journal,* 357. Referring to the similar declaration against the duc de Nevers in 1617, a royal official in La Rochelle noted in his diary for Monday, 6 February, "the declaration of the king in which M. de Nevers is declared guilty of lese majesty was read in an open meeting, as required by the king's attorney." Guillandreau, *Diarie,* 141.

taken up arms, delivered commissions [to officers in his rebel army,] and seized some of our towns." Although Condé's activities had been excused in the past, the declaration claimed, they could no longer be tolerated since his publication of a "scandalous manifesto" (the pamphlet *Manifeste* of August 1615) openly declaring his intent to interfere forcibly with the conclusion of the king's marriage. Therefore, the king personally, in his council, with the queen mother present, decided the following:

> We declare by this present declaration, signed by our hand . . . [Condé], together with the princes, officers of the crown, and all others who follow him and adhere to his designs, deprived of all honors, estates, offices, pow- ers, governments, charges, pensions, privileges, and prerogatives that they have from us, or preceding Kings. And in revoking these things we declare our said cousin the prince de Condé and all his adherents disobedient subjects, rebels, and criminals guilty of lese majesty. As such, we desire that legal action be taken against them personally and also against their prop- erty.[31]

This was the first in a series of such declarations.[32] They all followed closely the legal formulas and language used in the 1615 declaration, which was based on the form of an *arrêt* from the king's councils. Every effort was made to give these declarations the appearance of legal exact- ness and the force of sovereign judicial decisions, even though the pow- ers of the king's council as a court of law were vague. Following the normal legal procedure, the declarations were also sent to the Parlement of Paris for verification and registration. An obvious source for the exact wording, however, was the articles drafted by the Third Estate at the Estates General.

In the hope of public approval, the same formulas were used to justify Condé's arrest and imprisonment in a declaration that also charged with lese majesty those who had left Paris to protest his arrest.[33] This declara- tion of September 1616 was given the added legal authority of being

---

31. Ibid., 15–16.

32. The practice of issuing such declarations escalated sharply with the arrest of Condé and the disgrace of Villeroy in the fall of 1616. Included in the *arrêt* announcing Condé's arrest in 1616 was a pending declaration of lese majesty against all those who had left Paris in protest. Later, in January and February 1617, a charge of lese majesty was issued against the ducs de Vendôme, Mayenne, Bouillon, Nevers, the marquis de Coeuvres, president Le Jay, and all those still protesting the arrest of Condé. The duc de Nevers was also charged separately. These declarations were followed in March by an even more strongly worded declaration, *Declaration du roy, pour la reunion a son domain, et confiscation des biens des ducs de Nevers, . . .* (1617). All of these declarations were simply rescinded after the assassination of Concini in April.

33. *Declaration du roy, sur l'arrest fait de la personne de monseigneur le prince de Condé, et sur l'eslongement des autres . . .* (1616), and reproduced in the *Mercure françois* 4/2:217–227 (to which subsequent citations refer).

read and registered by the Parlement of Paris at a *lit de justice* attended by the king personally, his mother, the principal officers of the Crown, and many of the most prestigious individuals in the kingdom loyal to the queen.[34]

The declaration announcing Condé's arrest was the most strongly worded of any of the documents accusing the princes of lese majesty. It argued that Condé had not only been conspiring against the administration to capture control of the government but had also been conspiring against the person of the young king. The allegations reveal the advisers' nervousness about public reaction, but they were nevertheless reasonably confident that the "personal" dimension of Condé's alleged treason against Louis XIII would have the desired effect on public opinion.

The declaration made the sensational charge that Condé was conspiring to capture the king and to divide up the kingdom among the great nobles.[35] To threaten the person of the king or the integrity of his kingdom was, without any question, a capital offense. The very suspicion of such a treasonous intent justified extraordinary measures. The declaration therefore took pains to substantiate the charges, even if it required evidence of questionable value. The document cited the authority of "a princess" very attached to the queen who had overheard certain conversations and repeated them to the queen. The tenor of these conversations was that Condé was planning some sort of coup d'état. Next, the declaration cited the authority of one of the great nobles of France and "another of similar quality," as sources confirming the same information. A third source was alleged to be foreign ambassadors who had "officially requested" in "handwritten documents" that the king "be on guard" for his personal safety.[36] The personal threat to the king was held to justify the arrest of the first prince of the blood. Anonymous pamphleteers explained that when Condé returned to Paris in August 1616, he began to take over the functions of the king both socially and politically. His house drew more of the court than the Louvre. This was an insult to the dignity and authority of the king. Condé's actions in the *Conseil des Finances* had given him almost total control over the government's affairs. Thus, according to the declaration, Condé left to the king and the queen mother "only the name and image of sovereignty"—presumably usurping the substance for himself.

In early 1617 the administration's propaganda focused on the new association of nobles who were protesting Condé's arrest and Concini's

---

34. For the constitutional and symbolic significance of these events, see Hanley, "*Lit de Justice,*" 209–306.

35. *Mercure françois* 4/2:221.

36. Ibid., 221–223.

power. Again, the rebels' affront to sovereignty was portrayed as the central offense:

> It is unpardonable [of the rebels] to offend royal authority, which depends only upon God and the sword, and to want to control the King's actions in an affair [the detention of Condé] so important to the health of his person and his state. . . . Do you not know that subjects have no other legitimate arms than remonstrances and prayer, and that he who resists superior powers resists God, who established them?[37]

Another author wrote that the most important thing to keep in mind was that any kind of "resistance" to the king had to be considered "parricide."[38] The use of the term "parricide" was intended both to evoke general moral revulsion and to associate the rebels with the assassin Ravaillac, whose crime was widely called parricide as well as lese majesty.

THE REFUSAL TO CHALLENGE ABSOLUTISM

Condé and his allies devised a weak response to this onslaught of legalistic, absolutist rhetoric. From the beginning, the rebels had protested their personal loyalty to the king and queen mother, claiming their political challenge was directed only against a faction of the king's advisers and their evil policies. They also justified their actions according to the public interest, rather than their personal political rights. This strategy failed in part because it lacked a convincing theoretical foundation. The rebels were willing to argue that part of a general reform in the public interest would include restoring the great nobles to their proper places within the king's councils. But at no time during the 1614–1617 conflicts were they willing to challenge openly the prevailing notion of a perfect, undivided, unchallengeable sovereignty exercised by the king. They did not even champion very vigorously a notion of "fundamental laws" or of limitations on the absoluteness of royal sovereignty. Only a handful of pamphlets forwarded the notion of a monarchy in which the king was required to consult with and accept advice from subordinate political entities within the realm, including his council of great nobles.[39]

Condé and his associates called attention to their "rank," "condition," and "quality"—traditional concepts used in defense of noble privileges.[40]

---

37. *Remonstrances faictes à messieurs les princes* . . . (1617), 12–14.

38. Coeffeteau, *Response au manifeste* (1617), 15–16.

39. See *Union des princes* (1617), analyzed by Duccini, "Littérature pamphlétaire," 2:309–310.

40. The nobility may have been out of touch with both learned and popular opinion concerning their political role; see Schalk, "Appearance and Reality," 19–31; Chartier, "Noblesse et les États de 1614," 113–125; Clouatre, "Decadence of the Ancient Nobility."

As "princes of the blood," several of the rebels were in an especially strong position to press these claims. Although the princes and their supporters did not argue directly that Condé had a fundamental right to participate in the government of the kingdom, they did their best to imply this. One supporter asserted that the king's ministers ought to know "the rank that the princes of the blood must hold in the state."[41] Pamphlets supporting Condé frequently claimed that the prince's participation in government affairs was necessary for the health of the state.[42] But these vague claims were never sharpened into a clear argument that Condé and his confederates had a right to oppose their authority to that of the queen mother or the king.

Indeed, one of Condé's major rhetorical tactics throughout the struggle was to allege that he was working to maintain the authority of the king and his Crown by opposing those who had formed a secret monopoly within his councils. Such arguments were fully consistent with an absolutist position, and the propaganda of the princes was strikingly clear on Louis XIII's personal and absolute sovereignty. One supporter of the rebels claimed their primary goal was "the protection and conservation of the authority of our country, and the establishment and observation of the customary order in the management of affairs, until the king will have acquired the age to deal with these affairs as stipulated by our laws."[43]

After spring 1615 Condé and his allies complained openly that the queen mother's administration was acting as if it represented the royal will, when in fact her advisers excluded the king from any part in the affairs of state. In October 1615 Condé's party published a pamphlet under the prince's name that emphasized the distinction between the queen mother's administration and the will of the king. The rebels claimed to be in opposition, not to the King, but to those "enemies of the King and state" who had "usurped the sovereign authority and absolute government of the Kingdom."[44] The main point of the pamphlet was that those acting in the king's name had no sovereign authority; they were simply usurpers who had taken advantage of the king's youth to declare a private war on the great nobility. Condé and his associates were defending themselves against the tyranny of some of the king's advisers, not resisting the authority of the king. This strategy assumed that "absolute monarchy" was the normal state of affairs in France and that the

41. *Partisan royal* (1616), 7. For a somewhat different treatment of these issues in the pamphlet literature, see Duccini, "Littérature pamphlétaire," 2:304–312.

42. For example, *Justice que monseigneur le Prince* (1614).

43. *Noblesse françoise, au chancelier* (1615), 7, one of the pamphlets most hostile toward the regency.

44. *Declaration de monseigneur, le prince* (1615), 3.

authority of the central government was to be equated first and foremost with the personal will of the king.

The princes and their supporters also alluded to the personal, absolute authority of the king to discredit the charges leveled against them. How could the taking up of arms against the administration in power be construed as a challenge to the king? Were Concini, the Chancellor and his brother, Bullion, and Dolé (Marie's protegés) to be equated with the king?[45] In their propaganda protesting the arrest of Condé and the charge of lese majesty, the 1616–1617 confederation of princes complained, "It is a strange thing, Sire, to allow it to happen in your Kingdom, that we be esteemed criminals guilty of lese majesty for not wanting to submit to an infamous foreigner [Concini], and for not wanting to accept the final blow completing your destruction."[46]

The closest the princes came to arguing directly against the idea of perfect and undivided sovereignty was in defending their political authority and independence as royal governors. The ducs de Nevers, Vendôme, and Longueville, governors of Champagne, Brittany, and Picardy respectively, tried to stir up indignation against the administration by publishing accounts of the Crown's efforts to undermine their authority and to incite rebellion and sedition against them. Vendôme claimed that "his vassals" and his "own domestics" had been encouraged to rebel against him by misguided partisans of the queen.[47] Nevers claimed that by arming his own province against him, the queen was depriving him of the right to defend himself against the private armies of his enemies.[48] Longueville charged Concini with a long list of crimes designed to undermine the duke's authority as governor of the Province of Normandy and City of Amiens.[49]

In justifying such claims, however, they emphasized that their authority should not be challenged precisely because governors legitimately represented the king within their jurisdictions. They did not base their arguments on the assumption that they held personal rights to public authority based on "natural," customary, or hereditary claims. They argued for the necessity of procedural protection for those holding

---

45. For example, *Partisan royal* (1616), 5. This distinction was a constant refrain of most antiadministration propaganda beginning in 1615. Interestingly, this argument, rather than any of the more radical resistance theories, was also used by the Protestants to justify their taking up arms in support of Condé and their own political goals, *Discours sur les armes* (1616).

46. *Remonstrance envoiee au roy* (1616) 7.

47. *Seconde lettre de monsieur de Vendosme, au roy* (1614), one of the first of several such letters by Vendôme in the course of the conflict.

48. *Lettre envoyee au roy par monsieur le duc de Nevers* (1616); and *Lettre de monseigneur le duc de Nevers au roy, contre les calomnies* (1616).

49. *Lettre de monseigneur le duc de Longueville. Au roy* (1615).

royal offices. If other royal officials ordered people to disobey them, or even to rise up against them, these officials encouraged disobedience to the king, whose authority in the provinces was represented by his governors. The crime in the affront to them was the affront to the king. The line of argument assumed the absolutist position—admitting the legitimacy of a perfect, undivided, unchallengeable royal sovereignty. There was no attack here on the prerogatives of the sovereign, only on the usurpation of those prerogatives by those in his council who did not truly represent his will.

The revolt of the princes presented an opportunity for the deputies to the Estates General and the magistrates of the Parlement of Paris to press any claims they might have had against the principle of absolute sovereignty. Neither of them did so, despite their strong sense of participating in the governing of the country. In the spring of 1615 the Parlement of Paris began to press the Crown for some kind of a response to the *cahiers* drawn up by the Estates General. The magistrates were particularly concerned about what the Crown would do with the *droit annuel,* and they sent a deputation to the court to obtain information.[50] A brief political scuffle ensued in which the old issue of the Parlement's rights of remonstrance was raised. Marie and her advisers asked the magistrates not to meddle in "affairs of state." The magistrates responded that they were not meddling, but, rather, had a right to be heard.

One anonymous pamphlet, with no indication of the date or place of publication, mounted a theoretical defense for the Parlement's actions in this affair.[51] It claimed that the Parlement of Paris was indispensable to the kings of France because it was the "real depository" of the "justice" that God had charged the kings of France to administer. An explicit comparison was made to England's Parliament. The author argued for a "mixed" state because "when the full power rests on the will of a single man," the danger of his will becoming corrupted is too great.[52] But this

50. These events are discussed by Hayden, *France and the Estates General,* 166–171. A detailed narrative is provided in the *Mercure françois* 4:24–87. See also *Discours veritable de ce qui s'est passé au Parlement, en suite de l'arrest de la Cour du xxviii. Mars dernier, et des remonstrance* (1615); and *Arrest de la Cour de Parlement du vingt-huictiesme Mars* (1615).

51. *L'authorité royalle en son degré* (1615). The reference to "l'ancienne Monarchie d'Angleterre," in which "la puissance absolue des Roys" was "soubmise au judgment des trois Estats du Royaume, qu'ils appelent Parlement" (p. 30) was provocative rhetoric but did not represent a serious political goal. The pamphlet contains typical positions taken by defenders such as de la Roche-Flavin of the Parlement's rights. It acknowledges "authorité absolue" of the king but manages to argue at the same time that certain functions of "justice" exercised by the Parlement could not be suppressed by the king.

52. Ibid., 29. This pamphlet is a response to *L'authorité royalle* (1615), a curious pamphlet that advocates the ultramontane position with arguments referring to Bodin, du Tillet, and Machiavelli, as well as Cardinal Du Perron.

reservoir of constitutional notions was generally not tapped by other pamphleteers, and no larger campaign to press such ideas can be found in 1614–1617.

Nor does one find much constitutionalist rhetoric in the pamphlets devoted to the Estates General, in the *cahiers de doléances*, or in the fragmentary records of the meetings themselves. The Estates General was portrayed in all three contexts as an opportunity to air grievances and, possibly, to obtain specific legal and administrative reforms. In this respect, the deputies took their missions very seriously. Several times in the course of the sixteenth century, major reform legislation had followed from the recommendations in the *cahiers* presented to the king by the Estates. Many of the deputies clearly hoped this would happen again and for this reason often cited the previous legislation in the texts of their grievances.[53] The number of references in the 1614 *cahiers* to previous royal enactments—the edicts of Orléans (1561), Moulins (1566), and to a lesser extent Blois (1579)—is telling.

Partly because of this tradition of reform legislation, the entire discourse surrounding the Estates, in the pamphlets as well as in the *cahiers,* was one of supplication, not resistance. The Estates were not seen as a chance to agitate for political liberties, but as an opportunity to ask the king to turn his attention to this or that problem.[54] In fact, the royal government is portrayed as the major bastion of defense against local tyrannies of all kinds. The power of the sovereign was perceived, not as the problem, but as the solution.

Of course, there were many complaints about the royal government, the courts, nobility, church, and economic and social conditions in France. The king's tax officials were a plague. Local lawyers and judicial officials were corrupt. Local seigneurs exploited their tenants. Priests were absent from their parishes. Noblemen behaved like outlaws, while the wives of bourgeois dressed like queens. But such grievances were not articulated, either in the *cahiers* or the pamphlets, as fundamental political problems stemming from an oppressive monarchy. They were important but isolated problems, stemming from the immoral or irresponsible behavior of discrete individuals or groups. Some Frenchmen took advantage of their official positions, but this was not equivalent to royal tyranny.

Admittedly, we do not hear much from peasants and artisans. The local *cahiers* were drawn up by local elites, the vast majority of whom were

53. Chénon, *Histoire générale du droit français,* 2:346–357.
54. For analyses of the *cahiers,* see Hayden, *France and the Estates General,* 174–218; and the contributions of Chartier, Nagle, Richet, and Grimmer in Chartier and Richet, eds., *Représentation et vouloir politiques,* 63–174.

themselves royal officials of some kind. The evidence we do have concerning the grievances of the lower classes suggests that they were concerned primarily with basic economic issues, not with more abstract political matters.[55] It is also noteworthy that the elections of deputies had been heavily supervised by agents loyal to the queen mother's administration, a process that surely weeded out any political radicals—or, to use the language of the time, men suspected of not being "in the service of the king." Taking all of these factors surrounding the Estates into account, two things remain striking about the discourse it generated. First, despite the hundreds of complaints concerning the abuses of royal officials, no general ideology of regionalism or particularism was articulated. Second, the general direction of the recommendations of the deputies was toward strengthening, not weakening, the institutions of the royal government.

DOUBLING BACK: ABSOLUTISM AND THE COUP OF 1617

A final irony of absolutist rhetoric in the 1614–1617 campaigns was the way in which the arguments used to defend the queen mother's administration were turned against her in 1616–1617. This happened in large measure because Concini, known to the public at this time as the maréchal d'Ancre (after his most prestigious military office and his recently acquired marquisate of Ancre), began to be perceived as wielding a large share of the king's authority. Once this idea caught hold, it became impossible to effectively defend Marie's administration on the basis of her claim to be legitimately exercising the king's sovereignty. The arrest and imprisonment of Condé, at Concini's instigation, was thus seen as an act of violence perpetrated by Concini so that he could have his own way in the king's councils and thus exercise "absolutely" the powers of the sovereign. The remaining nobles of Condé's faction then went into revolt again, claiming they were constrained to challenge the administration because it was abusing the "name" and "youth" of his majesty. This time though, the charge stuck. Someone other than the king was exercising absolute authority and usurping the sovereign government of the kingdom.

The efforts of the administration to defend the arrest of Condé were weak. The queen mother's pamphleteers tried to revive the legalistic arguments about sovereign authority, but Concini's perceived role in the government appears to have neutralized the notion of lese majesty. Whereas people were willing to accept Marie de Médicis's representing

55. Chartier and Nagle, "Doléances rurales," 63–174, using *Cahiers de doléances*, ed. Durand (see sec. II of the Bibliography).

Louis XIII, no one would seriously place Concini in this role. The rhetoric of Richelieu and others who tried to characterize the arrest of Condé as "self-defense" on the part of the king backfired. Richelieu wrote a pamphlet that dripped with indignation toward those who criticized the arrest:

> Everyone knows well enough Condé's guilt. . . .
> His majesty is of an age to know right from wrong and desires so passionately to secure the one and to avoid the other that he will affirm without doubt to all the world that justice is the measure of his actions, and that one will never see his actions marked by violence.
> Who can say that he used violence in having arrested someone whose freedom placed his person and his state in imminent danger? There is no one in the world with any sense who could have such a thought.[56]

But the legitimacy of the government was no longer self-evident, and this line of rhetorical appeal avoided too many issues. The opposition argued that Condé had posed no real threat to the king, and that the king had not personally approved of the arrest. Was it not an even more disturbing threat, they demanded, to tolerate the tyranny of Concini over the king's councils?[57] This line of argument, pursued by the rebels throughout the winter of 1616–1617, eventually prevailed.

Concini was assassinated in April 1617 in a blatant coup d'état engineered by several of the young king's closest companions, including his falconer and friend, Charles d'Albert de Luynes, and the captain of his bodyguard, the sieur de Vitry. The assassination was justified after the fact in a flood of pamphlets celebrating the restoration to the king of his rightful and absolute power. The absolutist arguments reappeared in defense of the new government. The tone was set in the letter sent out to the provinces over the signature of the king announcing the death of Concini.

> You have easily observed how the maréchal d'Ancre and his wife, taking advantage of my young age and of the power that they acquired . . . over the mind of the Queen . . . , undertook to usurp all the authority [of the

56. As a newly appointed secretary of state, Richelieu responded in the name of the king to the manifesto published by those protesting Condé's arrest in *Declaration du roy sur le subject des nouveaux remuements de son royaume* (1617). Some evidence concerning Richelieu's authorship, in addition to the text of the pamphlet, is provided in Richelieu, *Lettres*, 1:301–17 (my translation is based on this text, 306).

57. See especially *Association of the princes of France, with the protestations and declarations of their allegeance to the King . . .* (London, 1617), an English edition based on *L'Union des princes* (1617). Cf. similar pieces, such as *Lettre de Monsieur le Duc de Buillon au roy sur la declaration publiee contre luy* (1617); and *Lettre de Monsieur le duc de Nevers. Au roy* (1617).

Crown], to dispose absolutely of the affairs of my State, and to prohibit me from having cognizance of them: a plan that they were able to push so far that until now nothing was left to me but the name of king.[58]

The language of this letter is also remarkable because of its emphasis on the king's personal involvement in the coup against Concini, highlighting his decision to arrest the marshal.

> God, through his great bounty, made me clearly aware of the eminent peril that threatened my person and my State [because of the unrestrained ambitions of the maréchal d'Ancre. However . . .] I was constrained to conceal my true sentiments, and wait for Him to provide the means and the opportunity to remedy the situation. . . . I resolved today to secure the person of the said Marshal, and commanded the Sieur de Vitry, Captain of my guard, to arrest him and place him in the Louvre as a prisoner. . . . Then I requested the Queen my Mother to find it agreeable that I take in hand the direction of my State, and try to extricate it from the extremity in which the bad advice that she followed has placed it.[59]

It is not easy to determine to what extent the public believed this transparently self-serving account. Having learned from Concini's mistakes, the eventual leader of the new political coalition, Luynes, purposely kept a low profile.[60] Whether people were ignorant of Luynes's role in the coup or simply wanted to believe the young king was now in command, they welcomed Louis as their absolute sovereign. The recall of several ministers (including Villeroy) disgraced by Concini also added to public confidence. In any case, the author of the *Mercure françois* reports that news of the change in administrations was welcomed by everyone. "The joy that the people experienced from this news cannot be expressed. Everyone shouted together, 'We have one King!' "[61]

At the level of printed discourse, the 1614–1617 challenge to Marie de Médicis's government did not generate a serious challenge to the principle of absolutism or to the form of the state from any direction. A significant discourse of resistance might have been mobilized by the radical wings of either religious party, by the Parlement of Paris, or by the deputies to the Estates General. None of these political interest groups, however, identified strongly with the revolt of the great nobility. The nobles themselves did not try to marshal any of the sixteenth-century resistance theories to justify their opposition to Marie's administration. Nor was

---

58. My translation is based on the text as reproduced in the *Mercure françois*, 5/1:201.
59. Ibid., 5/1:203.
60. Cf. Marvick, *Louis XIII*, 201–225.
61. Ibid., 200.

there even much rhetoric resembling late medieval views of the political rights of barons or peers of the realm. The political propaganda of Condé and his confederates remained fundamentally an attack on the personnel and policies of the ruling coalition.

The reasons for this apparent timidity were ideological as well as strategic. The rebels were overwhelmingly conservative. They initiated their hostilities against the queen mother's administration for essentially partisan political reasons. The prince de Condé and his supporters were not interested in changing the institutional power arrangement, but in gaining a greater share of existing authority. They recognized that power rested primarily on the ability to exercise certain functions of the royal government. Their role was defined more by practical concerns and tradition than by legal principles, and a more representative style of government would weaken this role. In the 1616 negotiations over Condé's entry into the king's councils, for example, the prince insisted that membership be restricted, not expanded, because such an arrangement would give him greater influence.

In short, Condé and his confederates believed a strong central government was in their interest; they simple wanted more influence over its policies. In this sense, *les grands* believed in absolute sovereignty in a different way, but just as strongly as legally minded magistrates of the robe. The rebels claimed they were interested in serving the king and in upholding his authority, not challenging it. What they were challenging, they said, was the usurpation of the king's authority by the queen mother's favorites.

Marie's propagandists recognized the broad support for the notion of absolute sovereignty, and they confidently characterized the challenge to her political coalition as an attempt to weaken and create disorder in the state. The corps of royal officials that constituted the leadership of the Third Estate seem to have been particularly receptive to the propaganda of absolute sovereignty. Heavily invested in their offices and dependent on normal social and economic activity for their incomes, they were anxious for law and order. They were particularly hostile to renegade military forces and the arbitrary power of military governors. Such people were naturally inclined to prefer "royal" authority to that of a regional tyrant. When the queen mother's propagandists simplified this choice to one between absolute sovereignty on the one hand and anarchy on the other, it was not hard for them to build a consensus around the former.

The success of this campaign was an important force in the conservation of the government's power in 1614–1617, but not because "absolutism" had been challenged and then defeated. The rebels based their claims to public authority on the "rank" conferred by their noble birth, the privileges conferred by their associations with royalty (such as the quasi-legal concept of peerage), and the need for "reforms." The political opposition of 1614–1617 was willing to use pamphlets to criticize the government's policies and to attack particular ministers, but they did not campaign for limitations on the king's authority or for changes in the basic structure of government. Pamphlets were a tactical, not ideological, weapon for the opposition. From the government's point of view, however, pamphlets were nevertheless dangerous because they threatened individual careers, politicized the public, and undermined the ability of king's council to function effectively. Thus, there was still good reason to undermine opposition by suggesting that political dissent of any kind was a challenge to the authority of the king, and by inundating the public with traditional divine right rhetoric and juridical notions of absolute sovereignty.

Conclusion

♦ ♦ ♦

Pamphleteering and the Development
of Absolutism

*This crime [of lese majesty] is committed in three different ways, namely, when
one defames the actions of the sovereign, when one makes an attempt on his life,
or when one enters into conspiracies against the state. . . .*
  *The first way of committing this crime was condemned by Moses [as a form of
impiety]. . . .*
  *But what increases further the atrocity of this sort of defamation is that it is
usually the forerunner of rebellion and of attempts on the life of the sovereign.*
—CARDIN LE BRET, *DE LA SOUVERAINETÉ DU ROY* (1632), 528–29

There was a public in seventeenth-century France, and its opinions
greatly concerned the men and women who tried to monopolize the
authority and power of the royal government. It is difficult to determine
the precise demographics of this public and impossible to quantify its
opinions and attitudes. But the volume of printed propaganda, the elaborate rhetorical strategies, and the mechanisms of censorship attest to its
strategic importance in political life.

The development of seventeenth-century absolutism has often been
associated with a broad shift in public opinion. The classic view is that,
following the wars of religion, a consensus supporting strong (but not
arbitrary) monarchy became a potent force in political life.[1] "The state
in its various connotations," observed William Church, "acquired new
meaning in the life of the French people."[2] There was a "widespread
belief," Church wrote, "that strong monarchy was the only instrument
that was capable of maintaining order among the turbulent French pop-
ulace."[3]

Our study of the 1614–1617 pamphlet campaigns helps to demonstrate that the notion of an absolute monarchy was something other than
a general evolution of *mentalité*. From 1594 onward French propagandists sought to defend the government by resorting to the rhetoric of
absolutism. Successive campaigns each made particular contributions to

---

1. Mousnier and Hartung, "Quelques problèmes concernant la Monarchie Absolue,"
1–55; and Church, *Constitutional Thought in Sixteenth-Century France*, 303–335.
2. Church, *Richelieu and Reason of State*, 21.
3. Ibid.

the growth of such rhetoric. The king's ministers consistently won this battle for public opinion in the early seventeenth century, not by defeating opposition to strong monarchy, which was generally insignificant, but by developing sophisticated ways to control the whole framework of public discourse.

The 1614–1617 campaigns helped to bring about the new era in several ways. Because the conflict was multidimensional and secular, pamphlets had to address specific political issues. Government ministers and other politicians followed very closely the public's reaction to signals of their political intentions. Their pamphlets were written and published to accomplish specific persuasive goals. The political opposition, which was both secular and factional, required censorship to go beyond the traditional suppression of religious heresy or seditious libel. The government tried to censor all clandestine pamphlet literature, but in the end it resorted more to the systematic production of its own propaganda. This pattern of attempts, first, to eliminate and, second, to overwhelm political opposition was an essential feature of French political culture in the seventeenth century. It was central to its historical development as well.

THE PUBLIC SPHERE RECONSIDERED

From the perspective of the later sixteen-hundreds, we can see that France entered the century with a relatively open public sphere that was free from direct state control. This situation was not the consequence of any commitment to freedom of expression (although Henry IV had a notoriously relaxed attitude toward censorship).[4] Before the 1630s the institutional means for comprehensive state control of the press and public political discourse simply did not exist. Even during the reign of Louis XIV, the government could not put a complete stop to the activities of the clandestine press.[5] But over the course of the seventeenth century censorship capabilities improved greatly. Opportunities to publish opposition political views were largely eliminated. Effective competition with the government in this sphere became more difficult and dangerous. What remained of public political discourse was distorted and manipulated either directly by government action, or indirectly through eco-

---

4. Soman, "Press, Pulpit, and Censorship," 444.

5. The general line of development during Louis XIV's reign is elegantly summarized by Klaits, *Printed Propaganda*, 3–57. For the state of the press, see Lanette-Claverie, "Librarie française," 3–44. On censorship see Birn, "Book Production and Censorship," 145–171.

nomic incentives and psychological mechanisms.[6] In addition to outright censorship, the public sphere was closed down through the granting, or withholding, of pensions and the formation of royal academies to privatize and otherwise restrict the expression of political ideas.

Throughout these developments, pamphlet campaigns were a focal point. High officials and leaders of political coalitions used pamphlets to win the support and cooperation of a broad spectrum of political interest groups.[7] And it was necessary for these same leaders, in order to maintain the effectiveness of royal government generally, to be broadly perceived as exercising the king's authority legitimately.[8] In its efforts to defeat challengers, the government had to mobilize favorable public opinion toward its ministers and their "official" policies.

Such policies gained momentum in the 1614–1617 conflict and continued to gather strength over the next two decades. From 1617 to 1621 the government of Louis XIII used similar strategies in its struggle against the exiled Marie de Médicis and French Protestants. A loose coalition of ministers, including Richelieu, gained control of Louis XIII's councils in 1625. At this point, there were new efforts by the king's council to increase the circulation of progovernment propaganda and to suppress publications by the political opposition. From 1626 to 1629 this group orchestrated a major military effort against Protestant autonomy, culminating in the seizure of La Rochelle.[9] This campaign too was accompanied by ferocious pamphleteering on both sides.

Increasing concern over control of the public sphere extended much further than the psychology of individual ministers and was certainly part of a general reaction in France to the many campaigns during the years 1610–1629. Nonetheless, the ministry of Cardinal Richelieu was an important turning point, and Richelieu's particular obsessions and policies played a fundamental role in the post–1618 developments. It is worth recalling here the passage from Richelieu's *Testament Politique*, in which he claims that a ruler can do more through manipulating public opinion than through armies.[10] Richelieu believed part of his mandate as a minister was to suppress all public political discussion that did not sup-

6. The psychology engendered by this artificial situation, and the writing strategies adopted to deal with it, has been explored by Ranum, *Artisans of Glory*, 103–277, and Marin, *Récit est un piège*, 15–34, and *Portrait du Roi*, 49–115.

7. On coalitions and control of the state, see Rule and Tilly, "1830 and the Unnatural History of Revolution," 49–77.

8. On power and legitimacy, see the classical view in Weber, *Economy and Society*, 1:30–40, 212–271. But cf. Habermas, "Hannah Arendt's Communicative Concept of Power," 3–24.

9. Parker, *La Rochelle and the French Monarchy;* and Clarke, *Huguenot Warrior*, 136–180.

10. See chap. 1, n. 4.

port a stronger royal government within France and a stronger France in the world.

Long before he was fully in power in 1635, Richelieu worked from various positions in the king's council to shape the flow of public discourse.[11] He was eventually able to curtail the pamphlet campaigns against his own administration and its policies and also to establish mechanisms for encouraging and sponsoring the publication of progovernment writings of all kinds. With his typical flair for administration and the skillful use of patronage, Richelieu made the existing organs of censorship and patronage more effective while putting new ones in place. By the mid-1630s antiadministration propaganda had been largely eliminated from France. In order to continue publishing, opposition pamphleteers such as Mathieu de Morgues had to flee the country.[12]

Richelieu's efforts to control French and international public opinion with respect to the monarchy are remarkable above all for their comprehensiveness. Not content simply to censor critical writings and encourage favorable publications, he also sought to set up a system of privileges and monopolies through which to discipline loyal printers and put others out of business. He recruited skillful pamphleteers and gave them salaried positions. He then worked closely with them and supervised their efforts to publicize and popularize his policies. One of the more innovative features of this undertaking was Richelieu's supervision of the periodical press. In 1624 he helped to engineer a change of editorship for the *Mercure françois,* perhaps one of the most important political publications of the time, which presented, more or less annually, a remarkably candid and comprehensive narrative of political events in France and Europe. Although information about the circulation of the *Mercure* is hard to obtain, early volumes were popular enough to have been republished several times, even in pirated editions.[13] The new editor of the *Mercure françois* was Père Joseph, one of Richelieu's closest collaborators and advisers, who used the *Mercure* to advocate Richelieu's foreign policy and to deflect criticism of his despotic control of the king's councils.[14] In a similar way, Richelieu protected and controlled Theophraste Renaudot's

11. Church, *Richelieu and Reason of State,* 82–101, 495–513; Thuau, *Raison d'état et pensée politique,* 169–178; and Elliot, *Richelieu and Olivares,* 3, 47, 85.

12. On the career of de Morgues see Bailey, *Writers against the Cardinal;* "Pamphlets de Mathieu de Morgues," 3–48; and "Pamphlets des associés polémistes de Mathieu de Morgues," 229–270.

13. The original editor and printer sued another printer for having had a pirated edition printed in Germany and sold in Paris; see B.N. Ms. fr. 22087, ff. 195–198. (See Introduction, n. 40.)

14. For Père Joseph's takeover of the *Mercure,* see Dedouvres, *Le Père Joseph Polémiste,* and Fagniez's review of Dedouvres, "L'Opinion publique et la polémique," 442–484.

Gazette, a weekly news sheet of several pages that began to appear in 1631.[15] In exchange for a legal monopoly on the trade, Renaudot obligingly printed material that was flattering to the cardinal and his policies as well as the king and his family.

CENSORSHIP RECONSIDERED

The history of the political press from 1618 onward is one of increasingly effective surveillance, censorship, and manipulation by royal officials. These efforts accomplished a great deal, especially after 1635, as Richelieu's government clamped down on booksellers, printers, and the literary establishment. The turning point in repression was the *Règlement* of 1618. This law was enacted in the form of *lettres patentes* from the king, verified in the Parlement of Paris on 9 July 1618. It was the first law to establish both comprehensive guild regulations for the publishing book trades and a workable system of royal censorship in Paris.[16] The legislation was designed explicitly, though not solely, to put a stop to the wild pamphleteering of the previous four years. Two of its articles contain the following provisions.

> Any printers, book sellers, or binders who may print or cause to be printed defamatory books or pamphlets will be punished as disturbers of the peace, and thereby deprived of all of their privileges and immunities and declared incapable of ever being able to engage in the profession of printer or book dealer. . . .
> And in order to avoid the abuses, disorders, and confusions that occur daily through the impression of an infinity of scandalous books and defamatory pamphlets, without the names of their authors, nor the publishers, nor the place where they were printed, because of the great number of book sellers, printers, and binders present in your said Realm, and especially in your good city of Paris where the abuses are so frequent, it will be expressly prohibited [for the community to receive more than one additional book seller, printer, or binder per year].[17]

Such passages confirm that pamphleteering, although not the only problem addressed by the *règlement,* was central. The preambles attached to repeated publications of the 1618 law confirm that pamphlets continued to be the principal target of the legislation.[18]

The 1618 law was, at first, only a limited success. Opposition pamphlets continued through the next decade to play a significant political

15. Solomon, *Public Welfare, Science, and Propaganda,* 100–161.

16. Cf. Martin, *Livres,* 1:54–57, and 440–470.

17. Articles 17 AND 18, Ms. Fr. 22061, ff. 209–220.

18. See the heavily annotated version of the 1618 *règlement* printed and published in 1621 at B.N. Ms. fr. 22061, ff. 241–252.

role for several reasons. The incessant struggle between Louis XIII's advisers and those of his mother, the religious wars of the 1620s, and the opening campaigns of the Thirty Years' War kept pamphleteers and presses active. At the same time, however, sentiment against pamphleteering hardened. Beginning in 1631 and extending up to the explosion of pamphlets that marked the Fronde, a new regime of censorship and tighter controls over the intellectual establishment all but eliminated the opposition press in France.

These developments under Richelieu have been a subject of interest since the nineteenth century, yet no study has emphasized strongly enough the pivotal role of the 1614–1617 campaigns.[19] The future cardinal was first exposed to the power of the political press when, as a young bishop, he participated in the factional politics of 1614–1615. His first appointment as a royal minister (acting secretary of state for foreign correspondence) ended dramatically in 1617 with the disgrace of Marie de Médicis and the assassination of Concini. This painful experience taught Richelieu a striking lesson about the power of pamphlet literature to shape opposition to the government, and, in so doing, to make a minister vulnerable. The sensational propaganda of 1616–1617 caused the queen mother's leading adviser to become an object of general public scorn and helped to legitimize his assassination. Richelieu's analysis of what had happened must have been close to that of his ally, Secretary Pontchartrain, who wrote in his memoirs that the general public hatred of Concini was the primary cause of the coup against the queen mother.[20] Along with the other ministers believed to have been protégés of the queen mother and her Italian favorite, Richelieu was removed from office after the coup. This was a major setback in Richelieu's career, and it took him nearly a decade of constant political intrigue and maneuvering to work his way back into the king's council.[21]

It is significant that Richelieu's first real experience in the central government came at a time of intense opposition pamphleteering. Although Richelieu's official duties focused on relations with the Protestant countries, he helped to defend the government against the propaganda campaigns of "the princes" in late 1616 and early 1617 by writing a pamphlet designed to justify Condé's arrest and discredit the new revolt of the rebel faction.[22]

Concini's assassination was a lesson that Richelieu eventually used to advantage, first to regain a place in the king's councils, and then to

19. Cf. Fagniez, "L'Opinion publique," 445–451, and Geley, *Fancan et la politique de Richelieu*, 18–35, where it is given limited importance.

20. Phelypeaux, "Mémoires," 380. See also Elliot, *Richelieu and Olivares*, 57.

21. Elliot, *Richelieu and Olivares*, 3, 35–38, 47, 85.

22. Richelieu was the author of *Declaration du roy sur le subject des nouveaux remuements de son royaume* (1617).

remain in power. Richelieu engineered his return in the early 1620s, as well-crafted propaganda campaigns undermined three successive administrations—those of Luynes, the Brûlarts, and La Vieuville.[23] Once in power, the cardinal gathered a stable of capable pamphleteers who helped foment support for his foreign policy and keep his governing coalition intact.[24] Richelieu continued to utilize the services of pamphleteers throughout his career, and was more successful than any minister before him in controlling the political press in France.

Thus the 1614–1617 campaigns were an important background for Richelieu's attitudes, his subsequent obsession with propaganda, and his efforts to shape the future of the public political discussion in France. And the *Règlement* of 1618 provided him with a framework for censorhip and control of the book trade and pamphlets.[25] Supported by the Crown, the Parlement of Paris, the Châtelet, and the tradesmen, the legitimacy of the 1618 law was beyond question. In practice, however, the new procedures were not as responsive to the perceived needs of the Crown as they could have been. Much of the policing power over the book trades had been left in the hands of the tradesmen's own syndics and the Châtelet.

A major royal edict of 1626 provided the means for Richelieu's more effective style of censorship, and is clear evidence of his intent to implement even greater royal control over the press than was spelled out in the *Règlement* of 1618. Richelieu desired a much more responsive, far-reaching, and effective system of political control, and the royal edict of 1626 (verified in Parlement on 19 January) marked the turning point in this regard. Unlike the 1618 legislation, which emphasized the self-policing of the publishing community, this new law sought to extend as much as possible the direct authority of the king's councils over the publishing trades.[26] The edict covered all forms of printing and publishing but was particularly intent on stopping pamphlet literature; *placards* and *libelles diffamatoires* were singled out as a serious problem. The pervasive antipublicity sentiment is obvious in the anachronistic preamble, claiming that printing "brought about great and dangerous difficulties in those States where it has been too freely permitted." The edict goes on

23. See Geley, *Fancan et la politique de Richelieu*, 35–239 and Deloche, *Autour de la plume du Cardinal de Richelieu*, 214–241.

24. See Fagniez, "Fancan et Richelieu," 107:59–78 and 108:75–87; Church, *Richilieu and Reason of State*, 383–504; Thuau, *Raison d'état*, 166–409; and Deloche, *Autour de la plume du Cardinal de Richelieu*, 245–511.

25. See chap. 3, "Censorship and Control of the Public Sphere." The text of this legislation was reprinted for circulation fairly frequently in the 1620s; B.N. Ms. fr. 22171 and 22061 contain various copies.

26. *Edict du Roy, portant defenses d'imprimer aucuns livres sans permission du grand sceau, et d'attacher et semer aucuns placards et libelles diffamatoires sur les peines y contenues*, a printed copy in the B.N., F. 46954.

to stipulate that printed material of all kinds, "books, letters, harangues, or other writings in prose or verse," must now be submitted for approval to the king's council prior to publication.[27] The law also stipulated that the penalty for publishing an anonymous book, posting a political placard, or disseminating an illegal political pamphlet was death by hanging.

A further indication of the government's attitudes in the late 1620s is an article in the *Code Michaud*, forced through the Parlement of Paris in January 1629. This was the work of a coalition of ministers, not of Richelieu alone.

> The great disorder and inconveniences that we see arising every day from the ease and freedom of publishing, in violation of our [the king's] ordinances and to the great injury of our subjects and the peace and tranquility of this State, [and tending to the] corruption of morals and the introduction of evil and pernicious ideas, obliges us to provide therefore a more powerful remedy than has ever been undertaken by previous ordinances. . . . We forbid any printer, whether from Paris or any other city of our Realm, . . . to print, and [we forbid] any book merchants or others to sell, any books or writings that do not carry the name of the author and printer, and are without our [written] permission. . . . Such letters shall not be executed unless a manuscript copy of the book has been presented to our Chancellor or Guard of the Seals, after which they will assign such persons as they see fit according to the subject and material of the book to examine it, . . . [28]

The direction of censorship was now mapped out, but full implementation of such policies was deferred until the mid-1630s. Control over the political press, especially over the nonclandestine branches of the press, was one of Cardinal Richelieu's major political achievements. His own experience with pamphlet warfare in 1614–1617 taught him that the elites likely to oppose the policies of the royal government—great noblemen, militant churchmen, and urban notables—made extensive use of political pamphlets to inform themselves, to build support for their causes, and to undermine ministerial authority.[29]

Richelieu's fear of pamphlets is nowhere more evident than in the

27. Ibid., 5–6.

28. *Ordonnance du Roy Louis XIII* . . . (Paris, 1629), article 52. Cf. Martin, *Livres*, 1:442. Because the registration of this edict was forced, the courts refused to acknowledge its authority.

29. Not only the widely read *Mercure françois* but also the more learned histories written by men such as Scipion Du Pleix quote extensively from pamphlet literature. In his account of the 1614–1617 years, for example, Du Pleix refers to or excerpts more than a dozen influential pamphlets, about half of which were published by the opposition; see his *Histoire de Louis le Juste*, 40–145.

passages in his *Mémoires* describing his sometime political ally, the pamphleteer Fancan-Langlois, a talented propagandist who had done much to help him into power.[30] Fancan supported Richelieu in the early 1620s as one who would help France resist the hegemony of Rome and Spain. When Richelieu's political alliances began to shift after 1626, Fancan turned against his former patron and ally. Because Richelieu was at this point working to form a stronger alliance with the ultramontane faction, it was probably Fancan's publications against the Jesuits that led to his imprisonment in 1627. The politics of this relationship were complex, which makes the unequivocal condemnation of Fancan in the emotionally charged language of Richelieu's *Mémoires* all the more significant.

> His ordinary practice was to compose libelous pamphlets to defame the government, to render the person of the king contemptible and the king's councils hateful, to excite people to sedition and seek out attractive pretexts with which to trouble the state. All of this was done in the name of a "good Frenchman" in an effort to destroy the kingdom. . . . As a follower of the devil, the truth was never on his tongue, and his lies had no other purpose than to bring about division among persons whose unity was necessary for the peace of the state.[31]

The cardinal's fear of Fancan's ability to read and manipulate public opinion vis-à-vis factional alignments is evident. The greatest danger was obviously that Fancan understood what kind of publicity would ruin the fragile consensus that Richelieu was trying to build around his less-than-popular foreign policy, and that he also had the literary skills and practical experience to mount a disruptive pamphlet campaign. The *Mémoires* try to camouflage these fears by alleging that Fancan had slandered the king and conspired against "the state." But the reference to bringing about "division among persons whose unity was necessary for the peace of the state" reveals that the real concern was rival political coalitions with dissenting views that might challenge Richelieu's policies.

The passages in the *Mémoires* also illustrate with remarkable transparency the cardinal's fear of a more open and public political process. Astonishingly, the *Mémoires* condemn Fancan not only as an idealist but also as a republican: "Nothing would make him content," writes Richelieu, "save unreal hopes for a republic, which he formed according to the disorders of his imagination."[32] Fancan had not advocated a French "re-

---

30. Fagniez, "Fancan et Richelieu," 59–87; Geley, *Fancan et la politique de Richelieu.*

31. As cited by Geley, *Fancan et la politique de Richelieu,* 4–5. Cf. Richelieu, *Mémoires,* in *Nouvelle Collection des Mémoires,* 2d ed. (1881), 21:452.

32. Richelieu, *Mémoires,* in *Nouvelle Collection des Mémoires,* 2d ed. (1881), 21:452. Cf. Fagniez observes that Fancan "cannot be placed in the ranks of those few partisans of popular sovereignty that still existed in his time"; "Fancan et Richelieu," 65–66.

public" in the sense that Richelieu clearly meant to accuse him, but he could well have wanted a more open political system in France that reflected a more representative body of political and religious opinion. This, the *Mémoires* state clearly, was to have opinions that made Fancan "an enemy of [his] times," and the victim of a "deranged" mind.[33] Fancan died in prison, accused of subverting royal authority. The lesson was not lost on other political opponents of the cardinal.

Fancan was perhaps the most sensational casualty of Richelieu's campaign to bring the political press in France under his control. But the most important features of the new regime of censorship were the thoroughness of its strategy and its overtly political purpose. The new system was particularly intent, as we have seen, on suppressing political pamphleteering. But Richelieu's program went even further. It was designed to eliminate all forms of uncontrolled, uncensored public political expression and to implement as much control over public opinion as possible in learned as well as more popular circles.

In 1631, with the Protestants brought low and his opposition within the council all but eliminated, Richelieu's administration enforced a system of pervasive censorship and established more elaborate economic control over the entire French printing establishment. He was assisted greatly in his efforts by the intellectual currents of the Counter-Reformation, and a new commitment on the part of the church to suppress subversive literature and control Catholic doctrine more carefully.[34] In October of 1631, Richelieu obtained the authority to establish an exclusive list of printers who could legally publish the official church literature.[35] He was now in a position to grant lucrative monopolies to printers who remained loyal to the Crown and who would cooperate with his publishing schemes.

Fully in control of Louis XIII's councils in 1635, Richelieu was enforcing throughout France many of the provisions of the *Réglement* of 1618 and the Edict of 1626. Through his faithful client, Chancellor Séguier, the cardinal organized a system of prepublication previw for *all* significant books. A letter from Pierre Mersenne to René Descartes attests to the effectiveness of the new regime: "Never has the censorship of books been more painstaking than at present. The Chancellor has faithful agents to examine books on theology, others to examine political writings, the Academy of Paris for literature in verse and prose, and the mathematicians for the rest."[36]

33. Richelieu, *Mémoires*, in *Nouvelle Collection des Mémoires*, 2d ed. (1881), 21:452.
34. Martin, *Livres*, 1:99–176.
35. Ibid., 1:451–452. See also 1:332–346 and 1:453–460.
36. Ibid., 1:443–444 (my translation).

A frank justification of the political motives behind the new censorship is found in the writings of the distinguished magistrate, Cardin Le Bret. In the 1630s Le Bret took up anew in his treatise, *On the Sovereignty of the King*, many of the issues explored earlier by Bodin and Loyseau. In his chapter on lese majesty, Le Bret explained that the crime could be divided into three major categories: (1)public criticisms of the actions of the sovereign, (2)attempts on the sovereign's life, and (3)threats and conspiracies against the state.[37]

Le Bret's explication of the first category, public criticisms of the sovereign, demonstrates that he and his patron had in mind virtually *any* publicly uttered criticisms, or even jokes, about the sovereign.[38] Moral considerations alone, went the argument, should prohibit such utterances because any insult to the sovereign was an affront to God. But the real danger of public criticism of the "prince" was practical and political. "What increases further the atrocity of this sort of defamation (*médisance*) is that it is usually the forerunner of rebellion and of attempts on the life of the sovereign."[39] Le Bret went on to explain that he did not just mean explicitly political slander, "published out of jealousy, hatred, and hostility," but even humorous banter and insults intended merely to entertain people.[40] Such views, pushed forward by Richelieu, were typical among many high royal officials in the 1630s and 1640s.

THE PUBLIC SPHERE AND ABSOLUTISM

The new environment nurtured "reason of state," an aggressive propaganda campaign supporting France's foreign wars and the glorification of the French monarchy.[41] Political pamphlets rationalized the use of royal power in more secular and pragmatic terms but at the same time continued to emphasize that political obedience was a traditional moral and Christian value. There was little need to defend in general the "absolute" authority of the monarchy, since this authority was rarely chal-

37. Le Bret, *Souveraineté du Roy* (1632), 528–529.
38. Ibid. The deleterious political effects of satire were an old theme. Both Le Bret and Bodin refer often to Roman authors when discussing satire, and both favor suppressing satires of a sovereign ruler. However, Le Bret's treatment of critical utterances in general as capital crimes—despite his allowances for clemency on the part of the wise ruler—is much more forceful and specific than Bodin's tendency to associate such utterances with the lesser crimes of disturbing the peace, sedition, and moral degeneracy. On Le Bret's relations with Richelieu, see Giesey, Haldy, and Milhorn, "Cardin Le Bret and Lese Majesty," 23–54.
39. Le Bret, *Souveraineté*, 529.
40. Ibid.
41. Church, *Richelieu*, 283–460; Thuau, *Raison d'état*, 33–102, 166–409.

lenged. Opposition rhetoric functioned in more specific ways, and government propaganda responded accordingly.

Pamphlets did not have to attack absolutism in order to destabilize the government and threaten political order. Attacks on the administration and policies of particular ministers could accomplish the desired ends. It was natural enough to challenge the political status quo by attacking a chief minister's claim to be acting "in the name of the king." In turn, the minister under attack might have to persuade the public that his authority came from the true source, the king's will, or suffer the loss of his authority on a national level. Paradoxically, such campaigns reinforced the rhetoric of absolutism (1) by emphasizing the unchallengeability of the king's political will, (2) by declaring illegal genuine debate on fundamental political issues, and (3) by systematiclly manipulating and distorting public political discussion.

Before Richelieu's time, the organized means for producing such propaganda were diffuse and decentralized, and throughout the pamphlet campaigns of 1614–1617 Marie de Médicis's government relied on a coalition of sponsors and authors over which it exercised surprisingly little direct control. In the years afterward, the government's control over such propaganda improved in the arena of public speeches and pageantry as well as in pamphleteering—a capability that was fundamental to the continuing growth of absolutism.

Regional uprisings and national eruptions, such as the Fronde, continued to occur in opposition to the government. But such movements were never able to mobilize an effective discourse of resistance. Censorship drastically curtailed the ability of factional movements to oppose particular ministers and their policies. At the same time, legal restrictions and practical impediments reduced the ability of broader opposition movements to resist government force and usurpation. This is all the more striking because locally based opposition was often led by the educated, argumentative, legal-minded officers of sovereign courts.[42] Opposition rhetoric continued to focus, as in 1614–1617, on the "abuse" of the king's authority by ministers and lesser officials.[43] Even the *mazarinades* contained relatively little serious political debate and had nothing like a campaign advocating the decentralizaion of royal authority.[44] Dissenting pamphlets demanded that the king's subjects be "heard," not that the monarch give up any of his authority to govern.[45]

The monarchy's great achievement was not that it silenced political

---

42. Kettering, *Judicial Politics and Urban Revolt*, 330–334.
43. Bercé, *Histoire des Croquants*, 1:379–395; Parker, *French Absolutism*, 108–115.
44. Jouhaud, *Mazarinades*, 237.
45. Carrier, *Mazarinades. La Fronde*.

opposition, but that it controlled its agenda and limited its access to the public sphere. Without any alternatives to absolute monarchy in view, the subjects of the Old Regime acquiesced in the growth of a strong, centralized government over which they had little control. In the long run, however, the forces that eliminated public dissent as a disruptive force also destroyed the public's ability to give the government authentic political support.

Louis XIV's legendary power rested on an increasingly artificial public consensus maintained in a cynically manipulated public sphere.[46] The quality of published writings on legal and political theory went into a general decline.[47] The artificiality of discourse and ritual finally led, by 1685 at the latest, to an erosion of public confidence in the idea that the king always acted for the good of his people.[48] The revocation of the Edict of Nantes, exposing Protestants to harassment and exile, illustrated to many observers that Louis XIV's government was little concerned with the "public good."

With this background more clearly in view, it is not surprising that the collapse of the Old Regime was preceded by an opening up of the public sphere.[49] The dissident intellectuals of the Enlightenment worked to rehabilitate authentic political debate in the salons and through their publishing projects. As the artificiality and incongruities of "official" public discourse were revealed, the power and authority of the monarch began to collapse. In the later eighteenth century, ministers and magistrates increasingly appealed to public opinion. Finally, the Revolution of 1789 gave birth to new kinds of public politics and to a new of form of politicial press—the newspaper. The new forms of communication provided broader and more immediate access to information and opinion and helped to channel revolutionary action. These developments marked the ultimate failure of institutions and policies designed almost two centuries earlier to enable the royal government to control the public sphere.

46. Mandrou, *France aux XVIIe et XVIIIe siècles*, 211–220.

47. Church, "Decline of French Jurists as Political Theorists," 1–40; and Bossuet, *Politique tirée des propres paroles de l'Ecriture Sainte* (see sec. II of the Bibliography).

48. Keohane, *Philosophy and the State*, 241–391; Kaiser, "Abbé de Sainte-Pierre," 618–643 (see Introduction, n. 3). See also the classic study by Rothkrug, *Opposition to Louis XIV*.

49. Baker, "Introduction," *Political Culture of the Old Regime*, xvii.

BIBLIOGRAPHY

♦ ♦ ♦

UNPUBLISHED PRIMARY SOURCES

Correspondence and Government Documents in Manuscript

Bibliothèque Nationale (Government and private correspondence, official papers, correspondence of the secretaries of state).
Fonds Clairambault (Ms. Clair.) 364–365, 647, 717
Fonds Dupuy (Ms. Dupuy) 92, 93, 558, 659, 661
Manuscrits français (Ms. fr.) 3712, 3713, 3260, 3653, 3713, 3801, 6379, 15581, 15582
Ms. fr. nouvelles acquisitions (Ms. fr. n. a.) 7171, 7260
Mélanges de Colbert (Ms. Colbert) 1, 12, 17
Cabinet des Estampes:
Collection Hennin, I–XX
Qb1 1612–1614, 1615–1617
Bibliothèque de l'Institute de France (Diplomatic papers collected by Godefroy)
Ms. Godefroy 112–114, 148, 267–268, 385
Bibliothèque Mazarine (Diplomatic papers, handwritten copies of pamphlets)
Ms. 2110
Archives des Affaires Etrangères (Diplomatic papers).
Mémoires et Documents, France. 770, 771
Musée de Condé à Chantilly (Papers of the prince de Condé).
Ms. 904, 910, 911

Records of Censorship proceedings, and regulation of the publishing trades

Bibliothèque Nationale, Ms. fr. 22061–22171 (Collection Anisson)
22061 (Legislation concerning the book trades)
22067 (Judicial proceedings against printers)
22078 (Copyrights and permissions to publish)

22087 (Censorship proceedings)
22115 (Colporteurs)
22171 (Notes on actions by Parisian courts involving the book trades)
Archives Nationales
X^{1A} 1870 (Register of the Parlement of Paris)
X^{2A} 189 (*Arrêts* from the Parlement of Paris)
X^{2A} 193 (ibid.)
X^{2A} 976 (Minutes from the interrogations of defendants before the Parlement of Paris)
X^{2A} 977 (ibid.)

Regional Archives

Archives Municipales de Dijon
  Series B: 187 (Register); 250, 251, 252, 253, 254
  (Deliberations of the Chambre de la Ville);
  463 (Correspondence)
Archives Municipales d'Angers
  Series BB: 60, 61, 62, 63, 65, 66, 67, 68
  (Deliberations of the Hotel et Maison de la Ville et Mairie)
Poitiers
  Bibliothèque Municipale, Ms. 74, 75
  Archives Municipales, (Register) 68
Archives Communales d'Agen
  Conserved at the Archives Departementales, Lot-et-Garonne, Agen, BB 42

PUBLISHED PRIMARY SOURCES OTHER THAN PAMPHLETS

Ardier, Paul. *L'Assemblée des notables tenue à Paris ès années 1626 et 1627.* Paris, 1652.
Arnauld, Robert, sieur d'Andilly. *Journal inédit d'Arnauld d'Andilly.* Ed. A. Halphon. Paris, 1857.
Aumale, Henri Eugene Philippe Louis d'Orléans, duc d'. *Histoire des Princes de Condé pendant les XVI et XVII siècles.* 7 vols. Paris, 1885–1896.
Bodin, Jean. *Les six Livres de la République.* Facs. of the 1583 French ed. Aalen (West Germany), 1961.
———. *The Six Bookes of a Commonweale. . . .* Ed. and intro. Kenneth D. McRae. Trans. Richard Knolles. Facs. of the 1606 London ed. Cambridge, 1961.
Bossuet, J. B. *Politique tirée des propres paroles de l'Ecriture Sainte.* Ed. Jacques Le Brun. Geneva, 1967.
Bouchitté, Abbé Louis-Firmin-Hervé, ed. *Négotiations, lettres, et pièces relatives à la conférence de Loudun.* In *Collection de documents inédits sur l'histoire de France.* Ser. 1. Paris, 1862
Correspondance de la Mairie de Dijon. Ed. Joseph Garnier. 3 vols. Dijon, 1870.
Cotgrave, Randall. *A Dictionarie of the French and English tongues.* Intro. W. S. Woods. Facs. of the 1611 London ed. Columbia, S.C., 1950.
D'Aubigné, Theodore Agrippa. *Les aventures du baron de Foeneste.* Maille, 1617.

D'Autreville, *Inventaire général des affaires de France, contenant les guerres et émotions civiles du royaume.* . . . Paris. 1620.

Des Lauriers, (pseud.?). *Facecieuses paradoxes de Bruscambille, et autres discours comiques,* . . . . Rouen, 1615

Du Pleix, Scipion. *Histoire de Louis le Juste.* . . . Paris, 1635.

Durand, Yves, ed. *Cahiers de doléances des paroisses du bailliage de Troyes pour les Etats Généraux de 1614.* Paris, 1966.

Du Vair, Guillaume. *De l'Eloquence françoise.* [1594]. Ed. René Radouant. Paris, 1909.

———. *Les Oeuvres.* . . . Rouen, 1617.

Duval, François, Marquis de Fontenay-Mareuil. "Mémoires. . . . " In *Nouvelle Collection des Mémoires.* Ed. Michaud and Poujoulat. Vol. 5. Paris, 1837.

Guillandreau, Joseph, sieur de Beaupréau. *Diarie.* In *Archives historique de Saintonge et de l'Aunis* 38 (1908). Also published separately, La Rochelle, 1908.

Inventaire Sommaire des Registres de La Jurade, 1520–1783. Ed. Dast Le Vacher de Boisville et al. 8 vols. Bordeaux and Castres, 1896–1947.

James I, King of England. "A Remonstrance for the Right of Kings, and the Independence of their Crownes, Against an Oration of the Most Illustrious Cardinal of Perron. . . . " In *The Political Works of James I.* [1616]. Ed. Charles Howard McIlwain. Harvard Political Classics. Cambridge, Mass., 1918.

Lalourcé, Ch., and Duval, eds. *Recueil des cahiers généraux des trois ordres aux Etats Généraux.* . . . 4 vols. Paris, 1789.

La Roche-Flavin, Bernard de. *Treize livres des Parlemens de France.* Bordeaux, 1617.

Le Bret, Cardin. *De la Souveraineté du Roy.* Paris, 1632.

L'Estoile, Pierre de. *Journal pour le règne de Henri IV.* Ed. L.-R. Lefevre and A. Martin. 3 vols. Paris, 1948–1960.

———. "*Mémoires.* . . . In *Nouvelle Collection des Mémoires.* Ed. Michaud and Poujoulat. Vols. 1–2. Paris, 1837.

———. *Mémoires-journaux.* Ed. G. Brunet et al. 12 vols. Paris, 1875–1896.

———. *The Paris of Henry of Navarre, as seen by Pierre de l'Estoile, selections from the Mémoires-journaux.* . . . Ed. and trans. Nancy Lyman Roelker. Cambridge, Mass., 1958.

Louis XIII, King of France. *Edict du Roy, portant defenses d'imprimer aucuns livres sans permission du grand sceau, et d'attacher et semer aucuns placards et libelles diffamatoires sur les peines y contenues.* B.N., F.46954.

Loyseau, Charles. *Cinq livres du droit des offices.* Paris, 1610. Bound with *Traité des Seigneuries* and *Traité des ordres et simples dignitez.* Lyon, 1701.

Machiavelli, Niccolo. *The Prince.* In *Machiavelli: The Chief Works and Others.* Trans. Allan Gilbert. 3 vols. Durham, N.C., 1965.

Mayer, Charles J., ed. *Des Etats généraux et autres assemblées nationales.* 18 vols. The Hague, 1788–1789.

Mayerne, Turquet de. *La Monarchie Aristo-democratique.* Lyon, 1610.

Mercure françois. 25 vols. Paris, 1611–1648.

Molé, Mathieu de. *Mémoires de Mathieu de Molé.* Ed. A. Champollion-Figeac. 2 vols. Paris, 1855.

Mouilhet, Pierre de. *Discourse politique au Roy par P.D.M.* Paris, 1618. Lindsay and Neu 4097.

Nouaillac, Joseph. "Avis de Villeroy à la Reine Marie de Médicis, 10 mars 1614." *Revue Henri IV* 2, no. 2 (1908): 79–89.

Nouvelle Collection des Mémoires pour servir à l'histoire de France. Ed. Joseph F. Michaud and Jean-J.-F. Poujoulat. 32 vols. in 34. Paris, 1837–1839. Also, *Nouvelle Collection des Mémoires.* Ed. Michaud et al. 2d ed. 34 vols. Paris, 1881.

Patte, Jean. "Journal historique de Jehan Patte, bourgeois d'Amiens, 1587–1617." Ed. J. Garnes. *Mémoires de la société des antiquaires de Picardie* 19 (1863): 183–374.

Phelypeaux, Paul, sieur de Pontchartrain. *Mémoires concernant les affaires de France sous la régence de Marie de Médicis.* . . . In *Nouvelle Collection des Mémoires.* Vol. 5.

Rapin, Florimond. *Recueil très exact et curieux de tout ce qui s'est passé de singulier et mémorable en l'assemblée général des Etats à Paris en l' année 1614,* . . . . Paris, 1651.

"Relation exacte de tout ce qui s'est passé à la mort du Maréschal d'Ancre." In *Nouvelle Collection des Mémoires.* Vol. 5.

Richelieu, Armand du Plessis, cardinal, duc de. *Lettres, instructions diplomatiques, et papiers d'état du Cardinal de Richelieu.* . . . Ed. M. Avenel. 8 vols. Paris, 1853–1877

————. *Mémoires.* . . . Published for the Société de l'histoire de France. 10 vols. Paris, 1907–1931. See also *Nouvelle Collection des Mémoires.* 2d ed. Paris, 1881. vols. 21–22.

————. *Testament Politique.* Ed. Louis André. 7th ed. Paris, 1947.

Rohan, Henri, duc de. *Mémoires.* . . . In *Nouvelle Collection des Mémoires.* Vol. 5.

PAMPHLETS

The major primary sources for this study were French political pamphlets, available in many libraries in France and in the United States. I used primarily the "Lb," "Lk," and "F" series in the Bibliothèque Nationale (B.N.), the Bibliothèque Mazarine, the Bibliothèque Municipale de Dijon, the Newberry Library in Chicago, and the libraries on the Berkeley campus of the University of California. I also made extensive use of the pamphlets available on microfilm in *French Political Pamphlets, 1547–1648* (Woodbridge, Conn., 1979–1980). In my list below, titles are arranged alphabetically by year. Index numbers and/or call numbers, e.g., [3047 and B.N. Lb36.305], have been provided in brackets. The same indexing scheme is used in the microfilm collection and in Lindsay and Neu's catalog, *French Political Pamphlets* (Madison, 1969). Following the style of Lindsay and Neu, orthography, diacritical marks, and punctuation have been kept as close to the original as possible.

Prior to 1614

Dialogue d'entre le Maheustre et le Manant. Cromé, François Morin, sieur de. (1593). Ed. Peter M. Ascoli. Geneva, 1977.

Response d'un bourgeois de Paris a la lettre de monseigneur le legat. (Paris, 1594). [1856].

*Remonstrances tres-humbles à la royne mere regente en F*₁*ance pour la conservation de l'estat pendant la minorite du roy son fils.* Nicolas Pasquier. [2608].

1614

A Messieurs des Estats. [Bibliothèque Mazarine, 34613].

Accueil au roy par Gabriel Bien-Venue: En faveur de MM de Poitiers. [B.N. Lb36.315].

Advis à monseigneur le prince. [2857].

Advis à tous les bons et fidels François de l'une et l'autre religion. [2858].

Advis au roy; sur la reformation generale des abus qui se commettent en son royaume. [2860].

Advis aux Trois Estats de ce royaume sur les bruits qui courent à present de la guerre civille. [2866].

Advis, remonstrances et requestes aux Estats généraux tenus à Paris, 1614. Par six paysans. [Bancroft Library, Univ. of Calif., Berkeley; Lindsay and Neu 2867 is a different pamphlet.]

Apologie pour monsieur le prince de Condé, sur son depart de la cour. [2877–2878].

Articles de la paix. [3007].

Le bon François. [2894].

Le Cabinet de Vulcan. [2910].

Le Caton françois au roy. [3027].

Conjouissance de Jacques Bon Homme paysan de Beauvoisis. Avec messeigneurs les princes reconciliés. [2895]. Also, ed. Charlier, *Revue du Seizième Siècle* 16 (1929): 209–218.

Le Conseiller fidele a son roy. [2943].

Copie de la lettre envoyee à la tres-chrestienne royne regente de France et de Navarre. . . . Henri II de Bourbon, prince de Condé. [2927].

Declaration du roy sur les edicts de pacification. . . . [3013].

Discours à messieurs les deputez aux Estats Generaux de France. [2953].

Discours de ce qui s'est passé à Mezieres. [2955].

Discours d'un gentil-homme françois à la noblesse de France, sur l'ouverture de l'Assemblee des Estats Generaux. . . . [2954].

Discours sur le traité de Soissons. [2960].

Discours sur les calomnies et medisances publiées contre m. les princes. [2963].

Discours sur les mariages de France et d'Espagne, contenant les raisons qui ont meu monseigneur le prince à en demander la surseance. [2964].

Double de la lettre escritte par monseigneur le prince de Condé, à la reyne regente, mere du Roy. . . . Henri II de Bourbon, prince de Condé. [2927–2933].

Double de la responce de la royne regente, mere du roy, à la lettre escrite à sa majesté, par monseigneur le prince de Condé. . . . Marie de Médicis. [3061].

Double de la response de messieurs du Parlement de Bordeaux, à la lettre de monsieur le prince. [2992].

Le Franc taupin. [2990 and Bibliothèque Mazarine 37279, piece 31].

La France courroucee sur la let[t]re de monseigneur le prince. [3025].

La harangue d'Achior l'Ammonite sur un advis donne à monseigneur le prince. . . . [2852, and Bancroft Library, Univ. of Calif., Berkeley].

La harangue d'Alexandre Le Fo[r]geron, prononcee au conclave des reformateurs. . . . [2872].

Harangue faicte de la part de la chambre ecclesiastique, en celle du Tiers Estat, sur l'article du serment. . . . Jacques Davy, cardinal Du Perron. [3328].

Le Justice que monseigneur le Prince demande a la royne, de la rebellion de Poictiers. [3047 and B.N. Lb36.305].

Lettre à monseigneur le prince de Condé. Th. Pelletier. [3097].

Lettre de Jacques Bon-Homme paysan de Beauvoisis: A Messeigneurs les Princes retirez de la cour. [2900]. Also, ed. Charlier, *Revue de Seizième Siècle* 16 (1929): 10–20.

Lettre de la Royne à monsieur de Roquelaure, . . . Touchant ce qui s'est passé n'a guieres à Poictiers, et en Bretagne. [B.N. Lb36.311].

Lettre de monseigneur le cardinal Du Perron. A monseigneur le Prince. Jacques Davy, cardinal Du Perron. [2970].

Lettre de monseigneur le prince de Condé, à la royne regente. [2937].

Lettre de Perroquet aux enfans perdus de France. . . . [3098–3099].

Lettre de Monsieur le Prince envoyée à la Royne. Touchant le refus à luy faict en la ville de Poictiers. [2939].

Lettres du sieur de Mazuyer, . . . écrites à la reine sur les mouvements arrivés en la ville de Poytiers. [B.N. Lk7.7938].

Libre Discours sur les mouvemens derniers de la France et particulièrement de Poictou. [B.N. Lb36.325].

Libre harangue faicte par Mathault en la presence de monsieur le prince en son chasteau d'Amboise, le seiziesme jour de Juin, 1614. [3078].

Le lourdaut vagabond. Pierre Beaunis de Chanterain. [2884–2885].

Mémoires à messieurs des estats, pour parvenir à oster la venalité des offices, tant de judicature que de finance, tirant gages de sa majesté. . . . [3080].

Procés Verbal de la revolte faicte par messieurs de Poictiers à leur gouverneur, monsieur le Duc de Roannes. [3151].

La rejouissance de Poitiers sur l'arrivee du roi et de la reine regente, mere du Roy. [B.N. Lb36.317].

Remerciement des poules. A monsieur de Bouillon. [3113].

Remerciment au roy par les habitans de la ville de Poictiers: sur le soing que sa majesté à eu de leur conservation. [3115].

Remonstrance aux mal contens. [3118].

Remonstrance faicte sur les esmotions de ce temps. A monseigneur le prince de Condé. . . . [3125].

Remonstrance de Pierre du Puis sur le resveil de maistre Guillaume. . . . [2978–2980].

Replique de Jacques Bonhomme, paysan de Beauvoisis. A son compere le crocheteur. Also, ed. Charlier, *Revue du Seizième Siècle* 16 (1929): 202–209.

Reponse du Crocheteur de la samaritaine a Jacques Bonhomme. [3141–3143]. Also, ed. Charlier, *Revue du Seizième Siècle* 16 (1929): 190–202.

Resolution à la paix et au service du roy. [3133].

Response pour la royne à monsieur le prince. [3144].

Le reveil de maistre Guillaume aux bruits de ce temps. . . . [3035].

Seconde lettre de monsieur de Vendosme, au roy. César, duc de Vendôme. [3173].

Le Serviteur fidelle. L'homme d'estat. Dialogue. [3154].

Utile et salutaire advis au roy, pour bien regner. Antoine Arnauld. [2879].

Le Vieux Gaulois. A messieurs les princes. [3176].

1615

Apologie pour messire Henry-Louys Chastaigner de La Rochepozay, Evesque de Poictiers . . . contre ceux qui disent qu'il n'est pas permis aux ecclesiastiques d'avoir recours aux armes en cas de necessité. Du Vergier de Hauranne, Jean. [B.N. Lk3.501].

Arrest de la Cour de Parlement, contre le prince de Condé, et autres princes, seigneurs, et gentilshommes, qui sans permission du roy, et contre son auctorité, . . . ont pris les armes, et commettent tous acts d'hostilité, qui vont à la ruine et desolation de son pauvre peuple. [3374].

Arrest de la Cour de Parlement, du vingt-huictiesme mars, 1615. [3380].

De l'authorité royale. [3287].

L'authorité royalle en son degré. [3214].

Avertissement à la France touchant les libelles qu'on seme contre le gouvernement de l'estat. [3185 and B.N. Lb36.441].

Le Bonheur de la France ou les allegresses publicques de bons François. . . . [3226].

Le Censeur, discours d'estat pour faire voir au roy, en quoy sa majesté à esté mal servie. [3245].

La chemise sanglante de Henry le grand. [3529].

Declaration de la volonté du roy addressee à nosseigneurs de sa Cour de Parlement. [3389].

Declaration de monseigneur, le prince. Contre les ennemis du roy et de l'estat. Henri II de Bourbon, prince de Condé. [3253].

Declaration du roy contre le prince de Condé, et ceux qui l'assistent. [3391 and B.N. F.46927, piece #24].

Declaration et justification, des actions de monsieur le prince. Henri II de Bourbon, prince de Condé. [3256].

Discours sur les conferences faites entre monseigneur le prince, monsieur de Villeroy, et autres deputez de leurs majestez. [3315–3316].

Discours veritable de ce qui s'est passé au Parlement, en suite de l'arrest de la Cour du xxviii. Mars dernier, et des remonstrance. [3320].

L'Espagnol françois. [3343].

La Grandeur de nos roys, et de leur souvereign puissance. Au Roy. Jerome Bignon. [3221.1].

Harangue de l'amateur de justice, aux Trois Estats. [3421].

Harangue faicte de la part de la chambre ecclesiastique, en celle du Tiers Estat, sur l'article du serment. . . . Jacques Davy, cardinal Du Perron. [3328].

L'Image de la France representee à messieurs des estats. . . . [3436].

L'Italien françois. [3437].

Lettre de monseigneur le duc de Longueville. Au roy. Henri II d'Orleans, duc de Longueville. [3461].

La Ligue renversee, ou response à la Ligue ressuscitee. [3473].

Le Manifeste et declaration de la France à ses enfans ligueurs et rebelles à leur roy, avec admonition à leur devoir. [B.N. Lb36.497].

Manifeste et justification, des actions de Monsieur le Prince. Henri II de Bourbon, prince de Condé. [B.N. Lb36.489].

A Messieurs des Estats. [3181].

La Noblesse françoise, au chancelier. [3502].

Le Protecteur des Princes. Dedié à la Royne. [3542].

Response de monseigneur le prince au roy. Henri II de Bourbon, prince de Condé. [3271].

Tres-humble remonstrances faictes au roy par les thresoriers de France et generaux des finances de son royaume, sur la continuation du droict annuel. [3601].

1616

Declaration du roy, sur la detention de monsieur le prince de Condé, le premier jour de Septembre, . . . [3689].

Declaration du roy, sur l'arrest fait de la personne de monseigneur le prince de Condé, et sur l'eslongement des autres princes, seigneurs et gentils-hommes. . . . [3686].

Declaration du roy sur les edicts de pacification. Verifié en Parlement le 4. Aoust mil six cens sieze. [3691].

Discours sur les armes n'agueres prises par ceux de la religion. [3657].

Edict du Roy pour la pacification des troubles de son Royaume. [3693–3697].

Lettre de monseigneur le duc de Nevers au roy, contre les calomnies qui ont este publiees contre luy. Carlo Gonzaga, duc de Nevers. [3631].

Lettre envoyee au roy par monsieur le duc de Nevers. Sur l'arret faict de la personne de monsieur le prince. Carlo Gonzaga, duc de Nevers. [3632].

Le manifeste et declaration de monsieur le duc de Guyse, sur son absence, au roy. Charles de Lorraine, duc de Guise. [3714].

Ordonnance du roy portant suspension d'armes et de toutes actions militaires par tout son royaume, . . . *durant le temps de la trefve.* [3702].

Le Partisan royal, sur la conferance de Loudun, au roy. [3733].

La Patience de Job, aux fidelles François. [3737].

Remonstrance envoiee au roy, par messeigneurs les princes, ducs, pairs, et officiers de la couronne, sur la detention de monseigneur le prince. [3748.1]

Tres-humble remonstrance au tres-chrestien roy de France et de Navarre Louys XIII. . . . [3765].

1617

The Association of the princes of France, with the protestations and declarations of their allegeance to the King. . . . (London) [3790]. English ed. of *L'Union des princes*. [4017].

Declaration du roy contre les ducs de Vendosme, de Mayenne, mareschal de Buillon, marquis de Coeuvre, le president le Jay, et tous ceux qui les assistent. . . . [3890].

Declaration du roy, en faveur des princes, ducs, pairs, officiers de la couronne. . . . [3896].

Declaration du roy, pour la reunion a son domain, et confiscation des biens des ducs de Nevers, de Vendosme, de Mayenne, mareshal de Buillon, marquis de Coeuvre, et president le Jay. [3897].

Declaration du roy sur le subject des nouveaux remuements de son royaume. Armand du Plessis, cardinal, duc de Richelieu. [3899].

Declaration et protestation des princes, ducs, pairs, officiers de la couronne, gouverneurs de provinces, seigneurs, chevaliers, gentils-hommes, villes et communautés, associés et confederés pour le restablissement de l'authorité du Roy et la conservation du Royaume. Contra la conjuration et tyrannie du mareschal d'Ancre, et ses adherens. [3826].

La Divine vengeance sur la mort du marquis d'Ancre. . . . [3851].

Lettre de monsieur le Duc de Buillon au roy sur la declaration publiee contre luy sous le nom de sa Majesté le xiii Fevrier 1617. Henri de la tour d'Auvergne, duc de Bouillon. [3801.2].

Lettre de monsieur le duc de Nevers. Au roy sur la declaration publiee contre luy, sous le nom de sa majesté. Carlo Gonzaga, duc de Nevers. [3806].

Lettre du roy aux gouverneurs de ses provinces. [3904].

Remonstrances faictes à messieurs les Princes pour leur reduction au service du Roy, contre les pretextes de leur desobeyssance. [3990 and B.N. Lb36.944].

Response au manifeste publié par les perturbateurs du repos de l'estat. Nicolas Coeffeteau. [3811].

L'Union des princes. [4017].

1618

Arrest donne par le roy en son conseil, avec lettres de declaration dudit seigneur sur la revocation du droict annuel. [4062].

Discourse politique au Roy par P.D.M. Mouilhet, Pierre de. [4097].

OTHER SOURCES

Adam, Antoine. *Du Mysticisme à la révolte: Les Jansénistes du XVIIe siècle.* Paris, 1968.

Altschull, J. Herbert. *Agents of Power: The Role of the News Media in Human Affairs.* New York, 1984.

Anderson, Perry. *The Lineages of the Absolutist State.* London, 1974.

André, Louis. *Les Sources de l'histoire de France . . . (1610–1715).* 7 vols. Paris, 1926.

Angenot, Marc. *La Parole pamphlétaire: contribution à la typologie des discours modernes.* Paris, 1982.

——. "Présupposé, topos, idéologème." *Etudes françaises* 13, nos. 1–2 (1977): 11–34.

Antoine, Michel. "La monarchie absolue." In *The Political Culture of the Old Regime,* ed. Keith Michael Baker, 3–24. Oxford, 1987.

Aquilon, Pierre. "Les Réalités provinciales." In *Histoire de l'édition française,* vol. 1. See Martin and Chartier.

Arriaza, Armand. "Mousnier and Barker: The Theoretical Underpinning of the 'Society of Orders' in Early Modern Europe." *Past and Present* 89 (1980): 39–57.

Aston, Trevor, ed. *Crisis in Europe.* Intro. Christopher Hill. New York, 1965.

Auerbach, Erich. *Mimesis.* Trans. Willard R. Trask. 1st German ed. 1946; Princeton, 1968.

Babelon, Jean-Pierre. *Henri IV.* Paris, 1982.

Bailey, Donald. *Writers against the Cardinal: A Study of the Pamphlets which Attacked the Person and Policies of Cardinal Richelieu during the Decade 1630–1640.* Ann Arbor, Mich., 1973. Microfilm.

——. "Les pamphlets de Mathieu de Morgues (1582–1670): Bibliographie des ouvrages disponibles dans les bibliothèques parisiennes et certaines bibliothèques des Etats-Unis." *Revue française d'histoire du livre* 18 (1978): 3–48.

———. "Les pamphlets des associés polémistes de Mathieu de Morgues: Marie de Médicis, Gaston d'Orléans et Jacques Chanteloube. Une bibliographie des fonds des bibliothèques de Paris et des Etats-Unis." *Revue française d'histoire du livre* 27 (1980): 229–270.

———. "Les recueils de Mathieu de Morgues: une bibliographie des collections dans les bibliothèques de Paris." *Revue française d'histoire du livre* 33 (1981): 553–592.

Bailyn, Bernard. *The Ideological Origins of the American Revolution.* Cambridge, Mass., 1967.

Bailyn, Bernard, and John B. Hench, eds. *The Press and the American Revolution.* Worcester, Mass., 1980.

Baker, Keith Michael. "Introduction." In *The Political Culture of the Old Regime,* ed. Keith Michael Baker. Oxford, 1987. Vol. 1 of Baker and Lucas, eds., *The French Revolution and the Creation of Modern Political Culture.*

———. "On the Problem of the Ideological Origins of the French Revolution." In *Modern European Intellectual History: Reappraisals and New Perspectives,* ed. Dominick LaCapra and Steven L. Kaplan. Ithaca, 1982.

———. "Politics and Public Opinion Under the Old Regime: Some Reflections." In *Press and Politics in Pre-Revolutionary France,* ed. Jack R. Censer and Jeremy D. Popkin, 204–246. Berkeley and Los Angeles, 1987.

Baker, Keith Michael, and Colin Lucas, eds. *The French Revolution and the Creation of Modern Political Culture.* 2 vols. Vol 1., *The Political Culture of the Old Regime.* Ed. Keith Michael Baker. Vol 2., *The Political Culture of the French Revolution.* Ed. Colin Lucas. Oxford, 1987–1989.

Bakhtin, Mikhail. *Rabelais and His World.* Trans. Hélène Iswolsky. Cambridge, Mass., 1968.

Barbiche, Bernard. *Sully.* Paris, 1978.

———. "Le Régime de l'édition." In *Histoire de l'édition française,* vol. 1. See Martin and Chartier.

Bardon, Françoise. *Le Portrait mythologique à la cour de France sous Henri IV et Louis XIII.* Paris, 1974.

Basdevant-Gaudemet, Brigitte. *Charles Loyseau, 1564–1627, théoricien de la puissance publique.* Paris, 1977.

Baumgartner, Frederic J. *Radical Reactionaries: The Political Thought of the French Catholic League.* Geneva, 1976.

Bayley, Peter. *French Pulpit Oratory, 1598–1650.* Cambridge, 1980.

Beauchet-Filleau, Henri, et al. *Dictionnaire historique et généalogique des familles de Poitou.* 4 vols. and 2 suppls. Poitiers, 1891–1912.

Becker, Howard S. "Culture: A Sociological View." *Yale Review* 71 (1982): 513–527.

Behrens, C. B. A. *Society, Government, and the Enlightenment: The Experiences of Eighteenth-Century France and Prussia.* New York, 1985.

Beik, William. *Absolutism and Society in Seventeenth-Century France: State Power and Provincial Aristocracy in Languedoc.* Cambridge, 1985.

Bellanger, Claude, et al., eds. *Histoire générale de la presse française.* Pref. Pierre Renouvain. 5 vols. Paris, 1969–1979.

Bendix, Reinhard. *Kings or People: Power and the Mandate to Rule.* Berkeley and Los Angeles, 1978.

Bennett, H. S. *English Books and Readers, 1558 to 1603.* Cambridge, 1965.

Bercé, Yves-Marie. *Histoire des Croquants: Etude des soulèvements populaire au XVIIe siècle dans le Sud-Ouest de la France.* 2 vols. Geneva, 1974.

Berenson, Edward. *Populist Religion and Left-Wing Politics in France, 1830–1852.* Princeton, 1984.

Berger, Günter. "Littérature et lecteurs à Grenoble aux XVIIe et XVIIIe siècles. Le public littéraire dans une capitale provinciale." *Revue d'histoire moderne et contemporaine* 33 (1986): 114–132.

Bergin, Joseph. *Cardinal Richelieu: Power and the Pursuit of Wealth.* New Haven, 1985.

Birn, Raymond. "Book Production and Censorship in France, 1700–1715." In *Books and Society in History,* ed. Kenneth Carpenter, 145–171. New York, 1983.

Biteaud, Philippe, and Bernard del Socorro. "Les Brochures politiques éditées à Lyon de 1601 à 1610 et conservées à la Bibliothèque Municipale de Lyon." *Revue française de l'histoire du livre* 26 (1980): 125–130.

Bloch, Marc. *The Royal Touch: Sacred Monarchy and Scrofula in France and England.* Trans. J. E. Anderson. London, 1973.

Bollème, Geneviève. *Les Almanachs populaires.* Paris, 1969.

Bonney, Richard. *The King's Debts.* London, 1981.

———. *Political Change in France under Richelieu and Mazarin, 1624–1661.* Oxford, 1978.

———. "Absolutism: What's in a Name?" *French History* 1, no. 1 (March 1987): 93–117.

———. "The English and French Civil Wars." *History* 65 (1980): 365–382.

Booth, Wayne. *The Rhetoric of Fiction.* Chicago, 1961.

Bourgeois, Emile, and Louis André. *Les Sources de l'histoire de France: XVIIe siècle (1610–1715).* 8 vols. Vol. 4, *Journaux et pamphlets.* Paris, 1913–1935.

Bowen, Barbara C. *The Age of Bluff: Paradox and Ambiguity in Rabelais and Montaigne.* Urbana, Ill., 1972.

Braestrup, Peter. *Big Story: How the American Press and Television Reported and Interpreted the Crisis of Tet 1968 in Vietnam and Washington.* 1st ed., 1977; abr. ed., New Haven, 1983.

Brandt, William J. *The Rhetoric of Argumentation.* Indianapolis and New York, 1970.

Brewer, John. *Party Ideology and Popular Politics at the Accession of George III.* Cambridge, 1976.

Briggs, Robin. *Early Modern France, 1560–1715.* Oxford and London, 1977.

Brink, James E. "Provincial Assemblies and Parlement in Early Modern France: A Review of Historical Scholarship." *Legislative Studies Quarterly* 11 (1986): 429–453.

Brown, Cynthia J. "Language as a Political Instrument in the Work of Jean Lemaire de Belges and Other Poets of the Rhétoriqueur Tradition." Ph.D. diss., Dept. of French. University of California, Berkeley, 1978.

Bryant, Lawrence M. *The King and the City in the Parisian Royal Entry Ceremony:*

Politics, Ritual, and Art in the Renaissance. Geneva, 1986.

Budd, Richard W., and Brent D. Ruben, eds. *Beyond Media: New Approaches to Mass Communications.* Rochelle Park, N.J., 1979.

Buisseret, David. *Sully and the Growth of Centralized Government in France, 1598–1610.* London, 1968.

Burke, Kenneth. *Counter-Statement.* 1st ed., 1931; rev. ed., Berkeley and Los Angeles, 1968.

———. *A Grammar of Motives.* 1st ed., 1945; Berkeley and Los Angeles, 1962.

———. *The Rhetoric of Motives.* 1st ed., 1950; Berkeley and Los Angeles, 1962.

Carey, John A. *Judicial Reform in France before the Revolution of 1789.* Cambridge, Mass., 1981.

Carrier, Hubert. *La Presse de la Fronde (1648–1653): les mazarinades. La Conquête de l'opinion.* Geneva, 1989.

———. "Souvenirs de la Fronde en U.R.S.S.: les collections russes de mazarinades." *Revue historique* 252 (1974): 27–50.

———, ed. *La Fronde: contestation démocratique et misère paysanne. 52 mazarinades.* 2 vols. Paris, 1982.

Cazauy, Y. "Essai de bibliographie des éditions de *La Satyre Ménippée,* publiée du XVIe au XVIIIe siècle." *Revue française d'histoire du livre* 34 (1982): 3–40.

Censer, Jack Richard. *Prelude to Power: The Parisian Radical Press, 1789–1791.* Baltimore, 1976.

Censer, Jack R., and Popkin, Jeremy D. "Historians and the Press." In *Press and Politics in Pre-Revolutionary France,* ed. Jack R. Censer and Jeremy D. Popkin. Berkeley and Los Angeles, 1987.

Charlier, Gustave. "Lettres de Jacques Bon-homme." *Revue du seizième siècle* 16 (1929): 1–20, 191–218.

Chartier, Roger. *The Cultural Uses of Print in Early Modern France.* Trans. Lydia G. Cochrane. Princeton, 1987.

———. "La convocation aux Etats de 1614: note sur les formes politiques." In *Représentation et vouloir politiques.* See Chartier and Richet.

———. "La noblesse et les Etats de 1614: une réaction aristocratique?" In *Représentation et vouloir politiques.* See Chartier and Richet.

———. "Pamphlets et gazettes." In *Histoire de l'édition française,* vol. 1. See Martin and Chartier.

Chartier, Roger, Marie-Madeleine Compère, and Dominique Julia. *L'Education en France du XVIe au XVIIIe siècle.* Paris, 1976.

Chartier, Roger, and Jean Nagle. "Doléances rurales: le bailliage de Troyes." In *Représentation et vouloir politiques.* See Chartier and Richet.

Chartier, Roger, and Denis Richet, eds. *Représentation et vouloir politiques: autour des Etats-Généraux de 1614.* Paris, 1982.

Chénon, E. *Histoire générale du droit français public et privé des origines à 1815.* 2 vols. Paris, 1910.

Church, William F. *Constitutional Thought in Sixteenth-Century France: A Study in the Evolution of Ideas.* Cambridge, Mass., 1941; rpt. New York, 1969.

———. *Louis XIV in Historical Thought.* New York, 1976.

———. *Richelieu and Reason of State.* Princeton, 1972.

———. "The Decline of French Jurists as Political Theorists." *French Historical Studies* 5 (1967): 1–40.

————. "France." In *National Consciousness, History, and Political Culture in Early-Modern Europe*, ed. Orest Ranum, 43–66. Baltimore, 1975.

Clark, Stuart. "French Historians and Early Modern Popular Culture." *Past and Present* 100 (1983): 62–99.

Clarke, Jack Alden. *Huguenot Warrior: The Life and Times of Henri de Rohan, 1579–1638*. The Hague, 1966.

Clarke, Peter. "Political History in the 1980s: Ideas and Interests." *Journal of Interdisciplinary History* 12 (1981): 45–47.

Clouatre, Dallas L. "The Concept of Class in French Culture Prior to the Revolution." *Journal of the History of Ideas* 45 (1984): 219–244.

————. "On the Causes of the Decadence of the Ancient Nobility." Paper delivered to the American Historical Association Annual Meeting, San Francisco, 28 December 1983.

Clouzot, Henri. "Notes pour servir à l'histoire de l'imprimerie à Niort et dans les Deux-Sèvres," *Mémoires de la Société de Statistique des Deux Sèvres*, ser. 2, vol. 7 (1867): 5–57. Published separately, Noirt, 1891.

Collins, James B. *Fiscal Limits of Absolutism: Direct Taxation in Early Seventeenth-Century France*. Berkeley and Los Angeles, 1988.

Constant, Jean-Marie. "Le langage politique paysan en 1576: les cahiers de doléances des bailliages de Chartres et de Troyes." In *Représentation et vouloir politiques*. See Chartier and Richet.

Coveny, Peter J. "Introduction." In *France in Crisis, 1620–1675*, ed. Peter J. Coveny. Totowa, N.J., 1977.

Culler, Jonathan. "Convention and Meaning: Derrida and Austin." *New Literary History* 13, no. 1 (1981): 15–30.

Cust, Richard. "News and Politics in Early Seventeenth-Century England." *Past and Present* 112 (1986): 60–90.

Daly, James. "The Idea of Absolute Sovereignty in Seventeenth-Century England." *Historical Journal* 21 (1978): 227–250.

Darnton, Robert. *The Great Cat Massacre and Other Episodes in French Cultural History*. New York, 1984.

————. *The Literary Underground of the Old Regime*. Cambridge, Mass., 1982.

Davidson, Hugh M. *Audience, Words, and Art: Studies in Seventeenth-Century Rhetoric*. Columbus, Ohio, 1965.

Davis, Natalie Zemon. *Fiction in the Archives: Pardon Tales and Their Tellers in Sixteenth-Century France*. Stanford, Calif., 1987.

————. "Printing and the People." In *Society and Culture in Early Modern France*, ed. Natalie Zemon Davis, 189–226. Stanford, Calif., 1975.

Decimon, Robert. *Qui étaient les seize? Mythes et réalités de la Ligue parisienne (1585–1594)*. Paris, 1983.

Decimon, Robert, and Eli Barnavi. "Débats sur la Ligue à Paris (1585–1594)." *Annales: E.S.C.* 37, no. 1 (1982): 72–127.

Decimon, Robert, and Christian Jouhaud. "La Fronde en mouvement: le développement de la crise politique entre 1648 et 1652." *Dix-septième siècle* 36, no. 4 (1984): 305–322.

Dedouvres, L. *Le Père Joseph Polémiste: ses premiers écrits, 1623–1626*. Paris, 1895.

Deierkauf-Holsboer, S. Wilma. *Vie d'Alexandre Hardy, poète du roi, 1572–1632*. Rev. ed., Paris, 1972.

Delalain, M. P. *Inventaire des marques d'imprimeurs et de libraires de la collection du cercle de la librairie.* 2d rev. ed., Paris, 1892.

Deloche, Maximin. *Autour de la plume du Cardinal de Richelieu.* Paris, 1920.

Denault, Gerard Francis. *The Legitimation of the Parlement of Paris and the Estates General of France, 1560–1614.* Ann Arbor, Mich., 1975. Microfilm.

Dent, Julian. *Crisis in Finance: Crown, Financiers and Society in Seventeenth-Century France.* Newton Abbot, 1973.

Desgraves, Louis. *Bibliographie bordelaise. Bibliographie des ouvrages imprimés à Bordeaux au XVIe siècle et par Simon Millanges (1572–1623).* Baden-Baden, 1971.

———. *Etudes sur l'imprimerie dans le Sud-Ouest de la France aux XVe, XVIe et XVIIe siècles.* Amsterdam, 1968.

———. *Les Haultin, 1571–1623.* Geneva, 1960.

———. *Les Livres imprimés à Bordeaux au XVIIe siècle.* Geneva, 1971.

———. *Répertoire des ouvrages de controverse entre catholiques et protestants en France (1598–1685).* 2 vols. Geneva, 1984–1985.

———. "Aspects des controverses entre catholiques et protestants dans le Sud-Ouest, entre 1584–1630." *Annales du Midi* 76 (1964): 153–187.

———. "Les 'bulletins d'information' imprimés à Bordeaux aux XVIe et XVIIe siècles." *Bulletin de la Société des bibliophiles de Guyenne* 79 (1964): 15–54.

———. "L'imprimerie à Agen au XVIIe siècle." *Revue de l'Agenais,* Congrès de Villeneuve (1962): 233–254.

———. "Supplément à la Bibliographie des ouvrages imprimés par Simon Millanges, 1572–1623." *Bulletin de la Société des bibliophiles de Guyenne* 76 (1964).

Desjonquères, Léon. *Garde des Sceaux Michel de Marillac et son oeuvre législatif.* Paris, 1908.

Deyon, Pierre. "A propos des rapports entre la noblesse française et la monarchie absolue pendant la première moitié du dix-septième siècle." *Revue historique* 231 (1964): 341–356.

———. "Sur certaines formes de la propagande religieuse du XVIe siècle." *Annales: E.S.C.* 36 (1981): 16–25.

Diefendorf, Barbara B. *Paris City Councillors in the Sixteenth Century.* Princeton, 1983.

Dompnier, Bernard. "Le Missionaire et son Public." In *Journées Bossuet: la prédication au XVIIe siècle,* ed. Thérèse Goyet and Jean-Pierre Collinet, 105–122. Paris, 1980.

Doucet, Roger. *Les Institutions de la France au XVIe siècle.* 2 vols. Paris, 1948.

Droz, Eugénie. "Antoine Vincent: la propagande protestante par le psautier." In *Aspects de la propagande religieuse,* ed. G. Berthoud et al., 276–293. Geneva, 1957.

Duccini, Hélène. "La Littérature pamphlétaire sous la Régence de Marie de Médicis." 3 vols. Thèse de troisième cycle, Université de Paris X, 1977.

———. "Pamphlets et censure en France au XVIIe siècle." *Lendemains* 13 (1979): 93–102.

———. "Regard sur la littérature pamphlétaire en France au XVIIe siècle." *Revue historique* 260, no. 2 (1978): 313–337.

Duncan, Hugh D. *Communication and Social Order.* London, 1962.

———. *Language and Literature in Society.* Chicago, 1953.

Dupriez, Bernard. "Où sont les arguments?" *Etudes françaises* 13, nos. 1–2 (1977): 35–51.

Edelman, Murray. *The Symbolic Uses of Politics.* Urbana, Ill., 1967.

Eisenstein, Elizabeth L. *The Printing Press as an Agent of Change: Communications and Cultural Transformation in Early Modern Europe.* 2 vols. Cambridge, 1979.

Elliot, J. H. *Richelieu and Olivares.* Cambridge, 1984.

Ellul, Jacques. *Propaganda and the Formation of Men's Attitudes.* Trans. K. Kellen and Jean Lerner, intro. K. Kellen. New York, 1973.

Fagniez, Gustave. *Le Père Joseph et Richelieu, 1577–1638.* 2 vols. Paris, 1894.

———. "Fancan et Richelieu." *Revue historique* 107 (1911): 59–78, and 108 (1911): 75–87.

———. "L'Opinion publique et la polémique au temps de Richelieu, à propos d'une publication récente." *Revue des questions historiques* 31 (1896): 442–484.

———. "L'Opinion publique et la press politique sous Louis XIII, 1624–1626." *Revue d'histoire diplomatique* 14 (1900): 352–401.

———. "Le Père Joseph et Richelieu." *Revue des questions historique* 48 (1890): 470–521.

Febvre, Lucien, and Henri-Jean Martin. *L'Apparition du livre.* 1st ed., Paris, 1958; rev. ed., Paris, 1971. See also Henri-Jean Martin, Lucien Febvre, and Paul Victor, *The Coming of the Book: The Impact of Printing, 1450–1800.* Trans. David Gerard; ed. Geoffrey Nowell-Smith and David Wooton. Atlantic Highlands, N.J., 1976.

Fessenden, Nicholas Buck. "Epernon and Guyenne: Provincial Politics under Louis XIII." Ph.D. diss., Columbia University, 1972.

Fish, Stanley. *Self-Consuming Artifacts.* Berkeley and Los Angeles, 1972.

Formon, Marcelle. "Henri-Louis Chasteigner de la Rocheposay, Evêque de Poitiers (1612–1651)." *Bulletin de la Société des antiquaires de l'Ouest et des Musées de Poitiers* (1955): 165–231.

Fossier, François. "La Charge d'historiographe du seizième au dix-neuvième siècle." *Revue historique* 253, no. 1 (1977): 73–92.

Foucault, Michel. *The History of Sexuality.* Trans. Robert Hurley. New York, 1978.

———. *Power/Knowledge: Selected Interviews and Other Writings, 1972–1977.* Ed. Colin Gordon; trans. Colin Gordon et al. New York, 1980.

France, Peter. *Racine's Rhetoric.* Oxford, 1965.

———. *Rhetoric and Truth in France.* Oxford, 1972.

Franklin, Julian. *Jean Bodin and the Rise of Absolutist Theory.* Cambridge, 1973.

———. *Jean Bodin and the Sixteenth-Century Revolution in the Methodology of Law and History.* New York, 1973.

French Political Pamphlets, 1547–1648. Woodbridge, Conn., 1979–1980. Microfilm.

Fumaroli, Marc. *L'Age de l'éloquence: rhétorique et "res litteraria" de la Renaissance au seuil de l'époque classique.* Geneva, 1980.

Furet, François. *Interpreting the French Revolution.* Trans. Elborg Forster. Cambridge, 1981. [Originally published as *Penser la Révolution française.* Paris, 1978.]

———, ed. *Livre et société dans la France du XVIIIe siècle.* 2 vols. Paris and The Hague, 1965–1970.

Furet, François, and Jacques Ozouf. *Lire et écrire: l'alphabétisation des français de Calvin à Jules Ferry.* 2 vols. Paris, 1977.

Geertz, Clifford. *The Interpretation of Cultures.* New York, 1973.

Geley, Léon. *Fancan et la politique de Richelieu de 1617 à 1627.* Paris, 1894.

Genette, Gérard. *Figures II.* Paris, 1969.

George, Alexander. *Propaganda Analysis: A Study of Inferences Made from Nazi Propaganda in World War II.* Evanston, Ill., 1959.

Giddens, Anthony. *Central Problems in Social Theory: Action, Structure, and Contradiction in Social Analysis.* Berkeley and Los Angeles, 1979.

———. "Jürgen Habermas." In *The Return of Grand Theory in the Human Sciences,* ed. Quentin Skinner, 123–139. Cambridge, 1985.

Giesey, Ralph E. "The Juristic Basis of Dynastic Right to the French Throne." *Transactions of the American Philosophical Society* 51. Philadelphia, 1961.

———. "Medieval Jurisprudence in Bodin's Concept of Sovereignty." In *Jean Bodin,* ed. Horst Denzer, 167–186. Munich, 1973.

———. "Models of Rulership in French Ceremonial." In *Rites of Power: Symbolism, Ritual, and Politics Since the Middle Ages,* ed. Sean Wilentz, 41–64. Philadelphia, 1985.

———. "State-Building in Early Modern France: The Role of Royal Officialdom." *Journal of Modern History* 55 (1983): 191–207.

Giesey, Ralph E., Lanny Haldy, and James Milhorn. "Cardin Le Bret and Lese Majesty." *Law and History Review* 4, no. 1 (1986): 23–54.

Ginzburg, Carlo. *The Cheese and the Worms: The Cosmos of a Sixteenth-Century Miller.* Trans. John Tedeschi and Anne Tedeschi. Baltimore, 1980.

Golden, Richard. *The Godly Rebellion.* Chapel Hill, N.C., 1981.

Goody, Jack, and Ian Watt. "The Consequences of Literacy." In *Literacy in Traditional Societies,* ed. Jack Goody, 27–68. Cambridge, 1968.

Goubert, Pierre. *The Ancien Regime: French Society, 1600–1750.* Trans. Steve Cox. New York, 1969.

Graff, Harvey J. *The Legacies of Literacy.* Bloomington, Ind., 1986.

Grand-Mesnil, Marie Noël. *Mazarin, la Fronde et la presse.* Paris, 1967.

Grendler, Paul F. *The Roman Inquisition and the Venetian Press, 1540–1605.* Princeton, 1977.

Grente, Georges, et al., eds. *Dictionnaire des lettres françaises.* 7 vols. Paris, 1951–1972.

Grimmer, Claude. "Conflits et doléances en 1614: le cas de la Haute-Auvergne." In *Représentation et vouloir politiques.* See Chartier and Richet.

Habermas, Jürgen. *Autonomy and Solidarity: Interviews.* Ed. and intro. Peter Dews. London, 1986.

———. *Strukturwandel der Öffentlichkeit: Untersuchungen zu einer Kategorie der bürgerlichen Gesellschaft.* Neuwied and Berlin, 1962; published in France as *L'Espace public: archéologie de la publicité comme dimension constitutive de la société bourgeoise.* Trans. Marc B. de Launey. Paris, 1978.

———. *The Theory of Communicative Action.* 2 vols. Boston, 1981–1984.

———. "Hannah Arendt's Communicative Concept of Power." *Social Research* 44 (1977): 3–24.

———. "The Public Sphere: An Encyclopedia Article." *New German Critique* 3 (1974): 49–55.

————. "What Is Universal Pragmatics?" In *Communication and the Evolution of Society*. Trans. Thomas McCarthy, 1–68. Boston, 1979.

Hale, John R. "War and Public Opinion in the Fifteenth and Sixteenth Centuries." *Past and Present* 22 (1962): 18–36.

Hanley, Sarah. *The "Lit de Justice" of the Kings of France: Constitutional Ideology in Legend, Ritual, and Discourse*. Princeton, 1983.

Harding, Robert. *Anatomy of a Power Elite: The Provincial Governors of Early Modern France*. New Haven, 1978.

————. "Revolution and Reform in the Holy League: Angers, Rennes, Nantes." *Journal of Modern History* 53 (1981): 379–416.

Harth, Erica. *Ideology and Culture in Seventeenth-Century France*. Ithaca, 1983.

Hatton, Ragnhild Marie, ed. *Louis XIV and Absolutism*. Columbus, Ohio, 1976.

Hayden, J. M. *France and the Estates General, 1614*. Cambridge, 1974.

————. "Continuity in the France of Henry IV and Louis XIII: French Foreign Policy, 1598–1615." *Journal of Modern History* 45 (1973): 1–23.

————. "Deputies and *Qualités:* The Estates General of 1614." *French Historical Studies* 3, no. 4 (1964): 507–524.

————. "The Uses of Political Pamphlets: The Example of 1614–15 in France." *Candian Journal of History* 21 (1986): 143–165.

Hexter, J. H. "Fernand Braudel and the *Monde Braudelien*. . ." *Journal of Modern History* 44 (1972): 480–538.

Hickey, Daniel. *The Coming of French Absolutism: The Struggle for Tax Reform in the Province of Dauphiné*. Toronto, 1986.

Higman, Francis. "Le levain de l'Evangile." In *Histoire de l'édition française*, Vol. 1. See Martin and Chartier.

Hill, Christopher. *The World Turned Upside Down*. Harmondsworth and New York, 1975.

Hirsch, E. D., Jr. *Validity in Interpretation*. New Haven, 1967.

Hohendahl, Peter U. "Critical Theory, Public Sphere and Culture: Jürgen Habermas and His Critics." *New German Critique* 16 (1979): 89–118.

————. "Jürgen Habermas: 'The Public Sphere' (1964)." *New German Critique* 3 (1974): 45–47.

Höpfl, Harro. "Fundamental Law and the Constitution in Sixteenth-Century France." In *Die Rolle der Juristen bei der Entstehung des modernen Staates*, ed. Roman Schnur, 327–349. Berlin, 1986.

Hovland, Carl I., Irving L. Janis, and Harold H. Kelly. *Communication and Persuasion: Psychological Studies of Opinion Change*. New Haven, 1953.

Howe, Alan. "Bruscambille, qui était-il?" *Dix-septième siècle* 38, no. 4 (1986): 390–391.

Howell, A. Lloyd. "The Political Thought of Charles Loyseau (1564–1627)." *European Studies Review* 11 (1981): 53–82.

Huguet, Edmond. *Dictionnaire de la langue française du seizième siècle*. 7 vols. Paris, 1925–1967.

Hunt, Lynn A. *Politics, Culture, and Class in the French Revolution*. Berkeley and Los Angeles, 1984.

————. "Review of Furet's *Interpreting the French Revolution*." *History and Theory* 20, no. 3 (1981): 313–323.

Huppert, George. *Les Bourgeois Gentilshommes: An Essay on the Definition of Elites in*

Renaissance France. Chicago, 1977.

―――. *Public Schools in Renaissance France*. Urbana and Chicago, 1984.

Iggers, Georg G. *New Directions in European Historiography*. With a contribution by Norman Baker. Middletown, Conn., 1975.

Iser, Wolfgang. "The Current Situation of Literary Theory: Key Concepts and the Imaginary." *New Literary History* 11, no. 1 (1979): 1–20.

Jackson, Richard A. *Vive le roi! A History of the French Coronation from Charles V to Charles X*. Chapel Hill, N.C., and London, 1984.

Jauss, Hans Robert. *Toward an Aesthetic of Reception*. Trans. Timothy Bahti; intro. Paul de Man. Minneapolis, 1982.

Jones, Colin. "The Organization of Conspiracy and Revolt in the *Mémoires* of the Cardinal de Retz." *European Studies Review* 11, no. 2 (1981): 125–150.

Jouhaud, Christian. *Mazarinades: la Fronde des mots*. Paris, 1985.

―――. "Le Duc et l'archevêque: action politique, représentations et pouvoir au temps de Richelieu." *Annales: E.S.C.* 41, no. 5 (1986): 1017–1039.

―――. "Ecriture et action au XVIIe siècle: sur un corpus de mazarinades." *Annales: E.S.C.* 38, no. 1 (1983): 42–64.

―――. "Imprimer l'événement. De La Rochelle à Paris." In *Les usages de l'imprimé*, ed. Roger Chartier, 381–438. Paris, 1987.

―――. "Lisibilité et persuasion. Les placards politiques." In ibid., 309–342.

Joyce, William L., et al., eds. *Printing and Society in Early America*. Worcester, Mass., 1983.

Kaiser, Thomas. "The Abbé de Saint-Pierre, Public Opinion, and the Reconstitution of the French Monarchy." *Journal of Modern History* 55, no. 4 (1983): 618–643.

Kelley, Donald R. *The Beginning of Ideology: Consciousness and Society in the French Reformation*. Cambridge, 1981.

―――. *The Foundations of Modern Historical Scholarship*. New York, 1970.

―――. "Murd'rous Machiavel in France: A Post Mortem." *Political Science Quarterly* 85 (1970): 545–559.

Keohane, Nannerl O. *Philosophy and the State in France*. Princeton, 1980.

Kettering, Sharon. *Judicial Politics and Urban Revolt in Seventeenth-Century France*. Princeton, 1978.

―――. *Patrons, Brokers, and Clients in Seventeenth-Century France*. Oxford, 1986.

Kierstead, Raymond F. *Pomponne de Bellièvre*. Evanston, Ill., 1968.

―――, ed. *State and Society in Seventeenth-Century France*. New York, 1975.

Kingdon, Robert M. *Geneva and the Coming of the Wars of Religion in France*. Geneva, 1956.

―――. "The Business Activities of Printers Henri and François Estienne." In *Aspects de la propagande religieuse*, ed. G. Berthoud et al., 256–272. Geneva, 1957.

―――. "Patronage, Piety, and Printing in Sixteenth-Century Europe." In *A Festschrift for Frederick B. Artz*, ed. David H. Pinkney and Theodore Ropp, 19–36. Durham, N.C., 1964.

Klaits, Joseph. *Printed Propaganda under Louis XIV: Absolute Monarchy and Public Opinion*. Princeton, 1976.

Kleinman, Ruth. *Anne of Austria: Queen of France*. Columbus, Ohio, 1985.

Knecht, R. J. *Francis I and Absolute Monarchy*. London, 1969.

Labatut, J.-P. *Les Ducs et pairs au 17e siècle*. Paris, 1972.

Labrousse, Elisabeth, and Alfred Soman. "Un bûcher pour un judaïsant: Jean Fontanier (1621)." *Dix-septième siècle* 39, no. 2 (1987): 113–132.

LaCapra, Dominick. *Rethinking Intellectual History: Texts, Contexts, and Language.* Ithaca, 1983.

Lanette-Claverie, Cl. "La librarie française en 1700." *Revue française d'histoire du livre* 2 (1972): 3–44.

Laswell, Harold D. *Propaganda Techniques in World War I.* Cambridge, Mass., 1971.

Leber, Constant. *De l'état réel de la presse et des pamphlets depuis François Ier jusqu'à Louis XIV.* Paris, 1834.

Lemaire, André. *Les Lois fondamentales de la monarchie française d'après les théoriciens de l'Ancien Régime.* Paris 1905; rpt. Geneva, 1975.

Le Roy Ladurie, Emmanuel. *Carnival in Romans.* Trans. Mary Feeney. New York, 1979.

Lewis, J. U. "Jean Bodin's 'Logic of Sovereignty.'" *Political Studies* 16, no. 2 (1968): 206–222.

Lewis, Peter S. "War-propaganda and Historiography in Fifteenth-Century France and England." *Transactions of the Royal Historical Society* 5th ser., vol. 15 (1965): 1–21.

Lightman, Harriet L. *Sons and Mothers: Queens and Minor Kings in French Constitutional Law.* Ann Arbor, Mich., 1981. Microfilm.

Lindsay, Robert, and John Neu. *French Political Pamphlets, 1547–1648: A Catalog of Major Collections in American Libraries.* Madison, 1969. See also *French Political Pamphlets, 1547–1648: A Supplement.* Woodbridge, Conn., 1981.

Lloyd, Howell A. "The Political Thought of Charles Loyseau." *European Studies Review* 11 (1981): 53–82.

Loemker, Leroy E. *Struggle for Synthesis: The Seventeenth Century Background of Leibniz's Synthesis of Order and Freedom.* Cambridge, Mass., 1972.

Lossky, Andrew. "The Absolutism of Louis XIV: Reality or Myth?" *Canadian Journal of History* 19 (1984): 1–15.

Lublinskaya, Alexandra D. *French Absolutism: The Crucial Phase, 1620–1629.* Trans. Brian Pearce. London, 1968.

Macdougall, Curtis D. *Understanding Public Opinion: A Guide for Newspapermen and Newspaper Readers.* New York, 1952.

McKennan, William. "Gaston d'Orléans and the Grands: The Opposition to Absolutism under Louis XIII, 1610–1643." Ph.D. diss., Brown University, 1972.

McLuhan, Marshall. *The Gutenberg Galaxy.* Toronto, 1962; rpt. New York, 1969.
———. *Understanding Media: The Extensions of Man.* 2d ed. New York, 1964.

McQuail, Denis. "The Influence and Effects of Mass Media." In *Media Power in Politics,* ed. Doris A. Graber, 36–53. Washington, D. C., 1984.

Magendie, Maurice. *La Politesse mondaine et les théories de l'honnêteté en France au XVIIe siècle, de 1600 à 1660.* Paris, 1925.

Major, J. Russell. *Representative Government in Early Modern France.* New Haven, 1980.

———. *Representative Institutions in Renaissance France, 1421–1559.* Madison, 1960.

Mandrou, Robert. *De la culture populaire aux XVIIe et XVIIIe siècles: Bibliothèque*

bleue de Troyes. Paris, 1964.
——. *La France aux XVIIe et XVIIIe siècles.* Paris, 1974.
Marais, Jean-Luc. "Littérature et culture populaires aux XVIIe et XVIIIe siècles." *Annales de Bretagne et des Pays de l'Ouest* 87 (1980): 65–105.
Marin, Louis. *Le Portrait du Roi.* Paris, 1981.
——. *Le Récit est un piège.* Paris, 1978.
——. "Pouvoir du récit et récit du pouvoir." *Actes de la recherche en sciences sociales* 25 (1979).
Marion, Marcel. *Dictionnaire des institutions de la France aux XVIIe et XVIIIe siècles.* 2d ed. Paris, 1969.
Mariéjol, Jean. "Henri IV et Louis XIII." In *Histoire de France depuis les origines jusqu'à la Révolution,* ed. Ernest Lavisse, vol. 6, pt. 2. Paris, 1911.
Markoff, John. "Some Effects of Literacy in Eighteenth-Century France." *Journal of Interdisciplinary History* 17 (1986): 311–333.
Martin, Henri-Jean. *Le Livre française sous l'Ancien Régime.* Paris, 1987.
——. *Livres, pouvoirs et société à Paris au XVIIe siècle (1589–1701).* 2 vols. Paris and Geneva, 1969.
——. "Classements et conjonctures." In *Histoire de l'édition française,* vol. 1. See Martin and Chartier.
——. "Culture écrite et culture orale, culture savante et culture populaire dans la France d'Ancien Régime." *Journal des savants* (1974–1975): 225–282.
Martin, Henri-Jean, and Roger Chartier, eds., with Jean-Pierre Vivet. *Histoire de l'édition française.* 4 vols. Vol. 1, *Le Livre conquérant: du moyen âge au milieu du XVII siècle.* Vol. 2, *Le Livre triomphant.* Vol. 3, *Le Temps des éditeurs du Romanticisme à la Belle Epoque.* Vol. 4, *Le Livre concurrencé.* Paris, 1983–1989.
Martin, Henri-Jean, et al. *Livres et lecteurs à Grenoble. Les Registres du libraire Nicolas.* 2 vols. Geneva and Paris, 1977.
Martin, L. John. "The Moving Target: General Trends in Audience Composition." In *Propaganda and Communications in World History,* ed. Harold D. Lasswell, Daniel Lerner, and Hans Speier, 3:249–294. 3 vols. Honolulu, 1980.
Marvick, Elizabeth W. *Louis XIII: The Making of a King.* New Haven, 1986.
Mastellone, S. *La Reggenza di Maria de Medici.* Florence, 1962.
Maza, Sarah. "Le Tribunal de la nation: les mémoires judiciaires et l'opinion publique à la fin de l'Ancien Régime." *Annales: E.S.C.* 42, no. 1 (1987): 73–90.
——. "Politics, Culture, and the Origins of the French Revolution." *Journal of Modern History* 61, no. 4 (1989): 704–723.
Mettam, Roger. *Power and Faction in Louis XIV's France.* New York, 1988.
Meuller, Claus. *The Politics of Communication: A Study in the Political Sociology of Language, Socialization, and Legitimation.* Oxford, 1973.
Mintz, Sidney W. "Culture: An Anthropological View." *Yale Review* 71 (1982): 499–512.
Mongrédien, George. *Les Grands Comédiens du XVIIe siècle.* Paris, 1927.
Moote, A. Lloyd. *Louis XIII, the Just.* Berkeley and Los Angeles, 1989.
——. *The Revolt of the Judges.* Princeton, 1971.
Mousnier, Roland. *L'Assassinat d'Henri IV.* Paris, 1964.

———. *Les Institutions de la France sous la monarchie absolue, 1598–1789.* 2 vols. Paris, 1974–1980.

———. *La Plume, la faucille, et le marteau: institutions et société en France du moyen âge à la Révolution.* Paris, 1970.

———. *La Vénalité des offices sous Henri IV et Louis XIII.* 2d rev. ed. Paris, 1971.

———. "Comment les Français du XVIIe siècle voyaient la constitution." *Dix-septième siècle* 25–26 (1955): 9–36.

———. "Le Conseil du Roi de la mort de Henri IV au gouvernement personnel de Louis XIV." In *La Plume, la faucille, et le marteau.* See Mousnier, 1970.

———. "The Exponents and Critics of Absolutism." In *The New Cambridge Modern History,* ed. G. R. Potter et al., 4:104–131. 12 vols. Cambridge, 1957–1975.

———. "The Fronde." In *Preconditions of Revolution in Early-Modern Europe,* ed. Robert Forster and Jack P. Greene, 131–159. Baltimore, 1972.

———. "L'Opposition politique bourgeoise à la fin du XVIe siècle et au début du XVIIe siècle." *Revue historique* 213 (1955): 1–20.

———. "La participation des gouvernés à l'activité des gouvernants dans la France des XVIIe et XVIIIe siècles." In *La Plume, la faucille, et le marteau.* See Mousnier, 1970.

Mousnier, Roland, and Fritz Hartung. "Quelques problèmes concernant la monarchie absolue." In *Relazioni del X congresso internazionale di scienze storiche,* vol. 1, 1–55. Florence, 1955.

New Catholic Encyclopedia. 16 vols. New York, 1967–1974.

Nouaillac, Joseph. *Villeroy, secrétaire d'État et ministre de Charles IX, Henri III, et Henri IV.* Paris, 1909.

Ong, Walter J. *Ramus, Method, and the Decay of Dialogue: From the Art of Discourse to the Art of Reason.* Cambridge, Mass., 1958.

Ouvré, Henri-François. "Essai sur l'histoire de la ville de Poitiers, depuis la fin de la Ligue jusqu'au ministère de Richelieu, 1595–1628." *Mémoires de la Société des antiquaires de l'Ouest* 12 (1855): 365–528. Published separately, Poitiers, 1856.

Ozouf, Mona. "L'opinion publique." In *The Political Culture of the Old Regime,* ed. Keith Michael Baker, vol. 1 of *The French Revolution and the Creation of Modern Political Culture,* 419–434. Oxford, 1987. (Also published as " 'Public Opinion' at the End of the Old Regime." Trans. Lydia G. Cochrane. *Journal of Modern History* 60 [1988]: S1–S21.)

Pagès, Georges. "Autour du 'grand orage': Richelieu et Marillac: deux politiques." *Revue historique* 179 (1947): 63–97.

———. "Le Conseil du roi sous Louis XIII." *Revue d'histoire moderne* 12 (1937): 283–324.

Pallier, Denis, *Recherches sur l'imprimerie à Paris pendant la Ligue, 1585–1594.* Paris, 1975.

———. "Les Impressions de la Contre-Réforme en France et l'apparition des grandes compagnies de libraires parisiens." *Revue française d'histoire du livre* 31 (1981): 215–273.

———. "Les réponses catholiques." In *Histoire de l'édition française,* vol. 1. See Martin and Chartier.

Parent, Annie. *Les Métiers du livre à Paris au XVIe siècle (1535–1560)*. Geneva, 1974.

Parker, David. *La Rochelle and the French Monarchy: Order and Conflict in Seventeenth-Century France*. London, 1980.

———. *The Making of French Absolutism*. New York, 1983.

———. "Law, Society and the State in the Thought of Jean Bodin." *History of Political Thought* 2, no. 2 (1981): 253–285.

———. "The Social Foundation of French Absolutism, 1610–1630." *Past and Present* 53 (1971): 67–89.

———. "Sovereignty, Absolutism and the Function of the Law in Seventeenth-Century France." *Past and Present* 122 (1989): 36–74.

Perelman, Chaim. *Le Champ de l'argumentation*. Brussels, 1970.

Perelman, Chaim, and L. Olbrechts-Tyteca. *The New Rhetoric: A Treatise on Argumentation*. Notre Dame, 1971; originally published as *La Nouvelle Rhétorique: traité de l'argumentation*. Paris, 1958.

Petit, Jeanne. *L'Assemblée des notables de 1626–1627*. Paris, 1936.

Picot, G. *Cardin Le Bret (1558–1655) et la doctrine de la souveraineté*. Nancy, 1948.

Pillorget, René. *Les mouvements insurrectionels en Provence 1596–1715*. Paris, 1975.

Poche, Jean [pseud.?]. *Quelques adresses de librairies, imprimeurs, relieurs, marchands, etc., du XVIIe siècle*. Paris, 1899. (In the Newberry Library, Chicago, Ill.)

Pocock, J. G. A. *The Machiavellian Moment*. Princeton, 1975.

———. *Politics, Language, and Time: Essays on Political Thought and History*. New York, 1971.

Porchnev, Boris. *Les Soulèvements populaires en France au XVIIe siècle*. Abr. ed. Paris, 1972.

Pye, Lucien W. "Introduction." In *Communications and Political Development*, ed. Lucien Pye. Princeton, 1963.

———. "Political Culture and Political Development." In *Political Culture and Political Development*, ed. L. Pye and S. Verba. Princeton, 1965.

Quinn, Arthur. *Figures of Speech*. Salt Lake City, 1982.

Rabb, Theodore K. *The Struggle for Stability in Early Modern Europe*. New York, 1975.

Ranum, Orest. *Artisans of Glory: Writers and Historical Thought in Seventeenth-Century France*. Chapel Hill, N.C., 1980.

———. *Paris in the Age of Absolutism*. 1968. Rpt. Bloomington, Ind., 1979.

———. *Richelieu and the Councillors of Louis XIII*. Oxford, 1963.

———. "The French Ritual of Tyrannicide in the Late 16th Century." *Sixteenth Century Journal* 11, no. 1 (1980): 63–82.

———. "Guises, Henry III, Henry IV, Concini—30 Years of Political Assassinations." *Histoire* 51 (1982): 36–44.

———. "Richelieu and the Great Nobility: Some Aspects of Early Modern Political Motives." *French Historical Studies* 3 (1963): 184–204.

Ravenez, L.-W. *Histoire du cardinal Sourdis*. Bordeaux, Paris, and Lyons, 1867.

Renouard, Ph. *Imprimeurs parisiens, libraires, fondeurs de caractères, correcteurs d'imprimerie depuis l'introduction de l'imprimerie à Paris (1470) jusqu'à la fin du XVIe siècle*. Paris, 1898.

Répertoire bibliographique des livres imprimés en France du seizième siècle. Ed. Louis Desgraves et al. 32 vols. Baden-Baden, 1968–1986.

Répertoire bibliographique des livres imprimés en France au XVIIe siècle. Ed. Louis Desgraves et al. 16 vols. Baden-Baden, 1978–1989.

Richards, Judith. " 'His Nowe Majestie' and the English Monarchy: The Kingship of Charles I before 1640." *Past and Present* 113 (1986): 70–96.

Richet, Denis. *La France moderne: l'esprit des institutions.* Paris, 1973.

———. "Autour des Etats-Généraux: la polémique politique en France de 1612 à 1615." In *Représentation et vouloir politiques.* See Chartier and Richet.

———. "Autour des origines idéologiques lointaines de la Révolution française: élites et despotisme." *Annales: E.S.C.* 24 (1969): 1–23.

———. "Paris et les Etats de 1614." In *Représentation et vouloir politiques.* See Chartier and Richet.

Roelker, Nancy Lyman. "The Impact of the Reformation Era on Communication and Propaganda." In *Propaganda and Communications in World History,* ed. Harold D. Laswell, Daniel Lerner, and Hans Speier, 2:41–84. 3 vols. Honolulu, 1980.

Rothkrug, Lionel. *Opposition to Louis XIV: The Political and Social Origins of the French Enlightenment.* Princeton, 1965.

Rothrock, George. "The French Crown and the Estates General of 1614." *French Historical Studies* 1 (1960): 295–318.

———. "Officials and King's Men. A Note on the Possibilites of Royal Control in the Estates General." *French Historical Studies* 2, no. 4 (1962): 504–510.

Rowen, Herbert H. " 'L'Etat, c'est moi': Louis XIV and the State." *French Historical Studies* 2 (1961): 83–98.

———. "Louis XIV and Absolutism." In *Louis XIV and the Craft of Kingship,* ed. John C. Rule, 302–316. Columbus, Ohio, 1969.

Rule, James, and Charles Tilly. "1830 and the Unnatural History of Revolution." *Journal of Social Issues* 28 (1972): 49–77.

Rule, John C., ed. *Louis XIV and the Craft of Kingship.* Columbus, Ohio, 1969.

Russell, Conrad S. R. "Monarchies, Wars, and Estates in England, France, and Spain, c. 1580–c. 1640." *Legislative Studies Quarterly* 7 (1982): 205–220.

Salmon, J. H. M. *Renaissance and Revolt: Essays in the Intellectual and Social History of Early Modern France.* Cambridge, 1987.

———. *Society in Crisis: France in the Sixteenth Century.* New York, 1975.

———. "French Satire in the Late Sixteenth Century." *Sixteenth Century Journal* 6, no. 2 (1975): 57–88.

———. "Gallicanism and Anglicanism in the Age of the Counter-Reformation." See Salmon, *Renaissance and Revolt.*

———. "The Paris Sixteen, 1584–1594: The Social Analysis of a Revolutionary Movement." *Journal of Modern History* 43 (1972): 540–576.

———. "Storm over the Noblesse." *Journal of Modern History* 53 (1981): 242–257.

Sawyer, Jeffrey K. "Jacques Bon-Homme and National Politics: Ethos and Audience in Seventeenth-Century Pamphlets." *Proceedings of the Annual Meeting of the Western Society for French History* 12 (1985): 23–32.

———. "Judicial Corruption and Legal Reform in Early Seventeenth-Century France." *Law and History Review* 6, no. 1 (1988): 95–117.

———. "Review of Christian Jouhaud's *Mazarinades.*" *Journal of Modern History* 58, no. 4 (1986): 933–935.

Schalk, Ellery. "The Appearance and Reality of Nobility in France during the

Wars of Religion: An Example of How Collective Attitudes Can Change." *Journal of Modern History,* 48, no. 1 (1976): 19–31.

Sedgewick, Alexander. *Jansenism in Seventeenth-Century France: Voices from the Wilderness.* Charlottesville, Va., 1977.

Sée, Henri. *Les Idées politiques en France au XVIIe siècle.* Paris, 1923.

Seguin, Jean-Pierre. *L'Information en France avant le périodique.* Paris, 1964.

———. *L'Information en France de Louis XII à Henri II.* Geneva, 1961.

Seigel, Jerrold. *Rhetoric and Philosophy in Renaissance Humanism: The Union of Eloquence and Wisdom, Petrarch to Valla.* Princeton, 1968.

Sennett, Richard. *The Fall of Public Man: On the Social Psychology of Capitalism.* New York, 1977.

Servière, Joseph de la. "Les idées politiques du cardinal Bellarmin." *Revue des questions historiques* 82 (1907): 378–412; 83 (1908): 56–90.

Shapiro, Barbara J. *Probability and Certainty in Seventeenth-Century England.* Princeton, 1983.

Sharpe, Kevin. "Crown, Parliament and Locality: Government and Communication in Early Stuart England." *English Historical Review* 399 (1986): 321–350.

Skinner, Quentin. *The Foundations of Modern Political Thought.* 2 vols. Cambridge, 1980.

———. "Hermeneutics and the Role of History." *New Literary History* 7 (1975–76): 209–32.

———. "Meaning and Understanding in the History of Ideas." *History and Theory* 8 (1969): 3–53.

———. "Motives, Intentions and the Interpretation of Texts." *New Literary History* 3 (1972): 393–408.

———. "Some Problems in the Analysis of Political Thought and Action." *Political Theory* 2 (1974): 277–303.

Small, Melvin, ed. *Public Opinion and Historians.* Detroit, 1970.

Smith, Jeffrey A. *Printers and Press Freedom: The Ideology of Early American Journalism.* New York, 1988.

Smith, Peter H. "Political History in the 1980's: A View from Latin America." *Journal of Interdisciplinary History* 12 (1981): 3–27.

Solomon, Howard M. *Public Welfare, Science, and Propaganda in Seventeenth-Century France.* Princeton, 1972.

———. "The *Gazette* and Antistatist Propaganda: The Medium of Print in the First Half of the Seventeenth Century." *Canadian Journal of History* 9 (1974): 1–17.

Soman, Alfred. "Press, Pulpit, and Censorship in France before Richelieu." *Proceedings of the American Philosophical Society* 120 (1976): 439–463.

Struever, Nancy. *The Language of History in the Renaissance.* Princeton, 1970.

Tapié, Victor L. *La France de Louis XIII et de Richelieu.* Rpt. Paris, 1967.

Thompson, John B. *Critical Hermeneutics: A Study in the Thought of Paul Ricoeur and Jürgen Habermas.* Cambridge, Mass., 1981.

Thomson, Oliver. *Mass Persuasion in History.* Edinburgh, 1977.

Thuau, Etienne. *Raison d'état et pensée politique à l'époque de Richelieu.* Paris, 1966.

Tilly, Charles. *From Mobilization to Revolution.* Reading, Mass., 1978.

———. "Reflections on the History of European State-Making." In *The Formation of National States in Western Europe,* ed. Charles Tilly. Princeton, 1975.

Tocqueville, Alexis de. *The Old Regime and the French Revolution.* Trans. Stuart Gilbert. 1st ed. 1856; New York, 1955.

Toulmin, Stephen. *The Uses of Argument.* Cambridge, 1958.

Trevor-Roper, H. R. "Fernand Braudel, the *Annales,* and the Mediterranean." *Journal of Modern History* 44 (1972): 468–479.

Tucker, Robert C. "Culture, Political Culture, and Communist Society." *Political Science Quarterly* 88 (1973): 173–190.

Van Kley, Dale. *The Damiens Affair and the Unraveling of the Ancien Régime.* Princeton, 1984.

Walker, Karl-Heinz. *Typologische und terminologische Untersuchungen zur französischen Pamphletliteratur des frühen 17. Jahrhunderts.* Papers on French Seventeenth-Century Literature, Biblio 17–29; Paris, Seattle, Tübingen, 1987.

Wallerstein, Immanuel. *The Modern World System.* New York, 1976.

Weber, Max. *Economy and Society.* Ed. Guenther Roth and Claus Wittich. 2 vols. 4th German ed., 1956; rev. ed., Berkeley and Los Angeles, 1978.

Westrich, Sal. *The Ormée of Bordeaux.* Baltimore, 1972.

White, Hayden. *Metahistory: The Historical Imagination in Nineteenth-Century Europe.* Baltimore, 1973.

———. *Tropics of Discourse.* Baltimore, 1978.

Winandy, André. "La Satire comme instrument politique au XVIe siècle." In *Culture et politique en France à l'époque de l'humanisme et de la renaissance,* ed. Franco Simone, 269–291. Turin, 1974.

Yardeni, Myriam. *La conscience nationale en France pendant les Guerres de Religion, 1559–1589.* Paris and Louvain, 1971.

Yates, Francis A. *The Art of Memory.* Chicago, 1972.

Zeller, Berthold. *Le connétable de Luynes.* Paris, 1879.

———. *Louis XIII: Marie de Médicis, Chef du conseil.* Paris, 1898.

———. *La minorité de Louis XIII: Marie de Médicis et Villeroy.* Paris, 1897.

INDEX

* * *

Compositor: ICC
Text: 10/12 Baskerville
Display: Baskerville
Printer: Braun-Brumfield
Binder: Braun-Brumfield